# *Green Hauntings*

### New &
### Selected Poems
### Volume One
### 2006-2016

# Alan
# Morrison

Caparison

First published in 2022
Reprinted in 2023
by Caparison
imprint of *The Recusant*
www.therecusant.org.uk


Printed by
Printondemand-worldwide.com
9 Culley Court
Orton Southgate
Peterborough
PE2 6XD

Typeset in SchoolBook by Caparison © 2022/3
Cover design © Caparison 2022/3

Alan Morrison is hereby identified as author of this
work in accordance with Section 77 of the Copyright,
Designs and Patents Act 1988

ISBN 978-1-8384966-2-3

# Acknowledgements

Many of these poems have previously appeared in variations in the following journals:

*Aesthetica, Aireings, Autumn Leaves (Canada), Awen, Bard, Cadenza, Candelabrum, The Cannon's Mouth, Carillon, Decanto, Eclipse, erbacce, Exile, Fickle Muses (US), First Time, The Fortnightly Review, The Glasgow Review, Great Works, Illuminations (US), The International Times, Jacobyte Poetry, The Journal, The London Magazine, Monkey Kettle, The Morning Star, The Once Orange Badge Poetry Supplement, Osprey, The Penniless Press, Pennine Platform, The People's Poet, Poetic Hours, Poet-in-Residence, Poetry and All That Jazz, Poetry Monthly International, Poetry Now, Poetry Salzburg Review, Poet Tree, Pulsar, Reading University Literary Magazine, Red Poets, The Seeker, Selene–Culturas de Sintra (Portugal), Snakeskin, Softblow (US), South, The Spleen, The Strix Varia, Stand, Voice & Verse, The Whistling Shade (US), The White Leaf Review, World Literature Today (US), The Writer's Muse, The Yellow Crane.*

And in the following anthologies:

*Soul Feathers—Poems in support of the Macmillan Cancer Trust* (Indigo Dreams, 2011), *The Reiver's Stone* (Ettrick Forest Press, 2010), *The Overdose* (Sixties Press, 2007), *The Real Survivors' Anthology* (Sixties Press, 2007), *Beyond Stigma* (Sixties Press, 2006), *Orphans of Albion* (Survivors' Press, 2005/8), *MEAN— New Writing* (The South, 2003), *First Edition—Don't Think of Tigers* (The Do Not Press, 2001).

My gratitude to the publishers of the volumes from which these poems are drawn: Paula Brown (Paula Brown Publishing, Portsmouth), Simon Jenner (Waterloo Press, Brighton & Hove), and Dennis Greig (Lapwing Publications, Belfast).

Special thanks to Matilda Persson for all English-Swedish and Swedish-English translations in *The Tall Skies*.

I am grateful to the Royal Literary Fund for its continued support which has helped me to spend the maximum time on my poetry.

*This book is dedicated to the memories of*

*My mother, Helen*
*(29th January 1949–31st October 2013)*

*and*

*my dear friend and poetic soulmate*
*David Kessel*
*(10th April 1947–8th March 2022)*

# Contents

from *A Tapestry of Absent Sitters* (2009)

from *The Tall Skies* (2013)

from *Blaze a Vanishing* (2013)

from *Shadows Waltz Haltingly* (2015)

## Supplemental Poems (1991-2021)

# Foreword

How to begin? With a warning to the curious? Approach with care, then, for this is indeed a book of hauntings. Morrison's work traffics in the spectral and the shadowy—there are over 120 uses of the word 'shadow' in *Green Hauntings*. His is a poetry concerned equally with and *for* people and histories hidden, obscured, peripheral to vision; with impoverished histories, those that persist and circulate in fragments or fleeting glimpses, carried on 'Thicketed whispers; oral aggregates of homecoming ghosts' ('Broomflower', p.226), and the dank ephemera of scent: 'a musty fume', 'a stain on the air' ('The Mark', p.232). Anxiety permeates these poems, an insecurity about both familial and cultural class identity. There exists a dissonance between the social and subjective dimensions of class, and Morrison is eloquent in distilling that unique sense of estrangement provoked by the downward mobility of the 'borderline *'shabby-genteel'* breed—/ *'The shock-absorbers of the bourgeoisie"* ('The Mark', p.233), who share the social condition of their class cohort, but whose intellectual and imaginative horizons exist painfully beyond their immediate and limited means.

Morrison's poetry is very much occupied with the essential ghostliness of such impoverished lives; lives that exist in—and are—shadows: lives that inhabit the dusty gloaming of poverty, a twilight of partial personhood, that is literally dark —as from the 'fasting electricity meter's/ Weekly Lent' (p.232)—and emotionally murky: 'I've lingered like a shadow where my own shadow should fall./ Sometimes I wonder whether I was ever here at all' ('My Life in the Shade', p.47). The poor are the pallid doppelgängers of more vivid and affluent lives, the 'cast-offs' of their 'material imagoes' (p.232). In such a guise they *haunt* middle-class imagination: an insubstantial yet persistent glitch at the edge of attention and conscience. They trouble the very idea of history as an enlightening ascent.

In '*Knoparmoj*' (p.173) a 'photograph of charred-faced Swedish chimney sweeps/ Circa 1900s, begrimed and brow-beaten by poverty' confronts the beholder

> Insolent-eyed with that special acrid proletarian pride
> So challenging to those who have never had to forge
> Their own dogged egos through the grind of growth-
> Eroding labour; barefoot in rags, cramped bags of bone.

The spectre of poverty—its filth, infirmity, and want—hovers over the living poor, whose bodies bear the material traces of class inequality; as tactile reminders of this grim disparity, the poor are everywhere ejected—from history, culture, civic space— until they become mere ciphers, an amorphous suffering, criminal mass in which no one face is distinct or memorable. The poor are an urban legend, a superstition: do not speak their name after sundown lest you invoke their malevolent spirit.

While the moneyed live on through their monuments—architectural and cultural—inscribing their legacy onto public space, preserving it through artistic canons and in historical archives, poor and working-class people have few enduring possessions; theirs is the posterity of small, slant things: as intangible as breath, as fallible and perishable as a single living memory. Against their erasure from consciousness and culture, Morrison performs an uncanny anamnesis, nowhere more so, perhaps, than in the poems from *The Tall Skies* (2013) in which '*Knoparmoj*' first appeared. In pieces such as 'Moa—The Lone Crow of Norrköping' (P.177), 'Now, Ivar Was a Traveller' (p.185) and 'Bastugatan 21 *A Séance with the Complete Bohemians*' (p.202) Morrison celebrates some of the great autodidacts of Swedish proletarian literature, not merely in tribute, but as an activation of proletarian literature's aims and ideals: Morrison's own autodidacticism becomes the vehicle through which an imaginative and intellectual solidarity is embodied, across generations, cultures and countries. These poems in *memoriam* do not strictly serve the monolithic and memorialising ends of bourgeois lyric production. They are, rather, relational, a calling into being of an intellectual and creative socialist community.

There is no proletarian literature separable from the working-class readers and writers who make it: they have no stable centre from which to establish and cement their creative lineage, their antecedents are scattered, and their textual practices routinely excluded from the accepted definition of "good" writing; they are seldom the implied audience for any work of culture. The literature of the poor is always emergent, requires serial acts of excavation and summoning. Morrison's homage to working-class writers and writing is, accordingly, part delicate archaeology and part inspired mediumship. In 'Moa—The Lone Crow of Norrköping' Morrison writes across the continuum of our exclusion:

> Her pen scraped on, her cramping hand,
> A blazing tumbrel of thumb and fingers, she had to try
> And empty her teeming brain, but the more she wrote,
> The more the questions heaped up on the paper, as if
> To fill the space of absent answers [...]
> [...] The answers never came... So she wrote on... (p.183)

While their literature is always emergent, it is also eternally deferred, impossible under conditions of class inequality. Morrison writes into the empty silence of those 'absent answers', interrogating both the treatment of the poor as citizens and their status as artists, projecting themselves into a future they seem destined never to occupy.

Throughout *Green Hauntings*, Morrison repeatedly signals the embodied act of writing and the effort required to bring it forth. The effect of this is two-fold: to enshrine writing itself as an act of proletarian labour, and to constitute the proletarian body as a site of creative and intellectual endeavour; proletarian lives as subjects worthy of literature. To put it another way, writing is work, and workers are writers. Art and labour, rather than being mutually antagonistic or exclusive, provoke and facilitate each other. As Morrison writes, towards the end of 'Moa': 'She poured out the shadows that she'd swept into/ Violent blooms of pounding prose' (p.186). In 'Bastugatan 21' we learn that 'Ivar Lo wrote only for posterity, so we are told,/ Not for worldly fame, wealth or popularity, but for/ A lasting place in the minds of those who followed' so that he might

> Be remembered, and, thereby, *he*, though not through
> Gauchely posed photographs with pipe and beret—
> But for what he wrote, and what he built up through
> The energy and industry of his iron-wrought words...' (p.209).

It is that 'energy and industry' Morrison is so adept at channelling: a writing that proceeds not from a scene of tranquil contemplation but driven by the peculiarly pressured contexts of impoverished lives, and by an animating sense of social urgency. Lo wrote—and Morrison writes, one feels—to challenge bourgeois notions of posterity as the vainglorious aftermath of the individual, in favour of an enduring supernatural fellowship between working-class and impoverished writers across time. The posterity envisaged by Lo is not predicated upon the preservation of his work within the hallowed precincts of literature. It imagines, rather, a collective and creative praxis with the potential to transform both culture and society. Lo's posterity is not one of static conservation, but of continuous and active struggle, something Morrison captures in these moving lines from 'Bastugatan 21' introducing the curator of the Ivar Lo-Museet as one 'of Ivar Lo's apostles: a living, breathing

> Barrel-load of his autodidactic ideals: for ordinary
> Working men to graduate from hand to brain,
> Fuse the anvil with the page, hammer out a mallet-thick
> Portfolio of furious prose; this manual man with artisan
> Hands has an artist's riveted head attached to his
> Lumberjack's frame: a proletarian man of letters... (p.205)

A deliberate ambiguity attaches to Morrison's description of this 'manual man': Morrison is writing about the curator, but because the curator embodies Lo's notion of the working-class autodidact, he is also speaking about Lo. By merging these two figures, Morrison creates a sense of both temporal glitch—making Lo, and by extension his ideals, vividly present in the present—and historical continuity. The intricate sonic work in this passage is typical of Morrison's use of sound to contour and extend meaning: the short, sharp vowels of 'barrel', 'didactic', 'mallet', 'manual', 'man', 'artisan', 'hands', 'attached' and 'jack's' create a sense of ceaseless labour between and across lines; interspersing these sonic hammer blows Morrison weaves the long, soft vowel sounds of 'Lo's', 'apostles', 'auto', ordinary', 'portfolio', 'prose' and 'prole', entwining notions of mental and physical labour, fusing in sound as well as image, the 'anvil with the page'. 'Manual', of course, refers to any work performed by hand, but it also describes a template or book of instructions for others to follow. More particularly, in its archaic use, 'manual' was a book of forms to be used by priests in the administration of the sacraments. A sacrament of a kind is being enacted in Lo's former apartment: a rite of impoverished communion.

Not all ghosts are holy. If the poor and marginalised are haunters of social and literary thresholds, they are equally haunted, by their collective past and familial histories; what was and might have been. This other, more personal engagement with ghostliness is particularly keen throughout the poems from *The Mansion Gardens* (2006) and those from *Shadows Waltz Haltingly* (2015). In the former collection the haunted or 'shunned' house is a significant and staple motif, in particular the derelict rural cottage, as in 'The House on the Rise of Reversion' (p.34). In this remarkable poem, Morrison uses the structural decay of the physical house and garden both to conceal and to communicate the misery of those who dwell within it. Morrison writes:

Eyes entirely detached survey
A shambling garden with scorn—
Instead of empathising they
Petition us to cut the lawn.

This short and tightly turned stanza pithily encapsulates an attitude—rife within English society—that treats the dereliction of poor houses as an effect without cause, as a cause in itself, figuring the poor persons who live there as equally contributing to the degradation of environment from which they suffer. The 'offense' given by the ramshackle homes of the poor provides an opportunity to mobilise class hatred and enact forms of social cleansing. In 'The House on the Rise of Reversion' this manifests in the pettiness of neighbours hand-delivering a 'a dearth/ Of signatures' through which they hope to coerce the occupants into tidying their property.

Morrison captures the layered complexity of this interaction through alert and original phrasemaking, evoking the 'trampled eyes' of the speaker's father, and his own 'anxious face of thwarted youth' twitching 'through reclusive curtains,/ Haunting a window's hidden truth.' The house and its squalor are supremely visible, obtruding onto the attention of the local community, yet this very visibility serves to obscure the personhood of those who live there, and to inoculate against an empathetic consideration of their lives. Morrison distils the meanness and futility of the petition; its normalising endeavour to sanitise the poverty of house and inhabitants alike. Such manoeuvres have little to do with improving the lives and conditions of poor persons, and much with evading responsibility for the systems that create and maintain those conditions. Against such willed inattention the house achieves a kind of dark victory: the flimsy instruments of collective spite are no match against the regressive anarchy of poverty, and the poem concludes with the ominous lines

Here a sham-lawn's been flung like a sheet
Over a bomb-shelter's furniture by
An idyll's betrayal to spaded defeat
For we who live in the house on the rise.

In the image of the 'bomb-shelter' Morrison merges the literal and the figurative to superb effect, conjuring at once the strange particularity of the speaker's garden while also gesturing towards the embattled and dubiously protected condition of the house's occupants. This blurring of physical and metaphorical elements is present throughout the poem: 'the rise' is both an actual location and a state of emergence or expansion; the poem taps into middle-class fears that the overrun haunts of the poor will themselves overrun their strenuously policed borders. The sprawling garden becomes a space of sinister revenant survival: like a b-movie zombie incursion, the poor aren't alive in any meaningful sense, yet they live, horribly and numerously animate. 'An idyll's betrayal' implies that such an invasion is both territorial and imaginative. Morrison's description of the cottage garden presents a perverse inversion of the pastoral, its idealised and apolitical rural spaces.

As William Empson notes in *Some Versions of Pastoral* (Chatto & Windus, 1935) 'good proletarian art is usually Covert Pastoral' (p.6). Empson suggests, and Morrison's writing would seem to illustrate this idea, that a narrowly prescriptive definition of "pure" proletarian literature, in which the writer is 'at one with the worker' is impossible because 'the artist never is at one with any public' (p.15). Rather, the pastoral form provides a space for exploring human relations without making pre-emptive assertions about absolute reality. Morrison's work, acutely class-conscious, but sensitised to the nuances of class and cultural identity, uses the rural space to explore a series of uneasy and class-inflected interactions. This uneaseis also interrogated through the Gothic trope of the haunted house. The haunted house is the traditional literary setting for an intersection of the past with the present, between the ghost and the future it cannot participate in except through its traces, through its aftermath, its effects of morbid repetition. A ghost, then, is a useful figure for trauma, for the destabilising *nachträglichkeit* of generational poverty. Morrison signals this through the conceit of 'reversion', which carries connotations of biological regression to an ancestral type, as well as that of legal inheritance.

The idea of the cottage recurs throughout *Green Hauntings*, but it resurfaces most explicitly in the poems from *The Mansion Gardens*, specifically 'The Cottage' (p.43) and 'The House of Sadness Past' (p.53). While both poems use the physical fabric of buildings to explore the emotional architecture of people, they figure the cottage in different ways and with varying degrees of tenderness. In 'The Cottage' Morrison writes of:

> Father's face hair-line cracked
> as the crumbly stone of the cottage walls;
> mother's nerves fragile as
> the shaky glass of the greenhouse grave—

Although the poem offers a gentle conjuration of 'misty summers' Morrison's use of 'hair-line cracked', 'crumbly', 'fragile' and 'shaky' suggest an underlying precarity; invisible tensions which trouble and subtly undermine the poem's seeming peace. In 'The House of Sadness Past' the cottage is described as 'the shrunken shack' and 'that tomb of stone' (p.53); 'our own little crumbled House of Usher' and 'a disgraced sight set back from the road' (p.54). The Poe reference in particular feels telling, evoking the original Gothic tale with its themes of long familial decay and claustrophobic entrapment. Transposing the Gothic grandeur of Poe's story to a small, dilapidated cottage in a Cornish hamlet is a playful subversion of genre conventions and a fine example of Morrison's wry humour, yet it is also suggestive: throughout the story Poe uses 'house' to refer to both the physical structure and to its inhabitants, both of which seem locked in a mutually corrosive and ultimately doomed interaction. Does the house exert a malevolent influence over the Ushers? Or does the malign character of the Ushers bring about changes in the structural stuff of the house? Are we shaped by an inescapable genetic destiny or by our surroundings? This interplay between heredity and environment is something Morrison is engaged with throughout *Green Hauntings*.

In 'Dole & Genealogy' (p.40) the speaker's father is caught

> mapping out ancestral pasts;
> in fogs of nostalgia he'll fumble
> through fictitious fasts.

Traces the line the light casts.

Dimming light. Dull evening glow
displays his only pride:
ancestors' names, row on row,
dead before his time although
he feels they're tutting by his side

In this complex poem Morrison manipulates and collides the multiple meanings of 'dole'—as unemployment benefit, as an individual's lot or destiny, as sorrow or mourning—to interrogate the notion of lineage in both its positive and negative aspects: while an imagined past provides consolation for an unliveable present, it also gives rise to an ideal to which that present is unequal. Nostalgia is a particularly dangerous and seductive form of haunting, and it is Janus-faced: composed of both voluntary memories—where the past is reshaped through an intentional and often distorting effort of recall—and involuntary memories, which superimpose themselves on present place in intense and overwhelming flashes.

The irony at the heart of 'Dole & Genealogy' is that the father's 'fogs' of ancestral nostalgia offer the only salve available to the misery provoked by these involuntary memories. Morrison's evocation of this tortuous bind is poignant and stark:

I find him foraging for childhood,
sleep-lost in stolen pasts
where memory graves are his mind-food
for hope... (p.41)

For the impoverished subject memory is often the only available repository of our history, our only 'mind-food for hope'. It can beguile and consume us, yet it might also anticipate and summon an elsewhere, an imaginary otherwise; provoking dissonance between the actual and the possible, and against the reductive and brutalising logics of late-stage capitalism, nostalgia can erect an alternative dialectical tenderness, can offer the restoration of dignity and alleviation of suffering that society can—or will—not. The ghosts, then, are also those of other pasts, of impossible futures and parallel socialist realities.

In the title poem from *The Mansion Gardens* (p.36), the narrator and his addressee walk through the house and grounds of a stately home, interlopers sanctioned by their clipped coupons, but not entirely welcome or at ease. Snatches of italicised text provide an unsettling commentary on the innocuous and curated 'past' presented to the visitors:

...There's the Lords
and Ladies, and their ancestors
hanging, framed and ashen-faced.

*But why are they ashen-faced*
*when they lives were so well-graced?*

While 'hanging' refers to the portraits on the wall, it carries—coupled with 'ashen-

vi

faced'—an ominous undertone of (potential revolutionary) violence. When Morrison's interlocutors are tempted to see more of the rooms than is permitted:

> Shall we stroll those dust-filled rooms—
> well, just alongside, take a little
> look at them, just peep inside?
> They're cordoned-off with blue rope...
>
> *just like our lives...*

we seem to get a comment on the peripheral position of the poor and working class with respect to the representation of English history as staged through heritage productions such as the stately home. The acidic sotto voce of *just like our lives* creates a moment of arrest inside the smooth, consensus doing of this history. The narrator and addressee operate through the poem like a species of spectral and uncanny glitch, flipping the convention of the haunted manor house, tenanted by ghostly figures of its illustrious past, and themselves becoming ghosts in the machine, potential poltergeists who threaten to cross the rope, walk on the grass, and generally upset the carefully managed order at any given moment. This is the secret power of the proletariat; this is a primary source of the superstitious fear to which they are subject.

While Morrison's poetic interaction with collective history feels profound, he is also an eloquent poet of personal and generational experience. *Shadows Waltz Haltingly* brings us familial haunting in a variety of guises: in 'Guns of Anguish' (p.253), war haunts the traumatised body and mind of 'Harold', a 'grandfather of the distaff side' who erupts erratically into

> [...] lunging gait, agitations, twitching thumbs,
> Sudden surges and beetroot-faced rages
> When he'd punch his own head, was barely held together
> By brown-rimmed glasses

Harold begins life haunted by 'our mother's ghost-uncle', killed in the First World War, after whom he was named, and whose doomed legacy he was able neither to live up to nor yet fully escape: suffering harrowing treatment as a prisoner during the Second World War, hit in the head with rifle butts, forced to 'to stand outside/ All night in the Bavarian snow, naked—naturally'.

While Harold's body is visited by a series of uncontrollable glitches and tics, his trauma resurfacing in often violent symptomatic episodes, he himself has been turned into a kind of supernatural transmitter, in constant 'cross-correspondence' with the spectral figure of his deceased wife. Morrison mobilises the metaphor of staticky radio communication here to superb effect—'During periods of poorer reception when lines/ Crackled and frequencies shifted' (p.254)—to convey the disorienting effects of Post-Traumatic Stress Disorder, and the sense of dislocation in time suffered by those who have experienced trauma. Further, Harold seems be a figure for exploring the way in which traumatic distress is imperfectly communicated between family members and across generations. Yet a traumatic reading of Harold's symptoms is further complicated by the discovery that he suffers from Huntington's disease, and the speaker questions the relationship between biological illness and psychological damage; these two forms of inheritance become the twin motors that drive this selection of poems: the grim hereditary of the Huntington's gene intersecting with other kinds of cultural inheritance and artistic legacy.

*Shadows Waltz Haltingly* is probably Morrison's most personal work; returning to these poems I am reminded of Melanie Klein's theory of haunting as a state of mourning, where the spectral figure is the mechanism by which loss persists and is amplified over time. A ghost, after all, is a strange kind of survival: the lost may return as the angel at our shoulder, offering comfort or protection but liable to disappear if we strain the pact of their magical existence too far, as in Harold's relationship with his beloved Beryl. The lost may return as a kind of phantom limb, irrevocably absent yet still acutely capable of perpetuating feeling; making the living world less vivid and less real, as in the 'wracked-pasts' and surges of involuntary nostalgia that visit the speaker in "Scorched Carpet': *Lepidoptera Chorea*' (p.264). The lost may return in the form of a mask or second skin, something we carry within us or feel destined to become. This last is chillingly present withing 'The Rage (an extended villanelle on Huntington's disease)' (p.256), Morrison's deft riff on Dylan Thomas's 'Do Not Go Gentle into That Good Night'. Here, the form's recursive qualities signal the rapidly cycling thoughts of the speaker, the jerky and repetitive progress of the disease, and the inescapable circuit of genetic destiny. The rage in this piece is manifold, belonging equally to sufferer and to speaker, who rage at the loss of their loved ones and the cruel fate visited upon them; they also rage for the hand they themselves have been dealt; their cards marked before they were born: 'Will my punished ears/ Prepare me more for when I disengage?/ Will augurs fail? Will *I* go out in rage?' (p.257).

The poems in *Shadows Waltz Haltingly* weave multiple levels and registers of haunting together into a layered reckoning with bodily illness, a confrontation with mortality, and a deeply moving work of mourning. Several of these poems deal with the loss by slow degrees of the speaker's mother, attentive to the exhausting practicalities of end-of-life care and to the emotional toll these exact. Morrison combines unflinching and visceral descriptions of the illness:

> A twitching-tissue hair-shirt stitched not to fit,
> But encumber, de-armour the motor, trip up
> Movement; insatiably itch like a bee-sting,
> Skin-crawling urticaria, allergy of the will,
> Inflammation of the soul, the Spirit's Hives,
> A riddle Sphinxing the tongue till it swells up
> Like Oedipus' curious foot, marble-numb...

('Night of the Pegasus', p.262)

with an anguished and tender regard for the aftershocks of suffering that it causes:

> Slumped by her barred bed, a peach crib,
> His fogged ghost struggles to decode her vague signals,
> Cryptic as Tongues; nonplussed, his blunt fingers
> Tapping indecipherable Morse on his scrambling brow

('Regal Margis', p.270)

Later poems are marked by an elegiac tone, and it is this adroit bracketing of loving homage and uncomprehending rage that gives Morrison's work of mourning its particular power.

In *The Mansion Gardens*, poems such as 'The Ring', 'The Coin Foragers' (p.43) and 'Old-Fashioned Sun' (p.44) perform similarly intricate emotional work, using the tokens and talismans of everyday life to bring moments into focus with a startling clarity. Inventively allusive and intertextual, 'The Ring' echoes the poem from Tolkien's Ring-inscription to refract through the lens of boyhood's literary preoccupations, an experience of family shame and almost bottomless defeat:

> No wizard there as our guide—
> Poverty's spell casts all else to one side.
> Father's face grey as Gandalf's gown.
> He always told himself he'd let us down.

> Love is its own darkness, slowly binding.

In 'The Coin Foragers' a family's hunt for small change from between settee cushions and the back of dusty draws is transfigured to a strange game, the 'winner: first to disinfect their treasure.' That these are not sentimental poems is a testament to Morrison's great skill as a writer, always balancing adult insight (and hindsight) with a clear child's-eye view of unfolding events. In the case of 'The Coin Foragers' this blurring of perspectives produces an ambiguous and troubling irony that the reader is unable to easily tease apart. It is this mixture of affection and unblinking realist witness that is at the heart of Morrison's poetic gift. There is no—in the words of Peter Davidson—'benign pastness' (*The Idea of the North*, London: Reaktion Books, 2005) to the recollections of Morrison's youth. Nostalgia does not soften the language of experience to become a tacit apology for the inequalities that produced it. Rather, Morrison's poems are sensitised to the hedged yet intense— intense *because* hedged—life and laughter of the poor.

What is affecting about Morrison's shorter family vignettes is their particularity: poverty is often conjured within the contemporary lyric through a series of tired tropes; it is frequently vague and nebulous. Morrison drills down into the individual moments that make up such an experience, not saturating them with straightened emotionality, but bringing a sharp attention to bear. 'Old-Fashioned Sun' is my favourite of these poems, in which Morrison's eleven-year-old speaker attempts to 'reclaim the past' through his father's books and records. It is a touching account of the portals art and culture can provide to another place and time; in stepping into and sharing his father's past, Morrison makes for himself a temporary refuge in the present. Although the poem ends with the frank admission that

> one can't stay absent from their age
> in the fusty clutter of historic shrine—
> so I parted the curtains, tripped the page
> to the post-imperfect future time,
> where pop lyrics strip the Kipling rhyme.

The poem's tight metrical structure disavows an *absolute* stripping, to acknowledge instead the persistence—and the ghostings—of early artistic influence. While the speaker ultimately forges his own path, a trace will remain of these prior preoccupations, and the unspoken intellectual and familial bond they represent.

Ultimately, what makes *Green Hauntings* such a compelling sampler of Morrison's work is the links it forges between personal, literary, and political history: what haunts Morrison the poet, and what haunts the 'Haunted Ghosts' (p.314) of the poor. In 'The Haunted Ghosts', Morrison's speaker lives the suspended, secluded life of a spectre: he and his father themselves are the uncanny objects of superstition (and judgement) for the more affluent community in which they exist but from whom they are estranged, at one remove. Surprised by a 'trespasser' in their 'rustic squat/ (The limbo we Shades haunted)', the speaker responds to his fumbling apology that he thought nobody lived there with a wry '& nor did we'. Poverty has rendered their existence so precarious as to be all but subliminal. Only in the act of being surprised, held by the hostile or discomfited regard of another, are they offered proof that they existed at all.

Morrison's merging of social and psychic concerns manifests in individual poems—such as the brilliantly Blakean 'The Corn Thresher' (p.37), again from *The Mansion Gardens*, where the agrarian conceit of threshing and binding corn becomes a figure for both social engineering and emotional cohesion—but also across poems and between collections, where Morrison traverses wide formal and thematic territories with approaches ranging from the epigrammatic to the polemic, and treating with equal care and attention both literary luminaries and society's most marginal members.

'Hauntings' is indeed the right word for this Selected Poems: the subtle undermining of social, familial and structural fabric: the termite teeth of poverty, burrowing into the psyche. Morrison creates a unique language to at once expose this process, but also to resist it. Resistance for the poor is itself ghostly, an ever-present prospect on the edge of emerging. That is the threat and the promise this poetry sings with.

In 'June Haunting' (p.319), the final supplemental poem that closes the collection, Morrison returns directly to the idea of ghostliness, to the speaker as a spectral presence who is somehow both pre-dead and revenant once, persisting beyond his allotted time to occupy the half-light of a grey and empty world, one which seems to offer little by way of escape or change. Perhaps, the speaker muses, his entire life has been a dream:

> [...] Or maybe that was all a dream
> & my father's Allan Quatermain mourning his son...?
>
> Isn't haunting just a sublime absentmindedness?
> A soul's shadow-throwing? Astral ruminating...?

Yet the speaker is seen by his father, as the aging father is seen—and held within the poem's space—by the speaker. They materialise each other in a touching act of filial solidarity. I wonder if a ghost—much like Adrienne Rich's definition of a poem—breaks a silence that needs to be broken? A ghost is a rupture to the homogenous structure of experience, an urgent interruption from another place and time, an exhortation to look and be aware, a way we might be shocked into better, more loving attention.

*Green Hauntings* leaves me with the feeling that it might just be possible for however fleeting a moment to accomplish this through language: to make those other others present in the present; to bring into life and into focus the history forged by singular individuals, and that 'lineage of suffering' ('Hell's Full of Early Risers', p.78) we all share in common. This is a book of hungers, spiritual and literal, and a yearning to establish the community and the canon of the outcast and the indigent, of anyone at odds or alone. *Green*, in the singing sap of its linguistic bravura and intellectual energy, Morrison's poetry makes such a canon momentarily visible and marvellously possible.

*Fran Lock, Jul-Aug 2022*

# Preface

Putting together a Selected Poems has been as much about selecting what to leave out as what to include, and a substantial amount of my oeuvre to date is excluded because I wanted—mostly for practical reasons—to only include shorter to medium-length poems (though my idea of the latter is probably what most other poets would think of as long). This means that my pamphlet-length poems from Sixties Press (both published in 2004), my verse play *Picaresque* (2008), and the two book-length poems *Keir Hardie Street* (2010) and *Captive Dragons* (2011), are not represented here (nor is the companion sequence to the latter, *The Shadow Thorns* —although a poem which only appeared on the jacket flap of that book, '*Inky-Dinky-Dink, Fleur de Lis, Fleur de Lis*', is included as a curio).

This is also intended to be the first of two Selected volumes. It charts much of my poetry from my first full volume *The Mansion Gardens* in 2006 up to 2016 which was a kind of watershed for me before I pitched into more openly polemical poetry. It has the prefix *New &* as it includes at the back some *Supplementary Poems*, most of which haven't appeared in any of my previous collections, except for 'Brown Studies' and 'The Lady in the Cabinet' (from *Gum Arabic*, 2020, though both were actually written around 2016). The latter is included due to its imageries linking back to several poems from previous collections which reference Charlotte Perkins Gilman's *The Yellow Wallpaper* as a fictional leitmotif in relation to my late mother's long battle with Huntington's Disease: the 'Tracing the Pattern' section in *A Tapestry of Absent Sitters* (2009), and a large share of the poems in *Shadows Waltz Haltingly* (2015)—as well as the Gilman acrostic 'Charlotte in a Different Light' in *Blaze a Vanishing* (2013). Regarding, too, the latter volume, which was suffixed *and The Tall Skies*, I have decided to split what was essentially a double volume and treat each part as individual volumes from the same year, since *The Tall Skies* is distinctly focused on Swedish culture and in particular its pioneering tradition of proletarian literature (the fruits of several stays in Sweden, including an Arts Council-funded research visit in 2012).

Additionally, I have not, for reasons of length, included the long eponymous poem that concludes *Blaze a Vanishing*—that will have to wait for a Selected Longer Poems, depending on whether there will be appetite for it. The *Supplemental Poems* also include some of my earlier poems written during the 1990s but not included in any of my volumes. 'June Haunting' was a poem composed during the lockdown of 2021 and published on *The Fortnightly Review* and is included due to its thematic and symbolic similarities to many poems in my earliest collections (it is the only poem which trips out of the temporal parameters stipulated on this book cover)— it has occurred to me that ghosts and phantoms, shadows and absences, crop up in much of my poetry but nowhere more so than in the first volume *The Mansion Gardens*. 'The Haunted Ghosts' dates back to around 2004 and previously appeared only in the anthology *Orphans of Albion* (2005). All these spectral poems came to inspire the concept of the title *Green Hauntings*: past poems haunting the present, and perhaps the future, like a gathering of typographical ghosts. The title also taps into Hauntology, as originally defined by Jacques Derrida (*Spectres of Marx*, 1993) and further explored in the works of the late Mark Fisher: as with most socialist writing my poetry is permeated by a melancholy, even morbid—or ghostly—nostalgia or mournfulness in part for things or states that never were, but which could have been, and which were anticipated, and which may yet come. Another way to view it is that my poetry is largely taken up by absences—a kind of haunted poetry (and what else are poets really but life haunters...?). This has been picked up on before: K.M. Newmann of the Irish Summer Palace Press remarked on the 'strangely haunting' quality of some of my early poems, while Geoffrey Heptonstall commented of one of my volumes under review, *Shadows Waltz Haltingly*: 'The poetry in this volume is haunted'. The *Green* of the title alludes to both the fact that much of this work comes from the pen of a younger self, while also alluding to my rural upbringing and the effect that the beautiful though often bleak, and mysterious, Cornish countryside had on my development as a poet. One working title for this book was *Haunted Pastoral*.

There are two main reasons why I decided to publish this volume under my Caparison imprint rather than approach any of my former publishers to take it on. Firstly, I wanted complete creative control, not only for the selection of poems, but editorially (so that I have been free to tighten up many of the poems, some extensively), and also in terms of overseeing the production, which seeps into the second main reason: I wanted complete autonomy on the design of the book, its 'look', which I didn't want to have to fit into the template of other imprints, plus I also felt it was a fitting time to branch into hardback. So this is a bespoke production. Being a seasoned book designer and typesetter it just seemed to make sense for this particular project to produce it myself. Much as being published by other imprints is confidence-boosting, there is nonetheless something deeply satisfying and immensely empowering about producing one's own book as a physical as well as spiritual object. (Indeed, it takes me back to the very beginning when, courtesy of some antediluvian apparatus in a local community centre, I hand-pressed my first chapbook of poetry—the sense of craftsmanlike achievement unlike anything I've experienced since). But limited funds inevitably necessitate that this is a very limited edition.

It is hoped this volume serves the purpose of showing my development from an earlier pastoral or 'Covert Pastoral' (see Empson)—even gothic—lyricism through to a more openly political, *impasto* poetry. Through the years, the lines have lengthened, the language grown more figurative—the metaphors ripened. My quondam publisher and editor, Simon Jenner, instilled in me the paramountcy of metaphor, that poetry depends on a heightened engagement with language and image, and any lapses into prose risk tipping it into verse, a very different medium where prosodic form often compromises poetic content—particular pitfall for rhyming poets (and at that time I tended to be one of those). That pitfall was at least temporarily nipped with the ruthless swipe of Simon's editing pencil as he struck out all unnecessary prepositions and conjunctions from my poems. The result of this Modernistic pruning is most evident in the more pared down poems of my first two volumes, though even those compositions stop short of the excessive sculpting which can end up reducing poetry to the Delphic—to presume the poetical must *ipso facto* be elliptical is a common pitfall of the opposite approach to 'verse'.

As to the spirit of my poetry, running through it all is a seam of something akin to New Sincerity: a tonal counterpoint to postmodernism. Simon would call this 'Naïf', his term for a variety of self-taught styles falling somewhere on the poetry spectrum between modernist and postmodernist. An implied lack of sophistication, however, places too much emphasis on the cerebral, when the composition of poetry is as much an expression of feeling as it is of thinking. Famous Naïf poet Stevie Smith had to have a certain amount of sophistication to compose unsophisticated poetry which nonetheless expressed profound thought. And many poets would probably agree it is far easier to compose 'sophisticated' poetry of the Eliotic kind than it is to produce the sublime lullabies of Blake's *Songs of Innocence*. One might have a sophisticated mind but an unsophisticated soul. In any case, for any apparent lack of sophistication to some of my early poetry, I have perhaps ended up overcompensating to the point that some of my later work has been criticised for its density and abstruseness. Certainly it has become, for better or worse, more erudite and didactic (common peccadilloes of the autodidact), though a quixotic aspect remains steadfast throughout. Hopefully there are periods on my poetic journey when I've struck the right balance. Perhaps all poetry is a pursuit of serendipities. Emotionalism, Expressionism, New Confessionalism, Naïfety, New Sincerity—any of these terms might describe aspects to the type of poetry I have attempted for the past three decades. What all my work certainly has done is go against the grain of what is fashionable and 'mainstream'—though this has mainly been down to creative instinct rather than conscious agenda.

Influences can no doubt be detected in the poems of each period—they include, in rough chronology of encounter: Blake (*Songs of Innocence and Experience*), Keats ('Ode to Melancholy' was the first poem to really give me the poetry bug), Shelley ('To A Skylark'), Coleridge, Wordsworth, Milton, Andrew Marvell, Byron, Emily Brontë, Tennyson ('The Lotos-eaters', 'The Kraken'), Thomas Hardy, W.B. Yeats ('The Song of Wandering Aengus'), D.H. Lawrence, Wilfred Owen ('Anthem for Doomed Youth'), Siegfried Sassoon, Gerard Manley Hopkins, John Clare, Horace, Pope, Walt Whitman, Robert Frost ('The Road Less Travelled'), W.H. Davies ('Leisure'), T.S. Eliot ('Prufrock'; *The Waste Land*; *Four Quartets*), Dylan Thomas (*Under Milk Wood*), Emily Dickinson, Stevie Smith ('Not Waving But Drowning', 'Do Take Muriel Out'), John Betjeman (almost entirely for his untypical poem 'N.W.5 & N.6'), W.H. Auden ('In Memory of W.B. Yeats'), Philip Larkin ('Aubade'), Sylvia Plath, Donald Ward, Arthur Rimbaud, Thomas Gray ('Elegy in a Country Churchyard'), Christina Rossetti ('Remember'), Isaac Rosenberg, George Barker, Louis MacNeice, Stephen Spender, John Davidson ('Thirty Bob A Week'—my favourite poem, a benchmark for me), Harold Monro (*The Silent Pool*), Walter de la Mare, Keith Douglas, Alun Lewis (*Raiders' Dawn*; *Ha! Ha! Among the Trumpets*), Sidney Keyes, Drummond Allison, Clifford Dyment, Bernard Spencer, Robert Lowell (*Life Studies*), John Berryman (*The Dream Songs*), Roy Campbell, Tony Harrison, Martin Bell, Peter Redgrove, Thomas Blackburn, Kathleen Raine, David Gascoyne, John Cornford, Christopher Caudwell, Ted Hughes, H.D., Wallace Stevens ('The Emperor of Ice-Cream'), Ezra Pound (*Hugh Selwyn Mauberley*), David Jones, Ivor Gurney, Harry Martinson (*Aniara*), ee cummings, Hart Crane (*The Bridge*), Anne Sexton (*The Awful Rowing Toward God*)... I'd whittle this list down to a handful whose work has had the most conscious influence on my own: Blake, Keats, Shelley,

Davidson, Monro, Eliot, Gurney, Auden, D. Thomas, A. Lewis, Larkin, Plath.

In terms of music: classical and orchestral is to my mind most closely related to poetry, though not a medium in which I pretend to be any sort of expert, nor even habitual listener. However, I would have to cite the soundscapes and sonic atmospherics of the following composers as having had significant influence on my poetry: Gustav Holst ('Jupiter' from *The Planets* in particular, *Somerset Rhapsody*), Ralph Vaughan Williams (*English Folk Song Suite*), Malcolm Arnold (*Symphony 1 & 5*, film music), Jerome Moross (*The Last Judgement, The Big Country, The Valley of Gwangi*), George Gershwin (*Rhapsody In Blue*), Claude Debussy (*Arabesques*), Erik Satie (*Gymnopédies*), William Walton, Manuel de Falla ('El Amor Brujo'), Stravinsky (*The Rite of Spring*), Rodney Bennett, Frederick Delius, Percy Grainger, Vladimir Cosma, Wilfred Josephs, John Barry, Béla Bartók.

In my teenage years, before I'd discovered poetry of the strictly literary kind, I'd been inspired by the lyrics of some popular songwriters, particularly Paul Weller (whose Jam B-side 'Tales from the Riverbank' struck a particular chord growing up in the countryside), John Lennon and Paul McCartney (The Beatles), Andy Partridge and Colin Moulding (XTC), Sting (The Police), Matt Johnson (The The), Kate Bush, Rick Wright and Roger Waters (Pink Floyd), Mark Hollis (Talk Talk), Roland Orzabal (Tears For Fears), P.D. Heaton (The Housemartins), Ian Dury. Regarding Weller again, it had been, ironically, on the back of The Jam's 1980 *Sound Affects* LP that I'd been first introduced to the immortal lines from Percy Bysshe Shelley's *The Mask of Anarchy* ('Rise like lions after slumber/ In unvanquishable number' etc.), a poem which would have considerable influence on my political poetry.

But it has been as much the writings of novelists, scholars, playwrights and philosophers that's influenced much of my poetry as it has the work of other poets —again, in rough chronology of encounter: H. Rider Haggard (*Allan Quatermain*), Rudyard Kipling, J.R.R. Tolkien (mostly for the mystique of his striking Germanic name and the strange worlds it signatured), Emily Brontë (*Wuthering Heights* first inspired me to write), Robert Louis Stevenson, George Eliot, Thomas Hardy (*Jude the Obscure*), Karl Marx (*The Communist Manifesto*), Max Weber (*The Protestant Work Ethic and the Spirit of Capitalism*), Émile Durkheim (*Suicide*), George Orwell (*Keep the Aspidistra Flying*; *Homage to Catalonia*), David Nobbs (*Reginald Perrin*), Lewis Carroll, James Joyce (*Ulysses*), Eugene O'Neill (*Long Day's Journey Into Night*; *The Iceman Cometh*), D.H. Lawrence (*Sons and Lovers*), John Osborne (*Look Back In Anger*), Edgar Allen Poe, H.G. Wells, Arthur Conan Doyle, Joseph Conrad (*Lord Jim*; *Nostromo*), Graham Greene (*The Heart of the Matter*), Samuel Beckett (*Waiting for Godot*), Shakespeare (*The Tempest*; *Richard II*), Charlotte Perkins Gilman (*The Yellow Wallpaper*), Henry James (*The Turn of the Screw*; *Wings of the Dove*), Angela Carter, Colin Wilson (*The Outsider*; *Ritual in the Dark*; *Brandy of the Damned*), Robert Tressell (*The Ragged Trousered Philanthropists*), Aldous Huxley (*Antic Hay*; *After Many A Summer*; *Brave New World*), Jean Rhys (*Wide Sargasso Sea*; *Good Morning Midnight*), John Wyndham, Susan Hill (*The Woman In Black*), George Gissing (*New Grub Street*), Daphne Du Maurier (*My Cousin Rachel*; *The Infernal World of Branwell Brontë*), Christopher Hill (*The World Turned Upside Down*), J.B. Priestley (*An Inspector Calls*; *The Edwardians*; *Angel Pavement*), R.D. Laing (*The Politics of Experience and the Bird of Paradise*; *Knots*), Al Alvarez

(*The Savage God*), Christopher Caudwell (*Illusion and Reality*; *Studies in a Dying Culture*), Michael Young (*The Rise of the Meritocracy*), Alasdair MacIntyre (*Marxism and Christianity*), Wal Hannington (*The Problem of the Distressed Areas*), David W. Petegorsky (*Left-Wing Democracy in the English Civil War*), Charles Rycfort (*Anxiety and Neurosis*), George Thomson (*Marxism and Poetry*), J.H. Plumb (*The Death of the Past*), Roland Camberton, Christopher Fry, Søren Kierkegaard (*The Concept of Anxiety*), Swedenborg, Annie Besant & C.W. Leadbetter (*Thought-Forms*), Bertrand Russell (*A History of Western Philosophy*), William Empson (*Some Versions of Pastoral*; *Seven Types of Ambiguity*), Edmund Wilson (*To the Finland Station*), Peter Shaffer (*The Royal Hunt of the Sun*; *Equus*), Caryl Churchill (*Light Shining in Buckinghamshire*), Erich Fromm (*The Sane Society*), Christopher Isherwood (*Prater Violet*), Robert Burton (*The Anatomy of Melancholy*), Cyril Connolly (*Enemies of Promise*), Rene & Jean Dubos (*The White Plague*), Albert Camus (*The Myth of Sisyphus*), Henry Mayhew (*Mayhew's Characters*), David Lockwood (*The Blackcoated Worker*), Richard Hoggart (*The Uses of Literacy*), Paul Roazen (*Brother Animal*), Harold Bloom (*The Anxiety of Influence*), Jack London (*Martin Eden*).

Some figures from fiction have become personified leitmotifs in my poetry, in some cases unconscious shadow archetypes of aspects to my personality—in particular, Emily Brontë's Heathcliff and his doomed son Linton, Hardy's Jude and his disturbed son 'Little Father Time', Dostoyevsky's Raskólnikov, Orwell's Gordon Comstock, Graham Greene's Henry Scobie, Conrad's Martin Decoud and 'Lord' Jim, Tressell's Frank Owen, Gissing's Edwin Reardon, London's Martin Eden. And real life figures who have held a fascination and affinity: John Keats, Vincent van Gogh, John Davidson, Vaslav Nijinsky, Kierkegaard, Gerrard Winstanley, John Lilburne, Robert Burton, Richard Burton (actor), Viktor Tausk, Oskar Werner, Tony Hancock.

Art has played its part too—no artist moreso than van Gogh for his sheer emotional intensity. Also: Manet, Millais, Holman Hunt, Henry Wallis, Walter Sickert, Matisse, Picasso, Munch, L.S. Lowry, Goya, Rembrandt, John Tenniel. The thick textural application of paint, *impasto*, as practised by van Gogh, and Sickert, is a term I've sometimes applied to my poetic technique of layered language.

It just remains for me to thank all those poets, writers, editors, publishers, critics, and other artists, including actors, who have helped me significantly in my poetic development, supported or encouraged my work, constructively criticised or critically praised it, or played parts in its public presentation: John Agard, Karunesh Kumar Agarwal, Jim Aitken, Robert Allwood, Sebastian Barker, Sarah Baxter, Brian Beamish, Larry Beckett, David Betteridge, Linda Black, Martin Blyth, Laura Boni, Denis Boyles, Jan Bradley, Leon Brown, Paula Brown, Alan Britt, J. Brookes, Norman Buller, Nick Burbridge, Jeanetta Calhoun Mish, Riccardo Capoferro, Pedro Carvalal, Debjani Chatterjee, Gillian Clarke, Cliff Cocker, Bernadette Cremin, Andy Croft, Alessandro Cusimano, Will Daunt, Dominique De-Light, Alan Dent, Matt Duggan, Alan Dunnett, R.G. Foster, James Fountain, Naomi Foyle, Greg Freeman, Jan Goodey, Wolfgang Görtschacher, Dennis Greig, Eileen Gunn, Peter Guttridge, Martyn Halsall, Colin Hambrook, Mary Hampton, Sophie Hannah, Graham Hardie, Bruce Harris, Geoffrey Heptonstall, Graham High, Martin Holroyd, Peter Holt, John Horder, Michael Horovitz, David Hunter, Michael Jayston, Mike Jenkins, Simon Jenner, Norman Jope, Tom Kelly, David Kessel, Prakash Kona, Katy Lassetter,

Fran Lock, Alexis Lykiard, Chris McCabe, Niall McDevitt, Maureen McKarkiel, Nick McMaster, Paul MacDonald, Munayem Mayenin, Christopher Moncrieff, Lindsey Morgan, Pete Morgan, Andrew Morrison, James Morrison, Julia Morrison, Paul Murphy, K.M. Newmann, Robert Nye, Steven O'Brien, John O'Donoghue, Thomas Orzág-Land, William Oxley, Matilda Persson, Mario Petrucci, David Pollard, Jody Porter, John Prebble, Alan Price, Mike Quille, Henry Ramadori, Peter Raynard, Jeremy Reed, Sally Richards, Kate Rigby, Peter Riley, Michael Rosen, Anne Rouse, Dave Russell, Phil Ruthen, Heathcote Ruthven, Vanessa Sadri, Clare Saponia, Kevin Saving, David Savoury, Michael Schmidt, Rachel Searle, Barry Smith, Sam Smith, Stephanie Smith-Browne, Steve Spence, Peter Street, Pauline Suett-Barbieri, David Swann, Barry Tebb, Michael W. Thomas, Frances Thompson, N.S. Thompson, Xelís de Toro, Xochitl Tuck, Ruth Valentine, John Welch, Julie Whitby, Brenda Williams, Gwilym Williams, Heathcote Williams, Colin Wilson, Ken Worpole, Nick Wroe, Dan Wyke, Wendy Young.

Finally, I would like to thank my late mother, Helen, who I think more than anyone else in my earlier life encouraged me to never give up on my poetry in spite of all the obstacles—she, above all, believed in me, even before I believed in myself.

*A.M., 2022*

# Green
# Hauntings

New &
Selected Poems
Volume One
2006-2016

# Alan
# Morrison

from

*THE MANSION GARDENS*

(2006)

## THE WATER SHALLOWS

As I was paddling in the water shallows,
the ripples turned to waves,
the paddling to a wade.

While I tried to shallow my tumbling mind,
the thoughts that swam in the water shallows
were chased as fish by the shadows of sparrows

## DANCE OF THE DRAGONFLIES

Around the still lake the dragonflies danced
In a flurry of cobalt & green—
They buzzed their glass wings & blindly chanced
Skimming the water-sheen.

One hit the water then hurtled & skidded,
Seemingly out of control—
A pilot was drowned where the lily pads lidded
The mantle which merged with the shoal.

The pilot's son cried as he tried to forget
But leapt up with a new sense of hope
As he spotted a dragonfly, wings stuck with wet,
Drag itself up the bank's sandy slope.

# THE HOUSE ON THE RISE OF REVERSION

Regarding the house on the rise,
Shabby, ramshackle, severe,
Of crabby stone & rustic gate,
Subjective views judge here.

Eyes entirely detached survey
A shambling garden with scorn—
Instead of empathising they
Petition us to cut the lawn.

Greeted by a worn, cracked face
A visitor digs up a dearth
Of signatures—Dad's trampled eyes
Merge with the judgemental earth.

Petition delivered, the visitor leaves.
An anxious face of thwarted youth
Twitches through reclusive curtains,
Haunting a window's hidden truth.

Inside: a tea-dripped radiator;
Kipling's *If* on a blanched wall fades
In a crack of sunlight through a broken pane:
Hide for spying listing spades.

Outside: a shoddy wire enclosure
Mangy guards limply patrol,
Possessive of a callous house—
Snouts in empty tins, they troll.

Forsythia's golden petals glow
Defiant, alone; the colour; the hope;
The island of life in a rough sea of weeds
Willing the rubble-bed garden to cope.

Here a sham-lawn's been flung like a sheet
Over a bomb-shelter's furniture by
An idyll's betrayal to spaded defeat
For we who live in the house on the rise.

# IN SEARCH OF THE HAGGARD GHOST

It flitted down the lane
past children's voices raised in play,
tracing its steps long ago
pressed into the mud,
trodden on a thousand times since.

The brief trek ended.

Returning up the lane, rain
in drips, hastened to penitent patters,
pelted on the muddy puddles
then intensified, sleeting—
bounced off clenched fists of grass,
pummelled flowers at the sides.

Standing silently, sullenly,
as the children ran out laughing
through a pasture gate, it stood there,
still and quiet, & they didn't see it.

A shabby, bedraggled, sopping ghost
orbited by a bulging black cloud
sagging in readiness to burst.

# NOSTALGIA

Even in those golden days
Life always left us wanting more—
Why we loathe ourselves today
Is why we loved ourselves before.

## THE MANSION GARDENS

Shall we stroll those mansion gardens,
baize on baize of velvet grass
so well-kept & un-walked-upon?
Come on, love, we've cut the coupons,
let's see those shouting flowers
round grounds of ivy towers.

Shall we walk those mansion cloisters
verged with portraits? There's the Lords
and Ladies, & their ancestors
hanging, framed & ashen-faced.

*But why are they ashen-faced,*
*when their lives were so well graced?*

Shall we stroll those dust-still rooms—
well, just alongside, take a little
look at them, just peep inside?
They're cordoned-off with blue rope...

*just like our lives...*

oh, we'll cope.

Shall we pace those mansion chambers
ringed by pasty-platted rope...

*easily unhooked & disobeyed...*

No—that would be to abandon
our law-abiding principles...

*what's wrong is always irresistible...*

Shall we recall those mansion gardens,
baize on baize of velvet grass
so well-kept & un-walked-upon?

*I'm not envious: simply a dreamer:*
*those lawns seemed so much greener...*

# THE CORN THRESHER

**1**

I gather the corn-strands from the field,
bind them together to force them to yield.
My act is assertion of mastery
over my nature—whatever that be.

**2**

A Confucian in my down-cast stare,
all green without spoil seems barren & bare
to my tampering eyes & grappling hands
that wrestle with Nature till She understands.

**3**

Onto my threshing-floor I step
binding tighter my thoughts like old men regrets—
or confessing Catholics the sums of sins
their intermediary's stale ear wins.

**4**

Then I wield my flail for the threshing
like the Father incense for blessing
the echoing house of his God on high,
to fumigate & purify.

**5**

When the job's almost done I grip
the bound corn tight in my fingertips
and perform the threshing manually—
with my chore I achieve true harmony.

**6**

My eyes, full of purpose as bales of hay,
roll about with an impulse like clouds during day,
as the grains of corn sheaves spill out free
like beads from a broken rosary.

**7**

I am a thresher of the corn
working the field in the chilly dawn,
I bind my thoughts tight in Belief
and thrash out all the grains of grief.

8

With every thresh of the flail I delve
into the Truth gripped in the helve;
my binding my thoughts is my will to believe
I shall resurrect like corn from its sheave.

## CHASING SHADOWS

Tipsy with nostalgia we
miss those times of Time's slower pass
when we were children trying to chase
our shadows on the grass.

## THE CHINA KINGFISHER

Dubbed useless for most of his days,
He saw himself in a similar light.
Counted hours in the window's haze;
Inert; a bird without flight.

Time tapered by, lost to a chair,
The nest from which he's seldom stirred;
From a window-ledge he flies the air
In an ornament shaped as a bird.

Imagines the wings that spirit away
Wishes set free from the mind of the wisher;
Pictures a lake on a still summer's day,
& flitting about it, a China Kingfisher.

## *MAKE WAY!*

*Make Way!* their banners gallop
In the choppy Cornish wind;
'*He Lives! He Lives!*' crashes on cramped
Coverack, Lilliput-twinned.

On the craggy harbour-side
They rejoice their Saviour's Risen!
& yet He's still invisible,
While their clammed evangelism

Is vivid & immovable
As Coverack shacks' limpet-cling
To granite rocks; or barnacles
On the moored hull of *Tamarind.*

Rustling tambourines displace
The shingle's cymbal hissing—
No footprints to be made out on
The sand because the tide is in.

In Chapel they all clap their hands,
Sing with palms splayed up in prayer
Spun by a cardigan-man on guitar
Strumming in a thumping chair.

In among the rocking pews
The Not-Yet-Born-Again's found out;
Someone nudges me: '*Come on,
Clap!*'—the spell to cast off doubt?

Into the street they pour their peal
Pounding on my doubting brow—
Bashing tambourines they dash
My faith like fish-brains on a bow.

# A HAMPER FROM LANDRAKE

In the creel of a slate-skied Cornish winter
we caught a scraping sound outside;
a huge mass landing, heavy as the weight
my father prayed would be lifted from
his jobless shoulders scraped & bowed—

cold wind shot through the hallway, lo!
we beheld a hamper packed with tins
& vegetables—no Christians,
just a scribbled note blown on the lino
saying *from the Parish*—my father scowled:
now he was obliged to let them Save him.

# DOLE & GENEALOGY

1
The fireplace littered with Carlsberg cans
he sits, disconsolate.
Concentration fills his hands:
his hobby gropes to compensate
for his neglected state.

From chair to chair he'll stumble
mapping out ancestral pasts;
in fogs of nostalgia he'll fumble
through fictitious fasts.
Traces the line the light casts.

Dimming light. Dull evening glow
displays his only pride:
ancestors' names, row on row,
dead before his time although
he feels they're tutting by his side

judging him. Tries to appease
their disappointment in him
by tracing ad infinitum
far into his fantasies,
fizzing cans, full ashtrays.

2

I find him foraging for childhood,
sleep-lost in stolen pasts
where memory graves are his mind-food
for hope; stale bread that lasts
till shattered like plaster-casts.

What use is love? Over us looms
a quiet Catholic God, aloof
from our penniless misfortunes,
old invisible heirlooms
flogged long ago to keep this roof
of poverty's brooding proof.

Can I convince my maltreated father
God is on our side
when our cramped prayers have scrimped an after
of comfortless dark?  Time & tide
long passed on the other side.

In creeps a torrid afternoon
of brief self-pitying;
more motherless sobs fill the room,
nothing can lift the casting of gloom
over the sound of a grown man crying.

3

I pity the prowess with which he heaps
more shame upon himself
as he lumbers his dad's damp-blotched books
onto the listing shelf—
sad tributes to a faded wealth.

More than any other member
of his leafless family tree
he personifies the motto
*Forgetful Of One's Own Interests*
warped through verdigris.

*'I've done my duty, I'd done my best'*
he mutters to a mirror
repeating this & all the rest
that still he is no winner
but definitely a sinner—
always self-accuser, never self-forgiver.


4
He slips to sleep & dreams of more
sleep; cuts adrift from the shore
of consciousness.          The more he copes
the more he reeks of cigarette smoke
that fogs the fact his nerves are broke—

& what chance did his nerves have
when at the age of three his skin
was blistered to the third degree?
Sixty years on his hands aren't ready
to keep their cigarette fingers steady.

I see his eyes are blurring again
back to blood-shot bleariness,
tired whites slowly yellowing—
I see him trace the family name
back to the safety of the past—
but how long can nostalgia last?

...long as lamplight puddles pages
of photocopied parish records
he trains his straining sights towards—
as the light begins to fail
his mind will slowly gather sail
& trace the print like mental Braille.

In the dark, he'll bite his nails.

## THE RING

No wizard there as our guide—
Poverty's spell casts all else to one side.
Father's face grey as Gandalf's gown.
He always told himself he'd let us down.

Love is its own darkness, slowly binding.

One day my mother had to pawn her ring,
But kept it secret till we'd finished eating;
Her finger as it was before their wedding.

## THE COIN FORAGERS

In darkling days of testing means
we found distraction in playing games;
one comprised four players,
rules always the same:
each foraged for mouldy copper tokens
hidden in the scrimping room,
collecting as many as they could find.

Some stuffed in the glooms & crumbs
of the settee's cushions; some
stashed in the clutter of the kitchen dresser.
The winner: first to disinfect their treasure.

## OLD-FASHIONED SUN

Eleven years old, I tried to reclaim
the past, inspired by cottage-gloom—
the countryside is always the same
no matter what time: I furnished my room
with my dad's dog-eared books caked in damp-stain
from *The Black Arrow* to *Allan Quatermain.*

On brumal mornings as a pale sun
lit thin curtains that filtered its rays,
I'd stick Holst's scratchy *Jupiter* on
summoning my father's schoolboy days—
Somerset, Nineteen Fifty-One,
in the ghostly warmth of an old-fashioned sun.

But there's a book-end to the shelf of time:
one can't stay absent from their age
in the fusty clutter of historic shrine—
so I parted the curtains, tripped the page
to the post-imperfect future time,
where pop lyrics strip the Kipling rhyme.

## FORGIVE-ME-NOT

Let go. Forgive. Forget the bitterness
That buttresses when love is dead:
Most of what's said isn't meant;
Most of what's meant isn't said.

## THE COTTAGE

For all the breath-smoked winter nights
we shared some misty summers
drifting off to light tunes' fall
like balsam on the garden
from my brother's bedroom window
jammed with grandma's *Iliad*;
sunbathed with mongrels at our feet;
plucked blushed apples from the tree beside
the cement-filled well, where we planted
hope for rescue from this rustic lull
false as our restless wishes were,
still yet to be weeded.

Father's face hair-line cracked
as the crumbly stone of the cottage walls;
mother's nerves fragile as
the shaky glass of the greenhouse grave—
I'm sure she's shrunken in this shade
all these faded years;
given the choice she wouldn't leave
this place for ties still tested like
the trembling washing-line.

This is where we first dug-up doubt
fossilized in the outhouse stone
like stories of our mythical home;
where we first came to believe
in not believing, with the countryside,
that simply is. How could we leave...

## INFATUATION: THE FIRST

Infatuation? It didn't last
Beyond rosy, rough-&-tumble days,
Gooseberry sweet, no sour aftertaste.
Time didn't intimidate the infant; time was sky.
The love, the bond that tore our hearts
Strained too far, sighed out to die.

*Time's the face you love*
*but are tired of looking at.*

Bitterness of callow apples, raw,
Windfall-bitten, sour out the tongue
With immature spices to subtle in
Its un-acquired taste—sap squandered on
Those who sample before ripe; spat out;
Wiped clean by sleeves it bruises on.

*Time's a face you love*
*but tire of looking at.*

Time takes long to trickle on; to traipse.
Rich spit of first kisses infiltrates the rest.
He: *life's not long enough for love.*
She: *love purses lips for death*;
Familiarity & death: the same.
We tied knots in our stubborn bond; our breath.

*Time's a face you love*
*but are tired of looking at.*

Feelings home in unhealed sores;
In lichened ruins bonds re-build
On slippery foundations—love clings on;
No shutting off till we're told—mistakes,
Only palpable once trampled past,
Form the pattern of the human face.

*Time's the face you love*
*but tire of looking at.*

## MY LIFE IN THE SHADE

Since I was sunburnt as a boy I learnt to love the shade,
Spared me from the heat where the other children played—
But I was tugged out in the sun & punished by its light
Turning from a shadow to someone in my own right,
& found that I'd preferred it when I'd felt invisible.
Sometimes I wonder whether I was ever here at all.

I've always loved so easily & pitied anyone
Who showed signs of remorse for the wrongs that they had done.
I've struggled & I've buckled under every thought I've had
As if the mere imagining of bad events was bad;
Pursued by Furies of my own phantasmagorical school.
*Sometimes I wonder whether I was ever here at all.*

The more I've lived I've lost myself & drifted far away
From the busy worlds of others & the places where they play.
As if I died some time ago & turned into a ghost
Haunting all the places that I used to love the most,
I've lingered like a shadow where my own shadow should fall.
*Sometimes I wonder whether I was ever here at all.*

I came to fear feelings of love for how they made me see
The image of myself through the eyes of those who loved me,
Until I was obsessed with being gone in all but mind
Sharing in the mourning with my loved ones left behind.
But I'm still here; still in the shade; trembling in its thrall.
*Sometimes I wonder whether I was ever here at all.*

## FEW NEVER ENVY

All I have: this shabby room
furnished grandma-style:
carpet muddy umber,
thin beige curtains pile
like luminous mosquito nets
over the draughty window-pane.
A lacquered table's centre-piece
where I eat cold meals, scrimp an aim

inkling in a typewriter.
Plastic clatter of tone-deaf keys
scores each curtained, fiction-night:
a blind mind tinkling ivories.
Breaks spent on a spineless bed;
fingers brush the woodchip Braille,
step across the blue-tack path,
trip to creak of banister-rail.

I stare up at a blanched van Gogh
by the toothpaste-spattered sink;
the ticking of the crippled clock
decides it isn't time to think;
I rise to wash: chalky water
chokes out to the rusty squeak
of the stiffer tap; over my shoulder
a back-to-front 'Thirty Bob A Week'

reflects in the mirror that traps me.
Smoking soothes as doubts unroll.
My only other luxuries: tea
& sleeping pills when I get my dole
of hardship maintenance that feeds
my lapsed Protestant shame
(though I was born a Catholic
I'm English all the same).

Few never envy others' lives
with their ambitions in arrears;
only thoughts that telescope
help one cope—focused years
blur the edges of fogged progress.
Lungs fangled for spearmint fags
purse their pockets. Abstracts heap
like half-p's in the money bags.


## DESTINY

She's push-chaired in on every shift
by a mother who sighs with coffee sips
cauterising suicide no doubt
or some other similar way out:
a bit more brown, another score
might push things on a little more.

Destiny sits there taking it in
with rag-doll's eyes, still, unblinking;
eyes no child should see with; no shine;
a grubby-faced Little Mother Time,
her mother's troubles sitting
on her marble brow's dark knitting.

I search for some sign in her eyes
of something like infant surprise
but the sharps of her mind are cluttered up
with images of her mother jacking up
in nightly attempts to numb the pain
coursing through syringe-thin vein.

Does Destiny deserve her name?

## TALES FROM THE EMPTY LARDER

I can't stand scant catechisms
of tremors in an empty stomach;
the stench of hunger-scented breath
where a full belly's the only tonic;
the famished itch in-between the teeth
where only food can feed relief.

The stain won't shift: mean-spirited strife
spoilt my appetite for living well;
splintered my spittle with bitterness;
chipped my shoulder with its scrimping chisel—
I taste it still in weak stewed blends;
in sickly stings of singed dog-ends.

I suppose the harsh lessons I scribed
inspired in me a need to dream,
to believe in insubstantial truths,
for you need a God when you can't keep clean
& hope, when your faith overspills,
socialism will cure most ills.

But it's often the morbid human way
to come to love what you should despise
just as, in depression, sadness comforts
with blessings of tears in tea-strained eyes;
so I feel perverse nostalgia
for those hours of hunger-fed neuralgia.

I've said to my brother, it's strange to think
amidst the dirt we found ideals,
a sense of justice in second-hand clothes
& transubstantiated packet meals—
the dark of a larder's empty shelves:
where we first found ourselves.

## THE FALSE CONFESSION

English Martyrs Primary School
Taught us hymns, Hail Marys, guilt;
On asphalt playgrounds, chalked pitches,
We played out innocence to the hilt.

One lunchtime, strayed to the other school
For handicapped children, sat in class—
As I froze over a moment's thought
My friends face-aped them through the glass.

Walnut-faced Miss Wall called us
Into her plimsoll-smelling office;
Pitting us against each other
x2 chances to confess.

Four denials later, our only escape
From standing shame in assembly
Was for me to say *Yes* on their behalf
(A revelation to me).

Now I stood, the guilty of the three,
Accused of betrayal by the other two
By confessing to what I didn't do—
But who did I betray? Them or me?

## THE FADE

Life's a string of mistakes—
the best ones, those
we don't know we've made.

Love's a dying high—
a favourite song
going into the fade.

## DEATH'S BREATHTAKING VIEW
*After Larkin's 'Aubade'*

We clutch the threads that stitch our seamless lives
Immersed in glass routines like black shark eyes;
A sentence hanging over all our heads;
The grimace of a clock face offering
No other explanation but its ticking;
A faceless wall at the foot of our beds.

All we can be sure of is powerless doubt
& the door we came in will invite us out
To nonsensical oblivion or bliss;
Or a frozen limbo while turning the bend.
So we burn the candle at both ends.
In the meantime all we scrimp is this:

Faith in the soul, a light that leads us on
Through the dark to terrifying perfection—
Anything but nothing, to be lost in the night,
The pitch-white mist of a fog-bound sea,
The unthinkable smallness of eternity—
Anything but the turning off of lights.

Some seek solutions in the superstitious;
Gregarious others simply drink like fish
Clinking glasses they can't see through—
Salvation: saliva of the garrulous.
Perhaps the only sanity is madness
When comprehending death's breathtaking view.

Some take the plunge, pre-empt the sea;
In spite of being contradictory,
Cancel dark with dark. Obviate
The inevitable? Impossible; we know
All we've come to love one day has to go—
But what could be more morbid than to wait

Until the darkness swallows us? & yet
No sense in stubbing out lit cigarettes;
Best to leave just ashes for the ashtray;
To try & come to terms long in advance;
Stretch perception of deceptive distance;
Put off the problem for an umpteenth day.

# THE HOUSE OF SADNESS PAST

After this fruitless time, the strife
of fifteen garbled cottage winters
dimmed in Trematon, I didn't
bid goodbye to the shrunken shack
bribed us to sojourn for time
unmarked by ageless slate West sky.

Chance missed to lay a lifetime
ghost to rest; leave behind
a difficult friend I fell out with
but stayed close to the bitter end;
a bond built on month-hours' foundations.

Too late to improvise goodbyes
in haunted stares, self-pity in rooms,
unrealised; plaster-pink walls,
unpainted; a damp-aired landing's
centre-reign, half-suggested...

*

I reassemble that tomb of stone
in its clump of weeds; hinge-creaked gate;
blue gloss door with Picksie latch;
derelict sunlight splintering where
twisted limbs of an apple tree
choked rotten spoils—soft crinkled skins
bruising to the touch: moth-thoughts,
hovering, tumbling numberless
as pebbled beds of crouching flowers
in those imprisoning mornings.
A cow-bell clopped to the overflow;
a carcass of glass spilt stinging nettles;
a cement-filled pebbledash well
pushed up shrubs of wishing petals.

Morbid, our umbrella word,
groping for a foothold in
laboured hours, weight of sadness
(there's the other word) as if
we lived our purgatory blurred in;
misting lives in suburbia.

Darkest nights I'd known;
moths, grotesquely outgrown;
hand-size spiders tapping on
peeling posters, clicking time
to the clock's taciturn ticks.

*

Bowed by the bent beam gazing over
warped books on the blistered sill
to the trampled sadness of our garden,
a tumble of nettle-tangled troubles
pouring from the house's mouth,
sculpting sorrows from sad panes—
a battered hat of buckling slates
trilbying its pockmarked face
of swollen stone: this house was ill.

Sold us as idyllic, white-washed,
it was a starker face: our own
little crumbled House of Usher
obscured by prouder abodes,
confiscated from the hamlet's view—
a disgraced sight set back from the road.

*

Stone-cool lounge, summer hung
thick outside, a fog of dream
struggling to wake the room,
bore in through the thought-sized crack
in the gloomy two-way pane;
the sooty cave of the fireplace,
focus of our shade—in winter,
of crackling logs' gooseberry-glow
spitting bilious flame.

Cuckoo-broken silence versed
with upstairs' floor-boards creaking
in an empty bedroom—a reassuring
ghost too shy to haunt us or
the panting scrape of earthly mother's
cobwebbed broom brushing the floor.

Some houses have souls, memories,
haunting them—this one had:
a sadness past remained, served
to feed ours with historic force.
I'll return, through the ghostly photo
of hollow windows' gormless glare—
an emptied relative's frozen stare;
grope up the slanting path into
its blossom-grey, cabbage-white
wintry circumstance, now time's
passed trace of us there…

## MOTHER MOUSE

My tiny mother in her tiny kitchen
Rinsing the washing up—
A poem warped above the sink
Entitled *Don't Give Up.*

But Greeting Card wise pearls aside,
Sentiments tire now;
Thirty-five years she's survived
Each wrung-out wedding vow.

For better, for worse, for richer, for poorer,
A shine for bees-wing eyes—
A sud-filled cup for a moment's doubt—
Some sparkle for disguise.

She scurries around her mental wheel
Like an obsessing mouse;
Spins her chores like effortless confessions;
Swallows her sobs as she tidies the house.

## LAST OF THE SPRAY CARNATIONS

Everything's through a haze today,
a nervy bleach, blurred photograph
exposed before developing
like a crippled Spartan baby;
a saffron-starched, sun-blanched album
family image, except it isn't
my family I mingle with, but a stunned
white drift of sun-paled faces probing
lychee-eyes into market bargains.

As if I looked at this bustling rock-pool
speculum of life through frosted glass
or a thick honey-coloured vase.

I trip on, lost to the fogged outside
of myself, part-deaf to the touting
shouts of the cod-eyed fishmonger,
the sun-flushed apple-shaped pink lady,
& lamb-shouldered butcher with
a scrag-end face, his white coat
pinking from bloodied meat.

Everything, poetic & pathetic
at once, in a burst of cheapside sunlight
scooping a pool on the scene.

Even the vivid spoils of the florists
appear pitiful: a cluster of pink
& white spray carnations,
green at the edges of thirsty petals
poking from a dripping bucket, a bunch
of scrunched-up tissues saturated
with tears of mustard sun.

## THE GOSPELS OF GORDON ROAD

In parroting streets the Parkers lived
in an outburst of spilt belongings
by a pet shop perched on Gordon Road,
No. 31—one score left to them;
muffled fluster of cockatoos
scratched the front-hall walls;
terrapins, tropical fish
splashed in a backyard aquarium
for a ghostly public, unforthcoming.

### I. THE GOSPEL ACCORDING TO BERYL

Obese-limbed Beryl, name the colour
of her bilious coat, avocados
she'd bleach with vinegar
supping on stories of Roaring Uganda,
kept a trove chockfull with spoils
of childhood paraphernalia:
a damp-spotted pith helmet,
one of her cast-off canvases
titled *Elephants in Jinja*,
ebony carvings, tusks, & tales
of a slate-eyed Scottish father
telegraphing the Savanna
& ivory white goddess mother
biting poison from Boy on the veranda.

Penner of eccentric green-ink letters
to all & sundry: from the star
of *The Flame Trees of Thika*
to Margaret Thatcher—Iron Beryl,
fulsome as lukewarm Stout.

Her mantelpiece of miniatures:
a small glass Buddha with an ochre flower
in its bloated belly, '*If you rub his tummy
it'll bring good luck*' she'd mutter through
cryptic lips, with other superstitious snippets:
'*Pray to St. Anthony if you lose anything*',
but he never recovered lost marbles.
Beryl believed in blonde baby Jesus,

cribs, clans, papacy, tooth fairies,
Clarabelle, Tinkerbelle, plaster saints
& table-salt superstitions—held
chair-ridden court cushioned in
upholstered throne, all swollen shins,
tortoise-shell glasses & netted hair.


## II. THE GOSPEL ACCORDING TO HAROLD

Her trilby-humbled husband Harold
limped in slump of self-belief,
stick to buttress his step,
stocky North Londoner, Gunners supporter—
shuddered at jellied eels, bow bells,
*'I'm not a Cockney'*, he'd maintain
but perhaps he was unconsciously:
fond of the phrase *'me old China'*.

A rifle-butt buffeted his spirit
in a German camp, buffered him
with fits of temper, trembling limbs—
from Corporal Parker of the Buffs
to Private Struggle pensioned off
to the tyranny of landlords
& the mush of meals-on-wheels.

A legacy of long-term concussion:
de-mobbed prompt in '45;
assembling dolls' limbs in factories;
spell as shopkeeper bankrupted off
to last stop by Balfour Road.

In mouldering, damp-walled winters,
bereaved by his worshipped wife,
coped through a series of botched episodes:
Catholic conversion, gulps of pills,
macabre bed-time reunions
with his spectral Beryl.

Harold went out like a flare in a trench,
refusing Last Rights in rabid-eyed rage,
leaving the Priest & the Pastor speechless
as the plastic Christ on his bedside table
he mistook for Mary as the beard had faded.

Four campaign medals, absent fifth
for a brave act screened off in gun-fog;
captured; tortured; frozen to snow
for escape attempts—never escaped
the stalking of the swastika's brand.

His prime predisposed to put him out in time:
namesake of his mythic brother,
killed 'spiking the guns' in the First,
smudged out with led like his last
pencilled scribbles blunt as his fate.

Harold rationed out his days,
guilt-inheritor, warped by self-blame
for the world's unanswerable blunders;
his prize: some debts & a pauper's grave.


III. THE GOSPEL ACCORDING TO GORDON

The Brighton Parkers played host to
a cadaverous bachelor, physsog threadbare
as his wicker sweater, also Gordon,
who lodged one ruptured flight beyond
obscure parameters of absent banisters
up a scupper of cuttlefish stairs.

A bachelor but for the merchant sea
he married, Gordon cut a skeletal shipmate
in his fisherman's cap & tweeds,
spruced on canine piss & bird seed.

Shut off in the trill & chirp of his
lemon-curd/sky-blue budgerigars
caging his company as a cancer-
growth his old dog Tony,
the gruff old lodger shrugged off thoughts
on gossip of souls & salvation:

*'I don't believe in Heaven; nothing*
*after this 'far as I'm concerned;*
*best make the most of your pension'*
he'd glibly comment if invited in
to give his shilling's worth of philosophical rent.

God scarpered from his dingy digs
in Gordon's head long ago to find
new lodgings in more malleable minds.

*How odd him not believing in God,*
I thought as a boy—my oblivion,
being alone—couldn't comprehend
his atheism, not knowing then
the dormant terms of my own.


IV. THE GOSPEL OF GORDON ROAD

We believe what we want to believe;
time buttresses us with splints of insight,
feeds us lies to starve doubts, to cope;
Gordon's tools, the mental present-ness of pets;
Beryl's, rent-book resurrection;
Harold's, ball-points on football pools.

*Some make themselves their own God;*
*some spend their lives fishing for stars;*
*some endure all with a humble hat's doff;*
*some keep budgerigars.*


# BEATITUDES

Today, everything's resolved: the man
with the rainy Sunday face has found
a smile's an inspiring beam of light
in his outlook; the senile lager-breathing
dragon of withered scales, forced to forgo
his habit for the day, is the better for it:
sober & brave; the two middle-aged
friends have let bygones be for a change;
the doubting housewife's found her faith
while vacuuming behind the chairs.

## OBVERBS

*MOTTO FOR THE MOUNTAINEER*
If you try to reach the summit
You're likely to become it.


*AGE'S HILL*
Young Puritans of austere will
Grow cavalier past age's hill.


*-ISMS*
Capitalism spouts from city walls;
Socialism mutters in draughty halls.


*DEATH'S DRESS REHEARSAL*
Romans called asthma rehearsal for death;
life was summed up as a shortness of breath.


*SLEEPY HEAD*
The man who looks like he hasn't slept well
has a face like a bed that's been slept in.


*THE GIRL WITH THE DIRTY HANDS*
She held out her hands, begged for a fag
she got from the boy with no jobs in the bag.


*FEAR OF BLINDNESS*
Believing in God for a dread of death
is living in darkness for fear of blindness.


*POETRY KILLS*
I read the warning in my short breath:
Poetry's a slow & painful death.

## ADAM'S NIB

It wasn't a woman tempted me
Into my fall, into my fall;
Just a piece of paper & a pen—
The imperfection of it all.


## THE BLACKBOARD

My first glimpse of oblivion:
the school blackboard, to me then
my life seemed like one scrape of chalk
smudging into the dark.


## INNOCENCE TWISTED

Too soon some said he spoke
with a sour taste,
& saw how innocence
twisted on his face.


## DEAD REMINDER

Thought-shelves list through lack of means:

book-binds losing stick split their seams,
prop each other up, nodding down-and-outs,
no one caring what they blurt about.

Tales aren't tall as bills, poems don't pay rent.
Pencils crack their points in tensing hands.

Tie a noose with plastic rubber bands:
find a dummy bouncing like his cheques.

## THE BUZZARD

At a safe distance its stare exacted me
from its golden hay-stacked throne,
shining with all the bravura of the sun;
big-limbed king of Cornish ramble-lands,
stubble-fields & ragged hills—
talons size of manly hands;
on prehistoric scale
to my eyes cowering their ground on a hay-bale
by the cottage back window for retreat if needs be—
the Buzzard kept still, its feather-crown's plumage
ruffled by the breeze-brushed sway of its dynasty.
I was too cautious to take a closer look,
could only guess if its royal stare
translated the thought: *What subject sits there?*


## IN THE LAPS OF THE GODS

I worship you because you give me love & warmth
with the magical touch of the strange white glow,
the smell of heat, wood-cool of ground
in summer, like outside, in the garden the air
blows our coats, fanning our stifled fur—
& the scent of the out: the leaf, the earth,
the language of dirt-tracks, the freedom, space;
the clinging scent of your hand as it strokes
my hair reassuring me with its familiar smell
when I grow lame & can't get around,
out of LOVE for me you'll put me down.

## THE POET TREE

We left to make home in a shell of stone,
garden left to ramble overgrown
making itself notoriously known,
overblown, wouldn't be mown,
as a mop of unruly hair won't stand a comb.

All dandelions & weeds; a sun-starved tree
couldn't bear fruits—we had to show it
by planting another in its shaded view.

But in time a home had grown;
daffodils twinkled; the shy, leafless tree
blossomed into a poet.

## MEETING THE PAINT EATER

I saw a man with candles in his hat
trying to capture the moon—
as I passed by I said to him
*'It's going to be supper time soon'.*

His foggy eyes acknowledged my words:
he brushed his stubbled chin,
put some crumbling paint to his lips,
smiled, & started eating.

## HELL OR A BETTER HAND

Some of us already suffer
torments of the damned—
but is this to prepare us for
Hell, or a better hand?

## GIVING LIGHT

When women give birth, the Spanish say
They're giving light—& it's said
The newborn child comes into the day
Armed with a loaf of bread.

## FIVE MINUTE FINITY

In the space of five minutes I held you, said,
half to myself, half to you, *'How did I
deserve you?'*, thought only of my fear
of dying, tried convincing you
of the soul while I wasn't convinced myself;
& you said you'd no fear of death only
of lingering suffering (that atheist chestnut)—
but why don't atheists fear death
when they're more certain of it?

Who fears death needs the crutch of faith;
who fears pain needs the crutch of death.

## INFINITE THINGS

I can't enjoy anything that must end;
Infinite thoughts & feelings with limit;
Mortality's labyrinth trails bend on bend
But leads only to what is in it.

## FOOTNOTES ON FAITH

*I've seen insane old men masturbating*
*until they'd drawn blood, wringing*
*their foreskins of every last feeling—*
*where are their souls? Where's their God?*

F.N. Their souls have long since departed.

*Since when? Since they last voluntarily farted?*
*Before their bowels broke down & went it alone?*
*Before their drooling & bedwetting set in?*
*There's no light within; no justice; no sin.*

F.N. Just a stubborn unwillingness to give in.

## FLOWERS IN THE VASE

Suddenly a fire stoked up inside me—
It was something someone said.
I thought the flowers were in the vase
But they were still in the flower bed.

Something someone said—*shhh*—
Or the sound of the fire fizzling out in water,
The dirty water which, hissing, said:
*The flowers in the vase are dead.*

## GRANDMA'S INGREDIENTS

I discovered at a tender eleven
Grandma was made of buttons,
Brooches, rings & leather watch-straps,
Gift-wrapped in cellophane for heaven.

## THE DRIVE

Either to be a premature dread-end
or terrible beginning, my thoughts juddered
in my darkening humid mind overcasting
with summer storm cloud maundering
from the blind east; tight eyes straining
to fathom detail of relentless hedgerows
cramping our car on narrow lanes
horribly idyllic in stretch—rain splattered
in harassing spits drumming the bonnet,
obsessing a web of drops on the windscreen—
the wipers screeched *Can't Cope! Can't Cope!*

## OBLIVIONS

The sun, the sky, the land, the sea—
*it's all been a bit too much for me.*

To smell, to taste, to touch, to see,
to think, to feel, to love, to be—
*it's all been a bit too much for me.*

By finding the oblivion in me
& the oblivion in you, might be
the end to my sensitivity—

but the need to belong, to be free—
*it's all been a bit too much for me.*

## TIMÉTATIONS

### I. THE BIN OF TIME

Browbeaten by routine's tyranny
ravages of wasted time
cuttlefish your luminous brow,
sleeping-pill white, marble eyes:
pay with daytime drowsiness
for nocturnal sedated bliss
numbing your mind, cushioning thoughts:
well-punched pillows supportable for once.

### II. TIME BITES

Hours hover, mothballing minutes
in static dust-clots, stick in the throat
as pills without enough water
to dissolve to flakes; time,
the irritable master it is, spits ticks
of rhetoric in gusts of stale breath
humming from a scoured tongue—
time bites like sharp radish,
a taste relished by the toothsome
while wisdom mints it out with gum.

### III. CLOSING TIME

In cigarette-mist of a smoke-filled pub
he sat hand on head, wrist on chin,
*'I'm trying to keep my brains in'*, he said.
Tears of snakebite streaming down
in lagered trace, misty eyes
disguised his tears, wasn't the place—
frozen, beered up, numbly waiting
for another round, dreading last orders
beckoning through tobacco smog—
could see his life half full, half empty,
clinging to his pint till closing time.

## IV. WHITE

Luminous cuttlefish sky stares pearly eye,
vast blank page, junket white winter sun
cocking a snook through parted clouds;
ghostly pale agoraphobic pate
parted by net-curtains' communion veil;
page of skin clinging, clinging;
sockets for eyes; cod-fish white glinting,
grinding nerves to powder, grinding
like the famished teeth of time.


## V. OUT OF CLOCK TIME

The soul knows no limits—I sense
this in my silent times—ticking
digits count only bodily lives—
but the soul, the self, the spirit lives in
its own domain outside clock-time—
ghosts, some think, cross to our side,
sometimes—a bit like obsessives popping
back to check they've remembered everything:
the gas; the keys; the watering of ashtrays;
or simply to remember to collect what they
forgot to the plodding tock of days.


## VI. OLD FATHER TIME

Time is a bitter, morbid old man
who can't hear what you're saying
or just can't understand.


## VII. TIME ANXIETY

Life without the anxiety of Time
Might prop us up in our tripping prime;
If we could cut down clocks like trees
We'd put the branches at their ease.

## VII. THE CLOCK THAT FORGOT THE TIME

*What Time is it?* asked the clock who'd forgot it.
*Well if you don't know, how should I?* replied
The Memory that couldn't remember. *What's the Time?*
Piped the poor Clock once again, then sighed.
*That's like asking. . .* said the Memory—*. . .no, I forget it.*
*I would have asked Death*, said the Clock, *but he's died,*
*& Life's far too busy regretting it.*


## IX. LITTLE FATHER TIME

Pallid offspring of future-minded parents,
torn too soon from nursery rhymes
thrown into dingy itinerancy
of rented tenements, uncertain tenancy,
a rag doll dragged through Christminster streets
by the scruff of the cockerel's neck,
son of two fugitives in limited times,
protector of wind-bitten little siblings,
windfall babies, daren't rock-a-by
them lest crimped cradles fall—
pale twisted innocent, twisted by love,
hair sweat-greased from compassion's damp fever,
all the world's troubles rub his marble brow
as if to polish off all infant fortitude—
*Is there nothing to do? Is there nothing to do?*
*Nothing* sounds out like a terrible blow
to his callow, cramped conscience, perilously raw;
nothing to do but sacrifice the lambs
then atone with immature martyrdom—
hung by shoe-straps, hands pillow-soft,
a crime of compassion in a child's despair;
a scribbled note slid under stool-wedged door:
*becos we are too menny*. How many more?

## THE NEED TO DREAM FOREVER

I remember I was barely fed,
Eleven or twelve, in a freezing bed
Damp with doubts, wanting outs,
Drift off & dream forever...
Thought I wanted to be dead—
*'Go to sleep'*, dad said.

## POEM ON EMPTY

Sat on the rag-&-bone sofa smoking
a singed dog-end in my ripped pyjamas,
staring at mug-stains on the lamp-lit table,
I said to my father, suppressing the groan
of my empty stomach, *'just to think
no one will ever know of this...'*

## THE SOUND OF EATING

My great grandfather, a Fabian,
never skipped a single meeting
to discuss best ways of feeding
empty bellies of the down-at-heel.

(Privately he ate his meals
in his study, apart from his kin:
he couldn't stand the sound
of other people eating.)

## DEATH OF A SOCIALIST

*'It's easy to be a socialist when you've only yourself to think about'*
muttered the veteran gargoyle of the left with bitter irony,
features crumpled as a rolled up *Morning Star*, front page
scanned, contents skipped by the masses it calls to arms
*'—having kids taught me how honour has to scrape & bow*
*for the sake of love. No greater cause. Socialism knows*
*no get-out-clause: Marx, like Christ, asks us to*
*sacrifice private interests for the public good;*
*turn our little families into big commun-*
*-ities. Well if everyone else did,*
*then I would.'*

## MIGHT

Why did some of us come to believe
The Left is in the right
When it has a massive clumsy body
& wings too small for flight?

## RIDDLE OF THE SPHINX

*Riddle*
What creature goes on four legs in the morning;
Two during the day;
& three in the evening?

*Solution*
The worker who begs on all fours for a job;
Gets up on two to paw for his pay;
Then limps with a stick when forced into leaving.

## SUI OBLITUS COMMODI

I came to know my father's parents
through dandelion recollections
scattered in their Crematorium.

Recognised John from a photo:
hook nose cushioned by strict moustache;
listened intensely to his crisp voice,
faint but distinctive,
slicing through hissing speakers
interspersed by clattering crockery
courtesy of his second wife's porcelain hands:

Saintly Lily, captured in sepia
snapshot from Heaven's after-flash;
those soft grey eyes epitomize
*Sui oblitus commodi—*
she lived a secret in their stark house at Rock;
father often found her knelt, a grounded angel,
scrubbing the floor, chained to chores
as a suffragette to railings:

she fluttered into strictness' ether;
groomed in Socialism by
her father Harold who dined alone
throwing Baptist scraps at the poor;
inherited his sentiments
(& sensitive stomach)
sweeping her Socialism
under a patch of carpet.

*My country right or wrong* rang hollow
from the pipe-propped mouth of her patriotic husband,
a splinter of rhetoric lodged in him
like a papery Kipling battle scar;
no stomach for Sassoon as he
had none for his son's *guts-ache* music,
Walton/R.V.W./Holst.

She: no stomach for selfishness
in her domestic soldiering;
strain of countryside seclusion
wrung her threadbare fibre dry,
manacled in phantasms;

her nerves took on the jolting force
of housebound bomb-shock (triggered by
doodlebugs she'd body-sheltered
her son from back in wartime Windsor);
no outbursts, just shattering silence,
obsessions cobwebbed about the morbid
cottage of her thoughts;

'My face has gone' she'd say in horror
before the mirror, 'I can't see it,'
or proclaim she'd lost her nose—
abstraction's Harpies plaguing her
with fears of blindness, formless impulse
throwing her from cliff edges
of thought, fed off her dread of dying,
her frightened love of life.

She laboured on to know one grandson,
witness the birth of a second, held him
in her thin, bone china arms,
hushabying under thundering breath.

Perhaps a little of the light in her
brushed off on me before it passed:

I share her sensitivities,
phobias, foibles, beliefs,
yet these in-grew as I grew out
from childhood's idolising of
her husband's disinterred ideas:
subordination of the self
for the nation—in that sense
a different ideal still deserving
*Sui oblitus commodi.*

[*Sui oblitus commodi = Forgetful of one's own interest*: motto of the Asgills, my
father's distaff side].

# VICTUALS

## I. TRANSUBSTANTIATION

First Communion: First Sin:
Forgot, God, forgot to go Confession:
No Absolution: maybe Damnation?
Incensed Him in initiation.
I open to receive His Body nonetheless,
Innocent to my callow sin's trespass.
They'd said the bread, unleavened,
Would taste a bit like Heaven:
Had my taste-buds given up at seven?
Confusion at the flavour of the Saviour:
*It doesn't taste of anything.*

## II. HOLY ROOFS

The roof of the church
caked in tasteless Salvation
like the roof of the mouth
at Holy Communion.

## III. ABSENCE OF BUTTERFLIES

I recall as an altar boy watching the priest
breaking the unleavened bread,
placing one half in my hand which I placed
on my tongue where it transubstantiated...

Now, as an adult, my doctor prescribes
a pill for my thoughts; nightly I break
a little white sleeping pill to attain
peace of mind & body; to slake
pins & needles of my nerves; numb
my stomach's downhill roll, steep rise—
but when I wake, like doubt from faith,
I feel the absence of butterflies...

## CATCHING SIGHT OF THE URBAN FOX

A bright May morning glows the supermarket bricks
Satsuma-orange, ambered by the sun
like blanching pages of sun-warped paperbacks
in Oxfam's hothouse racks, two doors down but one.

A more debonair of down-&-outs,
a tramp who's used to tramping about,
so does in a mature, dignified manner,
pushes his supermarket trolley of belongings
—as if a golf bag in the absence of a caddie—
piled full with plastic bags, empty *Coke* bottles.

Comes to a philosophical halt
in nice patch of sun, meticulously tips
trolley on side, flaps out his coat-tails
like a pianist, then balletically sits.
Checks himself, nose twitching, ears a-flicker,
in his vast shaving mirror, the glass wall *Waitrose*
politely provided him & those of his sort
who need to keep check on their manicuring.

A very true gentleman, truest of all:
less incentive than most to keep himself tidy;
looks most refined, gentleman's tweed
cap positioned in perfect symmetry
with his clean-shaven face; thinning grey
straw-like hair neatly combed out
of all its irritating mites.

Only thing letting his apparel down
is his hole-torn rain-mac, a dust cover for
his more dapper fox-brown overcoat—
he looks like a fox, not crafty & devious
as Beatrix Potter's, but pointedly razor-red
of face (burst vessels from cold,
not booze; no soberer man has tramped
in such immaculately un-scuffed shoes);
alert, sharp, proud; most of all, free.
Spit of an eccentric country gentleman
unaccustomed to hustle-bustle bristling city life;
quite out-of-kilter in a Mad Hatter-ish way—
used to see them all the time, swinging on lamp posts
in Nineteen Seventies' Goring-By-Sea;
Mad Hatters we labelled them Carrollishly.

It's rare to get so close to an urban fox
scrimping in its stubbly native habitat,
licking mitten-paws to wipe its side-boards clean—
but he can't see me, doesn't sense my stare
depicting him in my bus-window hide,
invisible as a flea in his itching hair.


## THREE SCORES & TEA

Elfin Stevie, flame-haired naïf,
frocks & socks at forty-odd,
stamping her iambic feet,
casting spells to filibuster Time
who shrugs Its shoulders, admits defeat,
lets her off all-tainting certainty
blanching the couch in the bay window glare.

Death comes even to suburbia.
Aspidistras wilt like sunless spinsters.
Doily wills curbed by window-sills
turn in on themselves for three scores & tea
in Aunt Lion's best-china-rattling tray—
one lump or two to spirit her away.

Poor jilted Freddy, cup-sipping pity,
might have patched one flesh together
had she pinched her nose, held her breath
but as wife she'd very little to offer
but bitter wit & junket;
an infantile infatuation with Death;
besides, her typist's fingertips
were only prone to wander keys.

Shelf-in Stevie, faded old maid,
her life, one long settee sit-in
on timeless catnapper, cigarette-
-singed verses to stimulate her mind
deeply morbid in the thundery gloom
of static parlour, crochet dull—
she'd have believed in God had He
not been a vengeful, damning one
but she could never reconcile
the Christian Doctrine of Eternal Hull.

## HELL'S FULL OF EARLY RISERS

I
In the dark time of whitewash light
Heaven was walled up from sight,
A jury of bills reigned on the mantelpiece
Obscuring ginger Jesus' stern brow crease
& sincere stare—*He looked at Peter
& Peter remembered*; the faulty heater
Stuttered its last, the flame turned blue
As Christ's resurrected aura: cue
For father to prise his slippers free
From dogs' worshipping jaws, slide the
Dying warmth away from its space
Sealing the empty tomb fireplace,
Scrunch newspaper into little balls
Stuffed with wet twigs & dampened coals,
Flick out a lighter run out of fuel,
Curse, sigh, flare at futility of rule;
Striking matches pinched out by the draft,
His fingers not nifty enough for this craft;
The wind pounding loud on the old cottage door
With gaseous fists—its dog-howling roar
Unsettles his spirits, sets his nerves a-jinx,
His mind cursed by riddles to fox a Sphinx;
Still barely morning, the Furies still sleep,
Dispossessed sons dream upstairs one flight steep,
His wife fights her shift at the nursing home
While his thoughts seek employment—nail-bites alone
Faith-destitute; at five he'll awake,
Resurrect sharp & abrupt for the sake
Of his sanity—can't lie-in:
Anxiety's heave sends his stomach plunging
Into early reveille—now a bit wiser:
He's learnt Hell's for the early riser.

II

Seems this intuitive wisdom runs through
Genes & traits of those who issue
From one's reproduction—few know this
Better than this slipper-footed genealogist:
A quirk in his youngest heir's mentality
Traced through a hiccoughing ancestry:
A chemical mutation behoves serotonin,
Gifting a spirit-level of coping.
Difficult forgetting days pre-diagnosis—
Dark age of tipping dubieties (: neurosis,
Obsessions, phantasms, intrusive thoughts),
School register crosses outdone by noughts;
Stomaching puberty in bottled-up Hell
(Hell I feel would describe it well
Depending on one's own patented idea
Of such an abstract place). Sharp fear
Would push him out of bed before break
Of day prised his eyes, clammed for the sake
Of his consciousness-shy head;
His mind tug back its curtains with dread
To behold another new day of old doubt,
Compulsions to somehow clamber out
Of himself & dead-end preoccupations;
A miniature saint bedevilled by temptations
His despairing father romanticised
Spying in his son, inhibited-eyed,
Chalk-white-faced, paper-thin-willed,
A glimpse of his wife when her thoughts spilled,
Before she found methods out through learning:
*Put a knob of butter on anything burning.*
The Furies chased his son despite his hesitation,
Elastic-stretched till the next generation—
His hunted offspring no longer foxed
By obsessions he borrowed, doubts he boxed
In mental attics, coaxed out by therapy,
Preventative spells of ERP*;
He learnt early on to be none the wiser:
Hell's reserved for the early riser.

III
Might be illuminating to cite one more
Dimension to genealogical law
(If you go in for the old forgotten gesture:
We all come from the same primogeniture):
One last strand to the lineage of suffering
Limbers absent-mindedly in the dim lighting
Of a white night shelter where his second son
Put on his Socialism as one
Puts on a shirt, combining dreams
With ham-fisted grabbling with shabby means,
Spill a little bit of idealism in
To reality's uninspiring reasoning,
Shake off his interests as if they were fleas
Bristling in his hair-shirt, take up keys
To forgotten doors while he could sustain
The daily weights of spiritual strain,
Try & scrape some happiness
For those Society deems to dispossess
Through factories that reject & replicate—
Squinted beyond knuckled *love & hate*,
Ravaging addictions, self-inflictions,
Blotches, rashes & fag-reeking fictions
To unspoken stories of glassy pasts
That trampled them into untouchable castes.
But the pain & frustration brought liberating
Insights in morning strip-lights scuttling
From flea-circus sheets, hermit crabs
Shedding linen shells, dandruff, scabs
& blisters, peeling on grime-stiff rags,
Strapping on rock-sacks, crustacean bags,
Blearily lining up for their tipping out
Into rock-pools of morning to dismally tout
Left-over *Big Issues*, or beg scraps from misers...
...Hell's full of early risers.


* ERP = Exposure Response Prevention

## RATS, CATS & KINGS
A Homage to George Orwell's *Homage to Catalonia*


1.

A Republic's crisis in striking distance
on the map of things, lightning not visible
but the purr of the rug-cat thunders the drums
of sensitive ears out-listening their nation's
deafness to all but cricketing meadows,
dull willow thuds & lily-white claps—
tub-thumping thunder tumbling near
from red earths of Aragón & Huesca.


2.

From Jerusalem's slums & coal-charred yards
to draughty halls of the ILP—
cheap soap & woodbine, chip shop & Brylcreem,
hard-grafted faces lit up with hope's politics,
journeymen, poets, dust-jacket dilettantes,
honourless prophets, clean-cuffed Quixotes
& flat-capped Panzas, united to joust
& oust the Fascist windmill giants;
leathery hands shake with white spiders
pale as the pamphlets of fingered polemic;
turpentine mingles with whiffs of fresh paper.

All differences left breathlessly behind
tousling chimneys of a frostier home:
heat-drowsed idealists enter their dreams
on chivalrous trains to mythologized fronts
(a tubercular scribbler's Burma's intact
on this clattering carriage of Socialist tract);
English, German, Italian, French
billeted together through exercise of will,
not sufferance of jingoistic blackmail:
our Captain says THEIR Country Needs You!
Man with beret displays deft marksmanship
with *porrón*: thread of red resuscitates flagging,
parched-mouthed Spaniard, stubble ruby-clagging.

3.

The Diggers, Keir Hardie & George Bernard Shaw
would have been in their elements in Barcelona:
no classes, differences, privileges here,
no profits, no tips for waiters or bootblacks,
a city collectivised, transport for all
in red & black taxis & trams on the Ramblas;
formalities, titles, traditional greetings
all levelled: *Senor, Don, usted* transposed
into *Comrade & thou,* even *buenos días*
replaced with *salud!* Now cats look at kings
straight in the eyes & square in the face,
Socialism in action—so much for the Church
of Spain, its capitalist altars: a trace
of deep-veined anarchy clots the character
of this Roman Catholic, Agnostic race.

4.

Green dreams of dust-jacket crusades
to battlefields of excrement & jagged tins,
bullet-rattled hills, birdless valleys,
villages sprawled like scattered dice,
crinkled hillsides like elephant hides
looming cold daunting—insect figures
shivering round flags, hugging flames
of pilfered Church candles they strike their lights by,
coughs for confessions in sandbag pews,
mortars sacred as plaster Madonnas
too precious to touch or use—
stagnation on the Aragón front;
heated exchanges of smoke-breathed views.

5.

The shabby freedom of a nation defended
by ragged children with sticks; greyed youth
greasing corroding scrap-iron rifles
with olive oil—*keep your powder dry*
cried Oliver Cromwell in a greener war,
now black & sea-green is black & blood-red
knotted in scarves round sticking necks
the colour of quail's eggs.
Don't tap the butt on the limestone ground!
Blunderbusses go off indiscriminately,
only guns are non-partisan here
along with the shakes & pneumonia—

not forgetting 'impartial' bombs that take out
the thrower as well as the target,
killing two stones with one bird.

A fag for a bomb worth throwing; a flag
for a trusty rifle; a cause for a clause
worth fighting for in this war against virus,
impasse against men; conflict postponed
for too distant pitching of camps & dug-outs
on honeycombed hillsides; sand-martins' nests.
The cracking of bullets on Fascist machine guns:
nuts hitting stones. These freezing soldiers
ache for battles & cigarettes
but night & the Jesuit return empty-handed.

6.
Shouting instead of shooting:
verbal bombs bounce from camp to camp;
starved cats have fasted for shouting duty
so hours of vocal volleys follow fuelled
on lack of tabaco, gut-rumpus of hunger
& spirits that scavenge glimpses of hope
on blue-smudged horizons, sights thrown amok
like a scamper of tramps scrimping fag-ends,
itching in lousy hair-shirts & goat-skins,
fleas hopping ship to & fro.
Futile mascots abound: a frozen
Moor in No-Man's-Land.
What gullible bribe brought him in the service
of Christians & Catholics? Should have fought
with us: raiders of gold-spoilt Churches;
we modern Roundheads; recusant hunters;
goosey ganders with highfaluting passwords
chiselling off Heavens from the headstones,
turning God's bullet-pocked Houses
into sanctuaries for smashed furniture & excrement.

7.
Casualties, the inevitable price of clashes;
competing with bombs, sirens caterwaul
from streams of juddering ambulances
that rescue the wounded, jolt them into corpses.
Sadly not as regular as faeces that spoors
in rank latrines, gifting rafts for rats,
is the infrequent trickle of Fascist deserters

inspired by catalysts of sparring polemic
ricocheting like cartridges through No-Tramp's Land:
*Viva el POUM—Fascistas maricones!* & so on—
arguments, like the spit of bullets, seem never-ending.
Damp trenches cause a passion for warm baths & clean sheets.

Polemic warms the farm house: heated politics
debated in freezing, rat-infested dug-outs
sandbags for soap boxes, bullets for ballots,
ideology in action on inactive battlefields
of barbed-wire –isms, shell-splintered wings;
pens dipped in blood; bayonets dripping ink.

8.
The battle-scene: a war-torn bed chamber
exposed to skies for a roof scooped by a bomb:
bedsteads for barricades; bed-pan latrines
filling with yellow water from urinating rains,
rats large as cats splashing in them like otters—
hardly the picturesque brocade crocheted by
fevered imaginings in rapt English bed-sheets
before the pan was spilt; & barely picaresque:
the only rogues here are rats & grenade-pins
& Catalan cats staring out Spanish kings—
who doesn't know the way to a monarch's heart
is through explosives? Cue Guido Fawkes,
the Catholics' last coup with grit & gunpowder
to blow down Parliament's pack of cards,
towers of matchsticks & ratified tricks.

Who will oust out this brute Franco?
The folk songs of Lorca? The buzz of de Falla's
swarming *El Amor Brujo*?
Not strums of flamenco, stamping fandango,
choreographed toreadors' pugilist ballet
in blood-coloured dust of the bull rings.

9.
On the Aragón front flares clash with the flash
of clean bayonets, white armlets & gritted teeth,
or the whites of the eyes of terrified sheep
herded by bullets in the still lunar darkness
black as liquorish-root cigarettes—
thanks to Franco's annexed Canary plantations—
on grounds pockmarked with shell holes like

the cratered moon. What contrast by day:
faces stained by white ferocious suns,
windburnt; sunbeaten. Gnarled-faced Andaluces
bask in anarchy of classless ranks,
prized for their deftness at tucking in ends
of cigarettes shovelled with brittle tobacco.


10.
On a chattering train anís-totting
leather-faced peasants reflect the drab palette
of conscripted cats' coarse brown & khaki
who naturally care only for a fresh packet
of fags: a day's wage for philanthropy
at ten pesetas, price of altruism
along with rice-leavened bread, consistency
of communion wafers; bread like putty;
screaming trams & milkless tea;
scourge of olive oil; cigarette famine;
pounding stomachs in tortuous streets.


11.
*¡Hola otra vez Barcelona!* The lights of this city
of labyrinthine intrigue pinched out like candles
in Church-like dark cast by Tibidabo,
hill from which el Diablo showed
Christ the countries of the Earth—Franco's
shadow obscures truth, inspires
Communist plots, Valencian papers
flaming with Fascism—the Fascist plot:
*Impeach the POUM—suppress the lot!*
Adios Maurín, la Confederación Nacional
de Trabajo, *La Batalla's* championing
of the Friends of Durruti. Nín disappears
like invisible ink while libellous blots
of lily-white foreign newspapers stain
red permanent slander on hearts & minds
of lamb; give the view of the Balaclava hill
through safe sights of picnicking opera glasses.

We are called Fascists behind our backs
& behind our fronts—*No hay tabaco*—
Quiroga, Barrio, Giral—Bilbao.
Communist policies of pin-pricks pummel
subtly away at the honour of the POUM,
turns freedom fighters into fugitives,

slams foreign crusaders into germ-ridden prisons
to die from their wounds & ideals—
in the meantime Franco's Spanish rats
spill in through the chaos & wobbling lines
of faction-split fronts: Madrid, Aragón,
Málaga, Bilbao, Huesca, Barcelona,
Valencia; all fall like dominoes—blood
pours into Spain like wine from a *porrón*...

12.
Rats large as cats nibbling scraps
in Republican pannikins: new rule of kings
sets in with the twitch of liquorish moustache,
stamp of black boots, a yellow/red flag,
rumpus of tub-thumping Fascist salutes,
*ustedes, Dons, Senores* restored
with classes & castes, tips, brothels, profits,
private monopolies—only the oranges
glow the same colour, like paraffin lights
in ink-spilt night's genuflected trees.
Oranges are oranges under Republicans,
Socialists, Anarchists, Fascists, all –isms;
they all taste the same to rats, cats & kings.

---

Notes: Stanza 2: ILP = Independent Labour Party. 'a tubercular scribbler...' = refers to George Orwell. *porrón* = Spanish drinking vessel for wine. Stanza 3: Ramblas = a mile-long promenade in Barcelona. *Usted* = formal version of 'you' in Spanish – the Republicans occupying Barcelona altered such formal addressing of citizens to the informal, to emphasize equality; the Fascists preferred formal addresses. Stanza 7: POUM = (Partido Obrero de Unificación Marxista) The Workers Party of Marxist Unification. *Fascistas maricones* = Fascist poofs. Stanza 11: *¡Hola otra vez Barcelona!* = 'Hello again Barcelona!' *Maurín* = leader of the POUM. Confederación Nacional de Trabajo = (CNT) National Confederation of Workers. *La Batalla* = pro-Fascist paper in Madrid. Friends of Durruti = anarchist militia opposed to militarization and governmentalism in the peoples' militia. Nín = co-founder of POUM who was falsely accused by the Communists of conspiring with the Fascists, and subsequently disappeared. *pannikins* = metal containers for warming up food rations in and eating them from.

## A LETTER FROM DAVID KESSEL

His crabbed handwriting scrawls
*poetry is a savage war*
& other spills of pub beer wisdom:
*in the destructive element immerse!*
straight from the disinherited Lord Jim
with a suicidal, sherbet-tasting bite
like the powder spilt out on the numbing tongue
from the split capsule of an anti-depressant.

*I'm still out of touch* the swatted legs
of letter-insects spell out on off-white paper,
*&, I believe, over-medicated!*
but not too much to date the letter—
*be in touch soon* the scribbles say
then his signature like a squashed spider appears:
*David*—makes arachnophobics flinch
& all the flies trapped in the spinning years...

## SHELL SHOCK

A huddled, bedraggled sand-bag,
eyes trembling with special fear
born from fatigue & lack of fags;
body crouched west but canny of rear
guns rattling from the unseen east,
Gatling chatter of bucolic bronchitis—
lungs concertina with grampus wheeze
of book-dust asthma, pen-hand arthritis—
in No-Fags-Land the casualties
of dregs-shovelled roll-ups scatter the carpet
of umber mud; battlefield teas
spill on the listing parapet
of warping pamphlets' ducking curves
under bombardments of battered nerves.

## ONLY ROSIE SMOKES

All rickety wood desks & chairs,
Garish matt-lemon pimply walls;
Unlit corridors that trail to stairs
Where a ghostly hum summons from the hall:
The irritable lift, grumbling empty—
Deep in this labyrinth of gingery glimpses
Into Hobbit-offices shut off like thoughts
On problems that haven't solutions
Bides faded, buck-toothed Rosie wrinkled
As a walnut, sole heir to the privilege
Of lighting up at work, poised with
Perpetual *Silk Cut* as she hunches,
Screwing her eyes at faceless audits
In the swirling vapours of her vice
Like Lewis Carroll's Caterpillar.
Fogs of rank fag-smoke for six hours
Percolate with the filtered coffee
Like the scent of hash in a Kashmir arcade.

## A MIGHTY ABSENCE

When she was fussing around him, throwing
Chocolate foil missiles while he tried to read,
Nudging his knee so his cradled book slipped
To his irritable sigh of '*Oh, Helen*',
His word-anchored gaze longed for solitude.

But when she was working an afternoon shift
His books became milestones of hours,
Grave-heavy weights that heaped on his mind
& his cattle-grid brow; he'd stare into space
& the empty lounge which after a while
Took on all the gloom of his thoughts in her absence;
He'd shuffle about like an abandoned schoolboy,
Biting his nails while the minutes
Traipsed by like a regiment of plodding doubts;
His fresh-polished shoes standing neatly to attention
For inspection by an empty fireplace;
His whole soul missing her, hanging grey
& desolate in his face.

# THE WELL & THE WISHER

There father sat, fishing for wishes
In the plastic tub filled with soapy water,
Face weighed down by cattle-grid brow,
Sad & thundery, a bedraggled angler
With nothing to show for patience & strain,
No bend on the rod, at best a mere morsel
At the end of his line.

Scrubbing the Queens' heads till they gleamed
As if freshly minted; ELIZABETH REG revived
Into sudded sparkle—regal tender
To bag & exchange for pentagon-shaped
Tolls to slot in the electric metre.
He gazed at the coins at the bottom
Of the shallow plastic well, frothing
With washing-up liquid bubbles, but silent,
No more fulfilling wishes, only see-through bubbles
Swelling & bursting on the limpid surface.

Then looked again through his wobbled reflection
At layers of coins & saw for moments
Glistening copper-coloured pebbles
He'd try to fetch out from the bed of the stream
Trickling down through the sloping meadow
At the foot of his father's hill, as a boy;
In that clouded time he'd stare back to
The smallholding summit on the crinkly brow
& think: *'I wonder where I'll be*
*Fifty years from now'.*

His dank reflection reformed in the pool
At his feet, now ditchwater green
For scum & mould shed from the coins
Like driftwood from a ship wreck.
His fingers fished the pebbles out
From the unreflecting stream.

## DADDY-LONG-THOUGHTS

Day of returns & returning, revisiting
overgrown rails of the mind
played as a tangible, metaphorical trip
to Bognor Regis, on rickety tracks
to difficult pasts, disguised in green-washed
terraces, sleepy, ghostly arcades,
a cramped museum of only two rooms
stuffed with Nineteen Forties' nostalgia,
haunted wireless sets, old record players
safely remote in chameleon cases,
cabinets filled with hisses & song,
mahogany mausoleums of ghost voices
caught for posterity on vinyl like life-lines
on faces; promising returns to muffled
yesteryears, *Take good care of yourself,*
*you belong to me*—& other legends:
*Anything is possible with a cup of tea,*
eternally-spiralling memories
caught in stylus-rut-tut of thought—
Dad taps into service days' airwaves
transported back to Signaller duties
tapping his name on the Morse-code generator,
last ditched attempt, unconsciously,
to communicate with his obsessive mouse-wife
cowering in a dark hole in the wainscoting...

Billeted at Barnham with baggage of years'
tortuous travelling to begin again
life's recurring evacuation
to flutters of breeze-leafed luggage tags,
tell-tale tickets of the soul—the mighty
distance lived, giant stones of vast,
towering things experienced,
time-manipulating milestones of minutes
morphing to trees, fields, hedges, clouds
in capitulation with the past,
pantomiming, re-performing moments
lost mostly in hope of non-remembering,
forgetfulness, vital blinkers of present-
seeking senses of cross-each-bridge-as-you-
come-to-it now; off-putter of tomorrow...

In the musty existing room of my parents,
crammed full with family mementos, books,
photographs, Styx's toll-fare tokens
or the hold of a Pharaoh's morbid tomb,
crouch Eden's forgotten descendants,
once giants, now shrivelled to earthly,
miniature size like two toy-scale figures
in a rented dolls' house hemmed between
a struggling back garden & windowed
partition to the outside world—ghosts
haunting progress's tumbleweeding suburbs,
eyes seamed with crow's-feet, stitched under-shadows
stewed-tea grey; old shoe-brown pupils
glistening tiredness, penetrating as nerves
jarred between contrapuntal cogs of thought,
strung out by crippling preoccupations
of the moment, terror's cryptic puzzles,
silent shouts skirting-board-shrunk inversely
in size to towering effect; nerves' stretched
piano wires creaking lost chords, lost notes,
lost times; eyes strained as recycled tea-bags,
marbled as milk-swirling tea, or egg-whites
bubbling in a frying-pan shrapnelled with shellsplinters;
ancestral tut-tut of out-of-kilter clock
stuck forever at Six—tea-time to starch-scented
Edwardians—illustrates to etiquetteless ear
what on some other plane struggles to be heard
in deafening, daytime, stuffy lounge silence,
dins of the taxidermist's inner-ear—
miniscule screams muffled under carpet slippers:
cork-creaking minutes, stone-scraping seconds...

Time is fed up, it's fretting, it's biting its nails,
until the next train comes... Tea brings lapsed
contentment, tings spirits presently depleted
to muster stimulation, stir peculiarly back
into being like pink-striped Bagpuss in his sepia shop,
caffeine-revivified, resuscitated to stammers
of nerve-edged conversations, verbal grabbling
for mental distraction, reiterated interests
stale with taste-betraying syllables, dull, insipid,
yellowed-eyed, watery weak; drained; stewed;
drunk on spurts of recaptured happier times
flitting fuzzily as bulb-clunking moths;
suicidal daddy-long-thoughts birthed by lullabies

of a moment's beyond self-soothing rocks
of tense torsos, time-tripping sighs, excruciating tocks...

Depending on mood my Dad's a Mad Hatter
postulating posterity's teatime scraps—
as the stained armchairs draped in sun-blanched covers
darken to monoliths, immovable doubts
in unexpected thunder-gloom cast by a cloud,
he turns to Mock Turtle, too life-tired to cry;
my mother alternates between March Hare
& Dormouse, depending on the hold of sudden
grope of hope or insoluble obsession
in the dimly gas-lit dolls' house of her mind—
we take our places in listless mummery
of past thoughts, feelings, imprisoning meanings
breathing back to life through thawing of sighs,
interminably frequent tripping of time...

*More dishwater tea?* asks Dormouse Mother
of Mad Hatter father to teapot patter;
she yaffles affirmations, *yawf—yawf—yawf*,
nearest her mouth comes to forming *yes*
since aeons of negatives; rings tea-strained eyes;
lapses back to doubt-muttered sleepy-byes,
rinsed of all energies; timeless tea-party
tripping with lethargy, rusting gentility,
frozen forever at Six-'O'-Clock,
stirring the stewed tea with a fob watch...

Angst-ridden glances grappling ungraspables—
tripped up by a thought's footstool—
go in circles round the centre table plinth—
casting story spells like the pacing Brontë sisters—
a jaundiced tomato plant implores its luminous
green buds to blush red, red of our tied blood
binding us together in eternal trinity
chains of pulsing wooden rosary beads
itching to hatch their polished shells
like November conkers; domestic mysteries
probed, unsolved, self-defining; ruby red
of veins rumbling into half-remembered,
half-abandoned branch lines divaricated
via wilderness-verged chronic tracks acrawl
with enervating, never-arriving trains...

from

*A TAPESTRY OF ABSENT SITTERS*

(2009)

# PRAISE WITH FAINT DAMNATION

*for Kevin Saving*

Don't damn with faint praise or admiration—
Drub our green words till they bruise at the smart.
Raze us to grain, praise with faint damnation.

Feel free to deflate with defamation—
Pick at the scraps of the amateur heart,
Don't damn with faint praise or admiration.

Anything but vague, blanched affirmation—
Rattle our talents with your crafty art,
Raze us to grain, praise with faint damnation.

We're not after plaudits or salvation,
Blast against the grain that splits us apart—
Don't damn with faint praise or admiration.

Trample us to our naïf foundation,
We'll grasp the straws at the pitch of your dart;
Raze us to grain, praise with faint damnation.

No time for hyperbole's temptation:
We'd sooner upset Fashion's applecart—
Don't damn with faint praise or admiration;
Raze us to grain, praise with faint damnation.

## THE CLATTERING CLASSES

Discarded on the curling pavement slabs
crouched the beetly dark grey UNDERWOOD,
shining levers stirruped in,
compacted as a swatted fly;
long-hammered keys, fingertip-blunted,
an eroded causeway of QWERTYU.

I claimed the decrepit old typewriter,
cradled it in my arms, careful
not to let it fall & shatter
as if it were my own dust-cocooned soul,
a little broken but still dormant;
reflexive; reactive against the bland
craven anvil of a hammering scene
crimped in brinkmanship, besotted by
sameness, an understated take
on what has to be said, by not saying it.

Suggestion needs a kick-start now & then
or it whimpers out to nothing. Roaring voices,
hardly audible for stacking attacks
on life-quarried lines; belletrist backlash
against fired minds' spined generations;
an anti-crusade for the sake of staking
vain claims on the creaming page,
buttered self-tributes, owing nothing
to a Blasting past. The Thatcherwrite hack.

They have it all wrapped up now;
creativity need no more question.
*We know this, we know this—but never show
we know, too obvious. Show don't tell.*
Deconstructing the poets, stripping their spell.

## ELOCUTION LESSONS

They sussed I scrubbed up from humble origins
by how my second-hand clothes wore me out
of pocket, kept up Sta Press pretensions
of 'well-heeled'; my clipped articulation—
practically accentless—betraying embarrassment
at state-school culling: too conscious of aitches
to pass for one above my fricative station.

Those old-tie school boys deloused my foibles
as psychiatrists their patients' phobias,
with lackadaisical lazy-lashed flicks—
*You lack that certain air...* didn't rattle me,
salted as I was with socialist distaste
for privilege-peppered classes. Though I
resented those tongues ironing out my creases.

Naturally snatches of taut consonants
& cavalier vowels rubbed off on my palette
but not that lofty atmosphere
orbiting moon-cool composure;
gravity-defying, gravitas-supplying,
tripping high to satellites of expectation.

# FANTASIA ON A THEME BY THOMAS HARDY

Never have ideas above your station,
    It'll only end poorly;
Remember that cloister-struck stonemason,
    Darkling Jude Fawley.

A greengage when he spied those skerries
    Of sandstone, & they spires
Sparking his eyes as blackest blackberries
    Unreachable on the greenbriers.

Those spires he saw were Devil's horns
    Leading him astray
From knowing's roses to knowledge's thorns
    That strip the heart away.

Time fleeced Jude's future—his wool eyes
    Unravelled from their books:
Lambs snagged on barbs by hushaby
    Box-cords tied to hooks.

He died in thrall of his tall vamps
    To peals of Trinity—
But tolling cow-bells, tumbril champs
    Chimed his varsity.

In their flowing gowns those dons n' deans
    They rascal jackdaws be:
Cawing in ruins cut out of dreams
    Of low-born boys as 'e.

The ink that stains their lily white
    Dainties b'ain't the dirt
That fills your fingernails a'night
    N' soils your patched-up shirt.

The only verse you'll plough verbatim
    Is the stump-jumped furrow there—
That plank for kneading bitumen:
    The only mortar-board you'll wear.

Those tasselled hats graduates throw
    To their Christminster sky:
Good as a cloud of cackling crows
    To the scarecrow's half-cocked eye.

## STONES & MORTAR-BOARDS

Intellect is catechised
Through tradition's tutelage;
Disciplined by licking cords,
Choristered on pristine sheets.

Blazered ranks are classicised
& classed in private cribbage—
Straw-boatered, tread springboards
Tripping footlight to staged feats.

*No surprise those scrolls are prized,*
*Prestige-steeped in steepled Oxbridge—*
*Streams of downcast mortar-boards*
*Millipede the chiselled streets.*

Those differently exercised
Towards the greater suffrage
Take the bench, or misericords
Of Parliament's selective seats.

Obscure scholars have disguised
As steeplejacks, scaffold-cortege
Of stonemasons' processions scored
By chisels' contrapuntal beats.

*No surprise those scrolls are prised,*
*Prestige-steeped in steepled Oxbridge—*
*Millipedes of mortar-boards*
*Stream the chiselled streets.*

Ambitions cracked as Latinised
Spines in peeling linage
Of Herodotus, over-pored—
Doomed as fox-prowled bleats.

The un-shepherded & ill-advised
In under-funded umbrage,
Cast sights & floater votes towards
Democracies' disguised elites.

*No surprise those scrolls are prized*
*In dream-spiring Oxbridge—*
*Gowned jackdaws in mortar-boards*
*Stalk the chiselled streets.*

## A STONE'S THROW

There goes Polyphemus,
Kerb-bound troglodyte.
He's got his one red eye on you
& on his Diamond White.

Here comes limping Oedipus
Dragging his swollen leg;
Guinea-pig of self-injecting,
Needle for a peg.

There's Medusa furnishing
Her flattened card-box home.
Every nickel chucked at her
Turns into a stone.


## THREE STREET SCENES


### I. THE METAPHOR ON THE PAVEMENT

There he exists on the pavement side
the knotted metaphor, worsted in a clump
of ripped & stained rags, soiled & piss-smelling,
yellow tongue flashing *'spare any change?'*

This ground-welded metaphor is an entire thing,
owns nothing, needs nothing but sustenance, a bite
to get him through another street-betrayed moment;
all he has is carried on his back, in his pockets,
is inside his shell, visible to all
in tortuous detail: sun-burnished skin,
stubble, odour, tattooed forearms, ear ring—
he is there, before us, existence distilled,
freed from the trappings of material things
into Hellish enlightenments: no need for
un-thirst-quenching objects, inedible
possessions, all hollow as his plunging gut—
so what use are those coins we chuck at him,
except to shed from our own shells
pennies that strip us of ourselves?
*The metaphor throws back*
*many copper eyes at us.*

## II. HIS EYES, EVICTED

A clotted youth has his greasy head down
on a step for a hard-worn pillow
outside the stucco Lodge, where, nearby,
keeping out of the sun, a secrecy of Masons
crouch in sweating suits, smoking.

An obsolete proprietor, cardiganed incarnadine,
lapses back into the tattered shadows of his stamp shop
that hasn't seen sunlight in the last dragged years.

The youth lifts up his face, skin scuffed & wrinkled
before its time, bruised by bad luck's knuckles—
young-in-kind, but less unlived-in than many his age;
a gutted squatter's scarpered digs; his eyes,
evicted, try to keep their shattered glass intact,
taped-up with patches, plasters, grubby bandages;
the puffing wolf blows his fag-paper life
into each stripped day, crutched on discarded cigs.

## III. THE PAVEMENT PIPER

Back against marble cold,
Sat on card,
The Pavement Piper plays;
A Tunnel Bard.

A passer by drops a coin
Into a cap
Then sits upon a bench
Paper in lap.

All the Piper has to sell
Is his pipe's song
But tunes cannot be bought
By anyone.

## THE STRAWBERRY THIEVES

*A man should put his heart into his work, and that work should be the kind that he can care about*

—William Morris

They filch my crust, lay waste my dreams,
But I'd not disturb them in their pursuit
Of robbing me of my only means
To bear any edible fruit,
Because the sight is beautiful as wallpaper

Blooming with flowers. Scamped in haste.
Creased over vaster walls of betters.
There to peel from porridgy paste
Steadily as grafting debtors'
Balsam-stripped hands. Time's itchy draper

Doesn't darn what it tears, just stitches
& glues the splitting seams;
Too busy counting its riches
To notice the fabric of dreams
Tangibly swirling, sprawling on paper.

Lowest of the low, I, decorator,
Pasting-up patterns from a blue-handed man
Of vision on blind walls. I, dumb curator,
Smoothing high sights with spattered tan
On vein-raised hands that crawl & taper.

There blushes the Strawberry Thief:
Brown-spotted thrushes on indigo set
Nestled in pouting calico leaf
Pilfering strawberries weals of my sweat
Ripen to gross for the gaffers' wage-caper.

But I can't begrudge them in doing so well:
They scoff the profits from the fruits of my labour:
They own the punnets my strawberries swell.

## THE RECUSANTS (1586–1986)

Our natures, frayed with sun-warped books
blanched khaki in the window beam;
cobwebbed in spider-hatching nooks
behind the hulking curtain screen
thick as the gown on plaster Mary
enshrined in the spare unpainted room.

Hood-souls, crouched in contrary
cottage-dark where doubts mushroom,
plunge the nicotined reredos
into outer blackness. —Biding
by altar-jambs, we ghost a cross
in the rigged ballot—then into hiding
opinions in empty larder priest-holes,
cowed by the blue torch Goosy-Gander.

Too strapped for brass, too bookish for proles,
our emblem, a grounded germander;
recusants of class—rubbed rosaries
for worry beads; drubbed socialism
waxing in candle-lit crannies.

Scrapers of coupon catechism
trampled by the Thatcher anathema—
snagged grants bar university
for familial fiscal asthma:
lapsed capitalists in bankruptcy.

Our stomachs howl hosts of weak refills
from stewed tea-bags: we fast past Lent.
Episcopacies of toast-racked bills
numb us to TV's otiose vent,
while our own obscure, un-broadcast soap
is watched by the set-top's porcelain Pope.

## THE PLASTER TRAMP

*for Sebastian Barker*

Gloomy morning, stewed from dreams
to an unclouded voice downstairs
drifting up through the ceiling beams
with a hint of incense, half-answered prayers.

I find my parents beatified on
respite from debt through alms; the fume
beading their heaped faces, briefly gone.
An aura of calm haloing the room.

Fear temporarily slopes into hope
as the plaster tramp seems to wink & grin
magically from its mantelpiece cope,
immortalised in glossed chagrin.

Through smudging years, that plaster tramp
caricatured our stony lot;
crinkled into bilious life like the damp
trumpeting the walls with rot.

The carrageen of repossession
stalked a clan of craned Canutes—
bracing wills at seas of recession—
neck-bent & pear-shaped as lutes.

Transplanted from that plaster tramp,
my adumbrated vagrant future:
captured bench-napping in the cramp
of a sculptor's time-trapped suture.

Indebted to days of alms & no phone,
insights of stripped-down poverty:
the tattered chair, no quixotic throne
had our house mushroomed commodity.

All material things appeared transparent
as the luminous fuse in me that frayed
my stripling grasp of tangible apparent;
toys turned to tomb relics, painted to fade

after my time. —Not the inanimate
tramp that matters in that plaster-past,
just the aura that haloed its insensate
sentiment; what the eye can't cast.

## THE CRACK ON THE VASE

*To be is to be perceived* —George Berkeley


'It's symbolic' murmured James,
my unknowingly Thomistic brother,
at the hairline crack crawled suddenly
on the dusty vase of poverty's salvage.
A sudden charge shone out from it
(not solely of it, projected *into* it
by our aesthetic artifice—
a reciprocal echo). It had
become something other
than a vase, now brimming
with sentiments in our animating
gaze. In a moment's enchantment we'd
cast an animistic spell, oblivious ourselves
to power ebbing from us—an outer *ents vital* (or
humming electricity)—now beaming something into
us we weren't aware of; a new-perceived significance;
*haecceity*. No more observers, now observed, as when hid in
the shadier pews to avoid serving on the altar, but still visible
to the priest's hunched helper, her vision all-observing as God's
(two genuflected trees pretending absence in empty quads);
haloed by holiness in objects obscured by style's crudity;
obfuscated by the surface (the material always nauseated
us, in spite of our catholic taste); the sudden emitting
shine on the vase ovaling our reflective faces. Was
that the collective soul we glimpsed in the
vase's vague glimmer? Connaturality
of all things we sensed, called it
compassion, socialism, this
airy quiddity, soul politic,
spiritual polish—but
it had no name, no
verbal tarnish, that
was its natural
poetry. All we knew
was the vase, ourselves, our
souls—none of them belonged to us.

## SPRIG OF THE BROOM

*Michael (Edward Lord) Abney Hastings,*
*reluctant Plantagenet Heir Apparent*


Apparently the last Plantagenet
capers obscurely down under,
indifferent as corks on a swagman's hat
to the outback's ancestral thunder.
Whence came his name? From an ancestor,
Matilda-waltzing Geoff of Anjou
whose branches snagged on *planta genista*:
his tag for donning the sprig of a broom.

Adopted by York to blazon his yolk
from Curtmantle, a superior claim
to the throne usurped by Bollingbroke
to accidental Lancastrian reign
through habit-forming throne-sitting
past incapacitated kith—
a thorn in the side of his prickly King,
neurasthenic Henry the Sixth,

sparking dynastic war (long-reckoned:
the branches had been rocking with tension
since the uncrowning of Richard the Second,
unable to tell his own reflection—
even in the mirror of his father-in-law,
fragile Charles the Sixth of France,
who had to be treated delicately or
he'd shatter into splinters of glass).

York was slain but the white rose bloomed
back into power through his son Edward
& in turn his sons, princes groomed
but nipped in the bud by Uncle Richard
(the Third), the last Plantagenet King:
a Pretender dismounted Crookback's reign
in a hacking glade. A disgraced sibling,
Clarence, transplanted abroad with the name.

Is it a genetic memory blade
jarred on the stabbing of Crookback
that the last Plantagenet prefers the shade
of a coolibah in the outback?
Crookback's crown snagged on a barb
of a broom, there plucked & donned
by an obscure dynastic valley arb
from the borders of bloodlines beyond.

& it's been borrowed since, for seven-
hundred odd years: through dour Tudors,
peruked Stuarts, rouged Georges, Wettins
of Saxe-Coburg-Gotha (Windsors)...
Monarchists might want to further take note
of a genealogical quandary,
when waving their Jacks at the Royal float:
of the alleged illegitimacy

of Edward the Fourth—the vital sliver
of blood-line between old & new:
that in the broom's absence a bowman's quiver
usurped the purple with Baylbourne blue.
If so, by primogeniture's lay,
Clarence's scion is—to use the Aus lingo—
our King *dinkum*: a Republican, blasé
as the bat, the kanga & leveller dingo.

[Notes: Baylbourne is the surname of the archer whom some revisionist historians allege may have been the real father of Edward Plantagenet, later Edward IV. If true, this would have made Clarence aka George Plantagenet, by the law of primogeniture, the legitimate heir to the throne. Michael Abney Hastings is apparently a direct descendant of Clarence. 'the bat, the kanga and leveller dingo' is a parody of the anti-Plantagenet rhyme 'the cat, the rat and Lovell our dog/ Rule all England under the hog', by William Collingbourne].

# ABSOLUTE BERLINERS

## I. NEUKÖLN

An English neurotic in Neuköln,
sore eyes soothed by painterly daubs
of pink cherry blossoms softening
Prussian grey terraces stiff as sentries
on the straight unbending will of the street,
interspersed with peach & pale orange
from subtler Ottoman palettes.

Berlin, self-denying; allied bombs
realigned you, cauterised your classicism,
like the fall, rise & decline of the
Holocaust Memorial's sable causeway
of ebony slabs. *That's where the Hitler youth
held their first rally* jabs the loud hailer
of the burly German tour guide
at an unassuming sun-blanched platz.

## II. THE WALL

The Wall: links of pocked concrete mural,
graffiti, scrawls, grotesques, statements
needing no translation, a tidal
wave of thronging faces spilling through
the parting bricks; a Curriculum
Vitae omitting all but dates—
spread on this canvas to Teutonic guilt...
...the East Side, still dismantling;
a Meccano hinterland; a mumbling
primordial suburbia limbering
on hind legs of dinosauric cranes—
West vestiges still tipping in,
sprawling billboards touting kitsch
pop icons beaming searchlight teeth
on the crumbled post-Communist bloc.

## III. ALEXANDERPLATZ

Marienkirche's weathervane
once compassed the highest view, now a
crouched casket of replicas & relics:
a Totentanz mosaic, baptismal
font wrapped with black dragons, two
melted bells—a third outside:
glowering Luther embattled in bronze,
gulped up by the craving shadow
of the cloud-pinioned Fernsehturm
spearing selective Heavens above
vast pavements of Alexanderplatz;
pewter Neptune & jade Dryads
fountain its centre with gushes of hands.

## IV. BRANDENBURG GATE

Brandenburg Gate: Doric columns
prop a vast stacked mantle, ground
to the galloping Quadriga: winged
Viktoria steering her chariot of four
turquoise horses stilled in charge,
holding aloft an eagle-tipped staff
cruciformed with tarnished brand.

## V. THE REICHSTAG

The Reichstag's stark face stares abashed
like a half-forgiven ancestor,
its pillared mouth yawning a trail
of steps flat-lit as platitudes,
haunted still by nightmare-footage
of fudge-brown tunics, sharply cut
Hugo Boss black uniforms
ascending Aryan infamy—
but Berlin won't be blighted by
detritus of long-stripped histories,
defies one fissure in pantheist past
with splinter-bitten liberties
casting light no Titan shadows
of Führer, Kaiser, Bismarck can dark.

## VI. GALLERIES OF THE DEAD

The silences between the headstones
in the writers' cemetery
lengthen with the scrolling shadows;
arcades of painted mortuaries;
freshly dug graves groaning humps
of cocoa-coloured loam: molehills
marking spots where poets &
philosophers have gone to earth,
or had their works newly exhumed.
Posterity mingles with fresh fumes
of coffee-ghosted galleries:
daubs of browns, greys, pale blues
in inked outlines by posthumous
Paula Modersohn, an almond-eyed
nocturnal kobold caught by night.


## VII. AN ABSOLUTE BERLINER

A gypsy lady kneads a dowdy
gap-toothed accordion,
grins in the beating sun bearing
her yellowed ivories, adjusting
a polka dotted head scarf, flattered
I camera-frame her face carved out
of walnut-shell: her tawny skin
countenances all of time's
page-gnarled mistakes. Her bright
miraculous smile forgives my gaze
its rarely travelled greenness. She
busks in the dust of indifferent traffic,
moulding back into slow brown burn,
beaming, beaten, hopeful, vibrant
            as her absolute Berlin.

# TALL THOUGHTS IN GAMLA STAN

*for Matilda*

*Många bäckar små gör en stor å/ Many small brooks will form a river*
—Swedish saying

*From my graspless hand/ Drop friendship's precious pearls* —Coleridge

Shadows stand tall in the Swedish light.
Lashes blink unaccustomed to
Gamla Stan's autumn stamina:
acrylic haven after England's watercolour.
Solar spots on the ocular halo,
retinas dazzled to sundogs arced
over Stockholm's huddled mushroom-patch
in Vädersolstavlan.
Takes time for clouds to acclimatise
as Sixteenth Century converts to
King Gustav Vasa's vision.
Scandinavian suaveness amazes
in stark light tricks of dark & day.
The silhouetted cityscape
prickly with contradicting spires,
inking alternative views.

Near Norrköping, a pavilion
stands haloed in gold & copper leaves.
Cathedrals of heady chardonnay light
pour royally down on a yellow & white
icing & marzipan palace.
Looming above, pillars of trees
impaled with bark-nailed Swedish Kings
flood Golgotha shadows on
the sloping cloudberry ground.

In the chilled haze of Lotorp's pines
ice-mists comb the forest floor,
web the trees in aspic of dewfall.
We forage for scatterings of Chanterelles
careful not to tramp them to
squashed trumpets on the greasy leaves,
boot-trolling toadstool villages.
*The moment's all we have* breathes Berit

in sanguine owlish gasps
as she pours coffee from a flask,
*coffee dark as the day is short*
(says Matilda); I basket these
chance aphorisms in creaking wicker
as the Chanterelles compare themselves,
yellow-trunked & charcoal-roofed,
to sentry-boxes on Stadsholmen.

*O to bribe Kronos with a krona.*
But mortality gifts me Matilda
& light that accidents, distracts
time's fractured stare, transcendental
thought-patterns graspless as air.

Lakes sit piercing quiet, elliptic—
no birdsong, no tree-creak, no sound—
perhaps this is Valhalla?
Longship clouds row splashless oars
across the lake-reflected sky...

Long thoughts stand demure as stones
or introspective trolls...

        ...tall in the Swedish light.

[*Vädersolstavlan* 'The Sundog Painting' painted on the morning of April 20th
1535 depicted sundogs (small incomplete rainbows) over Stockholm—some at the
time thought this meteorological phenomena to be a sign that God was displeased
with the then King Gustav's conversion to Protestantism. *Stadsholmen* an island in
Stockholm on which the Royal Palace stands; it means, literally, *Island of the City*].

## SEEING THE NIGHT ENTIRELY

I.

On the train from Norrköping to Stockholm
I trundle from Sweden's unadulterated sun
back to England's vaguer skies
& watery countryside. As I
leave this sprawling, laky kingdom
I'm already returning, struck sights snagging
on pines, spires, standing stones poised in
smooth postures amid a wood-carved carriage,
carpentered to share while travelling.
An absence of classed compartments; a view
afforded everyone, not just a kept few.

Sweden is shared: you see this in its vast
rambling green, un-hedged, unfenced—perhaps
how England once was before the land grab
chequered it—sprawling boundlessly, verged
only by polite interruptions of trees,
pine forests sprung in orderly numbers
knowing the pastures need space to breathe
& gather their luminous green.

II.

Norrköping, no in-grown provincial town,
but blossoming post-industrial
with flowering warehouses, trickling wharfs,
paper mills, factories transformed
into old-world curiosities:
the mustard-yellow Museum of Labour,
shaped like a steam iron, stands miraculous
on a canal; a tall brick chimney
sprouts from the calm waters; nearby
a man-made falls rustles its applause.

A stone-grey building mumbling a sign
Rättvisa Solidaritet Socialism
levels the eye on a pavement corner,
a provincial feature—polls apart
from every drawn-curtained English town's
backstreet-crouched Conservative Club:
Sweden has ever held the evener view,
politics & skies of a very different blue.

III.
I've come to see through the neighbourly
ease of fey Sweden—its yellow, blue, green
& russet wood hobbit-houses, white-decked
verandas; friendlier, less forbidding forests
soft-carpeted in moss; its wakeful nature's
summer insomnia, burring crickets
in the salmon-pink twilight of small
enchanted hours—that in vaguer England,
our clouded eyes have invented night:
a soupy stupor rinsed of ancient magic,
fairies, trolls, elves—conjured still in
Sweden's shadow-dappled woods where
elks' antlers crack like moving branches
through the brindled trees; our own folkloric
roots ploughed to cloddish logic & chronic
clocks... in Sweden, this summer, there was
no starless darkness, I saw the night
entirely in pinks, whites, violets, & now
I wonder if dark isn't just another form of light
to which our eyes have yet to adjust...


# DRIVEN IN SUNDSVALL

*...life is only comprehensible through a thousand... local gods. ... Worship...*
*all you can see... and more will appear...*

—Peter Shaffer, *Equus*


I.
Vast skies of Sundsvall sunder open,
sun shafts in, banishing shadows,
wrenching me from the comfortable dark
of thoughts' mushroom patch, cool introspection,
into sunburst of possibilities
petrified as the clutching trees,
the jagged stones, the terrible beauties,
the intensifying green in a staring unabashed sun,
that boundless sky, an atlas of sculptured cloud
depicting Nordic deities, storm-browed forebears,
billowing gods with sinewy limbs

in a tableau of grappled Giants,
mapped arbiters with epic brows,
translated mortals trumpeted
by raven-winged Valkyries.


II.
*& should I take that tumbling sky*
*& fold my arms around it*
*& scrunch the clouds into cotton balls*
*& stuff them in my sockets?*

*Should I, as a faint pain burrs inside*
*as if a poker skewers my brain,*
*throw out my arms & gather up*
*the tumbled sky, & start again?*

*Should I cauterise the beating sun*
*& pour its gold yoke down my throat?*


III.
Or maybe I should calm my mind
with thoughts on bed, its pillow-cold
cushioning solace, soft douse of fire
& fever searing through my boiled
metabolism like the over-heated
engine furring my hemmed-in feet
with burning vibes, a barely pent
polite insanity
fuelled on Englishness & tea—
what is this urge, this energy
vibrates through me but isn't in
my power to harness or determine?
Limp in the passenger seat, driven
by an unreasoning intensity
I have to create to alleviate.


IV.
*On & on the storm-thoughts go.*
*We pass a turning to a town called Limbo.*

V.

Your Scandinavian face aglow
in the gold sun of a sunlit churchyard;
a flash of the camera, a flash in me,
wanting to capture the moment for certain,
capture certainty, beat away
ambiguity; be lifted above
dead-ends, mazes & labyrinths leaning
in on themselves like beaten ambitions;
be freed from the sentence we all must bear;
drift into the light that is & isn't there.


VI.

In a second's camera flash you capture
panic in a snapshot, distracted
by your shining hair, blonde as a Bauer
angel, falling straw in the balm. I root
my thoughts once more in the ground, plant my
mind in the stony loam, lime-green, ragged.


VII.

I focus on the magic chapel
in a slate cap with a slatted steeple,
its rough-carved curvatures,
plain daubed white striated stem—
it's not been built but grown from the soil
like a toadstool, grown out of worship;
sprung up from nothing with the graves'
drunk tributes to planted spirits. Graves
they once called memory stones—I wish
my memories could be etched in stones
so I could put them down & walk away.


VIII.

Nothing grows from nothing, yet it does.
No thought outlives itself, yet it tries.
A thought is an overgrown instinct, swollen
to poisonous ripeness like a ruby bane,
soon souring, overpowering its patch
till it has to be cut back... Calm again.
Mind drives away. Shadows & chapels
mushroom the pastures, patches of worship
spring all around on the rag-tag hills.

## WHERE BANSHEES BROUGHT ME

Gusts hurled blustery fists outside
  & threw, with sweeps, the rain
That lashed against the draughty glass
  Of the sunken window-pane;

I caught the squalling croon
  Of a thousand drowning choirs;
The bawling caterwauled across
  Plunging downs & dipping mires—

I heard them beckon me outside;
  Their morbid song, lifting in pitch,
Led me from a restive mood
  To the turbid depths of a ditch;

The wails turned to watery gasps—
  Into the ditch I tripped & fell;
The rain filled in the dug-up grave
  & there's little else to tell...

Except that here I drowned with ease—
  My thoughts, the bricks around this well.

# CHARLESTON PHARAOHS    *A BLOOMSBURY BROCHURE*

*Ours was an elastic home, it never broke* —Quentin Bell

## I. THE FARMHOUSE FACADE

A farmyard's straw & manure fades
as a painty fragrance wafts out through
the door to cool summoning glooms
of grey-faced Charleston's bracketed treasures,
glowing *Black Brook* shallows—warren
for a Singer Sargent protégé
eloping with her brush & lover
to unfashionable chic *a la rustique*.

## II. THE TOUR

A whispery guide, reverential as if
curating relics of venerated Saints,
leads our trespass into the stilled head
of a dead Arts Hydra, up rackety stairs,
through corridors of paint-faded spoils left
by the Bloomsbury dynasty—Pharaonic
breed in turbans & flannel suits.
Their rooms, art deco tombs, assembled
by impulse, thrown like artists' parties;
colour-clashing slapdash affairs; rag-tag
gallimaufries—lamp-stands ad-libbed
from wastepaper bins in smoke-easy boudoirs
where writers, painters & flappers played.

Each crack, crease, crook, cross-stitch,
mismatched heirloom—Thackery's Dutch-
walnut bureau, & a marquetry table—
damned to stilted smalltalk like awkward
party guests: a ramshackle backlash
at wallpaper pa's & gossamered aunts.
Duncan's nude sinuous in oils
on an easel in *The Studio*, incarnadine
as the slapmark on *'good taste's'* volte face.

## III. PART OF THE FURNITURE

Maynard stayed so much a bedroom mushroomed
around him, where he moonbeamed on
macroeconomics on the *Morpheus' Bed*;
& in spite of mattress-spring ballerinas
(though he had Lopokova tucked up at home)—
the Bloomsbury bedroom farce—finished
*The Economic Consequences Of The Peace.*
A Delacroix pencil sketch & a Cezanne
offloaded like luggage in a hedge at the end
of the lane—*'what a hoot'*—equated to rent.


## IV. DISTINGUISHED GUESTS

A laquered red cane decade clustered round
that dining table, a Camelot
of Brylcreemed intellectuals rubbing
shoulders like the Staffordshire Figures,
gaudy Clarice Cliff & Charlotte Rhead
on the mantelshelf; sprays of caryatids
& stencilled chalk flowers on ash-black walls,
always alterable.　　　　What arty tattle
they'd have ruminated through, freckled in
the rusticated light of an upturned strainer.

Taking cakes & ices in a glooming
garden room where saturnine Tom
first purred *'April is the cruellest month...'*
　　　　Myopic Aldous tripping through
French windows of perception. The set's
sitting circle: Messrs Strachey & Saxon,
Miss Sitwell—lugubrious Virginia,
fidgetiest of sitters, captured
more lifelike in clay than in photograph:
a Gorgon bust *sans* snake-hair.
　　　　　　　　　　What paper
tales crackled in that rickety library
by the flickering *Cockerel & Dog*?

## V. THE AVANTE-GARDEN

Out in the avante-garden, chipped-nosed gods
cast marble stares from cobbled-flint walls
over statued lawns; a limpid pond
round as Omega dappled by lily pads
& dragonflies; a mossed ghost glowering up
from the rambling reeds at windows gulped
in shadows, walls scrawled with wisteria.

## VI. MORPHEUS' BED

The last-ditched front parlour, quieter than
its riotous cousins, where evenings grew.
A grubby Sickert miniature scowling on the wall
for a hint of urban grit. A pipe-&-slippered
abstract armchair against a pampering
of pastel lozenges along a makeshift mantle.
A book-cooled refuge of embrasured shade
from sunburned bohemian bonhomie...

Its reclusion shattered in a telegram:
the loss of one son besotted by poetry
& left-wing politics—dopes of the proles
& lower-middle-classes: taken out
in *'that blasted Spanish thing'*; now, demobbed
& bootless upstairs on the Morpheus Bed.

## VII. AFTER-FACTS

Heady days of painting, writing, thinking—
a rented farmhouse camouflage disguising
a singed paradise of otherworldly rooms,
now, wowing samplers for makeover vogue;
a museum of giving & letting go;
tombs to hoarded after-facts of empty-palmed Pharaohs
embalmed in objet d'art, sarcophagi
of jumble & white elephant paraphernalia
absorbed back into the ebb & flow
of egoless objects: to be, but not to know.

## LETTING GO

Being: a long, surprise-filled haul
Of struggling, painful, slow—
Of coming to terms with coming to terms;
Of letting go of letting go.

## THE MARBLE GRAVE

He put a bit away for a rainy day,
His dictum, *It's always good to save*—
& when the rain came it pounded down
& marbled his marble grave.

## ARTIST'S LOT

The lot of the artist
Has always been rotten:
Be dead & remembered,
Or alive & forgotten.

## THE END OF THE METAPHOR

*Should I, after tea & cakes & ices,*
*Have the strength to force the moment to its crisis?*

—*The Love-Song of J. Alfred Prufrock*, T.S. Eliot

The leaky pipe of the basement flat
boarded-up across the road
squeals & rustles like a tattle of rats.
I've stopped by the hand-spurned railings trailing
steps of rattling leaves to listen,
be convinced of no infestation.
An un-haunted mustard dark where ghost
recluses make their absence felt.

My nerves are elastic these rubbery days.
Scrap-paper trees stab antlers in the street
arcing the cat that talks by itself;
barbed shadows snag on the blistered beige
of terraces' burnt meringue.

*Black tarmac glistens like a smoker's tongue*
*night-lit by lampposts that stub out the stars.*
*Where's that throaty singing tumbling from?*
*Something threading under the rain-pounded cars,*
*bobbing down the gutter like a buoy to the beat.*
*Ah! It's my head floating down the burst street.*

O for thoughts to curl away
as coiled arabesques from a cigarette's stem.
Arbitrary light blasts the daily battlefield again.
Inner-enemies reassembling;
smoke-trolls amassing from ash hinterlands.
Thunder in the chest rumbles like an organ,
churns emphysema-hymns in the bronchia's
cathedral. In spite of distant artilleries
I roll & drill my rank-&-file
slim white infantries—then send
them one by one into the splutter of lungs.
There the metaphor must end.

Phantasms drag into partitioned day's
cramped flat: a gallery of damp & fags.
The goblin-green ghost of Harold Monro
hovers over my shoulder. I hope in time
ruminations' rioting patterns detach
from the thump of the mind, the spirit's split-
level; be separate as imprints, stripling
poems poured out in long bloomed youth.

*Tonight I wrestle metaphors,*
*unlock inkhorns of Minotaurs.*

The brain, a garbled labyrinth of honeycomb
abuzz with bee-thoughts stumbling by their stings
bumping off walls like balls of string.
As long as there are ropes, one copes. Dreams bland
unbearable day. The sinking pillow
whispers escape but morning gropes
soon one un-puffs its battered cloud.
One vague future day all there'll be is the bed
sighing your imprint: a urine shroud.

Since a child I've plunged in imponderables,
dabbled in abstractions the brain can't contain:
eternal light, blindness, oblivion. Nerves'
swell peddles pump purple dread at unending
dark, the sealed lid. —But I begrudge
the blind man's cloak of peacock tones; his wombed
solipsism. The heart's fleshy clock beats time;
each tock-thought, a sweaty-palmed haul up the bend
in slippery banisters, a hesitation
on the stairs. There the metaphor must end.

## VINTAGE

Nose-bleed spoor of an awful wine,
uncultivated, vindictive, cheap,
with a hint of the plummy unmentionable
puddles my lamp-punished desk,
moats the plinth of an ashtray charred
by black thumb-prints—this vicious wine:
*perfect complement to blue*
*cheese, red meat, fluoxetine.*

My parched throat's tickled by nicotine,
voice rasping; ash-blasted tongue
brackish with tar. Corked thoughts clogged
with bottlestops of doubt. Sour tang
of phlegm emerges cramping breaths
while lungs like flapping mackerels
gasp to understated deaths.

Posterity's bottle may mature to adage;
& a dusty vintage.

## ACQUIRED TASTES

Being: a temperamental, appley wine,
Its effect, not instant, takes bearding time
To filter through: first nausea sets in,
But the more one sips, a seeping-in
Of warmth, hope, berried resignation;
Then acquire its taste, peregrination
Of sapping buds—leads to a wander
Round rich fruits; pained asunder
Of flesh. The business of existence based,
Not on instinct, beliefs, desires—but taste;
That bittersweet tang came from an apple—
Or grape? All fruits windfall in chapel...
Some sip the wine, keep sipping still...
Some, after one, know they've had their fill.

# SUDDENLY THUNDER

*for LMB*

Suddenly, it ended like a heatwave:
a sky's impermeable blue bruised by
one thunderburst ousting the heaviness
so long stored—struck in a flash to muggy
concussion. A narrative built up to
patter out to limp impasse on the page.

Now I wake to a sun's cloudy yolk
casting faint albumen on light-bulb days;
draw the curtains until night shrinks in.
Oh, I go out—but only to trace back. I'll
turn the corner, or think I have, gaze
up at a gap-light in the drapes of the flat,
half-expecting to find you curled upstairs
in the couch, *mi gata*, like a cat.

I haunt the faded afternoons
of traceless past, once tangible
as these vague laughterless rooms
I grope in through gradual marbling pain,
clouding to dull rumble, purring to dark.

Absently, I replace your traces
with ill-matched miniatures, bric-a-brac
to stamp a heart's dismantling; things
only *my* sentiments have invested in.

Nights scratch nests from under-cliffs
of pillows, for the thousandth forgetting
before plunging to sleep. You'll appear
in dreams imparting small details of your
new life; we'll reflect, merge tones once more
like colour-echoes in a daubed Cezanne;
your tapering hands will brush mine for last
as a shadowy warmth waves us apart.

Feels like only yesterday, last week:
you reaching the end of a novel in bed—
*buenos noches y dulces sueños* said
as I kissed your quail-egg cheek—
you turning the pages in your head,
whispering, *how suddenly it ended*.

## OXIDE YELLOW MINOR

*...it is one of the chief purposes of decoration... that it has to sharpen our dulled senses:*
*for this end are those wonders of intricate patterns interwoven, those strange forms*
*invented*

—William Morris, *The Decorative Arts*, 1877

Behind closed lids deep indigo night
(Reflections from veins in the retina?)
I see William's crawling wallpaper,
Unfathomable foliage, cerebrum-white:

Tortuous intricacies; inner-sight
Inverted: blue-touch tendrils taper,
Lobed leaves sprout like the brain's cauliflower—
Optics lost to Catherine-wheels of light:

Acanthus, raging Marigold, sharp bite
Of Apple, fiery Honeysuckle, Larkspur,
(Ripostes to Brinton's rioting of Kiddiminster)
Tangible slide effects from the Bakelite

Sanity of Lustral, its coursing sertraline—
Vegetable palate of the dye-refiner:
Weld yellow, red madder, indigo carmine,

Iron oxide black—produces a shiner
For bruising senses: the brilliantine
Curlicues of Oxide Yellow Minor.

[Note: Brinton of Kiddiminster was a contemporary designer of Morris's, whom the
latter considered the producer of tasteless patterns].

# GULLIVER HEAD

*for Sally Richards*

When I broke out from Lilliput
Escaped my giant thrall
& found my way back to five foot seven small
I found that oddly my mighty thoughts
Had remained the same size as in Lilliput
Where an accident of scale by chance
Had aggrandized my stride in all things
Having to be careful not to tramp cities
& people on my wanderings—
As, when a baby, I'd crawled across my
Brother's cardboard castle, crushing its turrets;
My thoughts had outgrown vicinities
I once fitted into, & were growing still—
Things would never be the same size again;
Looking at everything around me
Through the wrong-end of the lens
As when an adult you drift to revisit
Those vast haunts of childhood's stomping grounds
Now suddenly seeing how small & cramped
& easily trampled they really are.

## KINK KNUT

Rootless, since memory imprisoned me:
at ten loosed from ties into superstitious
Cornish backwaters. Ten month's off school
for intrusive thoughts, driven reclusive.
Innocent to the stamp of stagnation
gathering to darker fantasias:
picturing posthumous futures, absent
but aware, a ghost among my mourners.

*The waters lash in & I lash back.*

Melding identity with lumpen parents,
aping a father's Somerset past
as a boy at Rock; cramming my room
with peeling barks of crinkled spines
crookbacked on the speckled shelf;
paper knights galloping allegro;
Holst's striding *Jupiter* thumping in
the stirrup-spiriting afternoon.

*I lash at the waters & they lash back.*

Deep-slipping, absenting bliss;
tadpole circling out of pond-context,
brined in frogspawn of pause; aspic
of limbo. Buried in undefined
countryside's timeless rolling rills.
Blurring boundaries: day, night, youth, age—
tumbling into one on the page.

*The waters lash in & I lash back.*

Happy in absolutes, absently bartering:
'If I sacrifice this, I can have that...'
balancing scales, tilting at tipping
into soul-floored slump. Haunting the day,
a contented shadow in intrepid strides
of an older sibling. Solo, unschooled
but for thumbprints on sprays of uniforms
or ghostly plates' static chivalries.

*I lash at the waters & they lash back.*

An Anti-Knut: a kink in my thinking,
hand raised to halt mutating waters,
stall time's tide wrapping round the legs
of my capsizing chair, convinced
I'm still King of my thinking, Prince
of scraping precocities, while my
courtiers see me knotting, sinking...

My mind pulled under, I grope through leather
sargasso for sturdier ties to take root—
new title to tilt with: Kink Knut.

## KNIGHTS IN TAUT CASTLES

[adj. obsessed from the Latin *obsessus*: besieged]

Thoughts cram the taut castle.
Over-sized Knights & Knaves jostle
cluttering tiny turrets,
cramping miniature battlements...
towers, so out of proportion.

Claustrophobic chivalry.

Sword & shield pyramid
in slopes to absolutes—
scrunched by tempests to crumpled tents
but still incarcerating sense.

The enemy gathers invisibly.
The oil boils over the battlements
relentlessly under siege...

*Obsessing Room Only, my liege.*

## BOSHAM TIDES

Rebounded, in mumbling summer
to Bosham, your favourite bygone haunt,
that last stop on our move to Cornwall's
dark, back in Nineteen Eighty-Five...
Today, a nostalgia trip, sipping tea
in that same 'olde-worlde' café
with pillars crimped like pasty crusts
& walls patterned like marble cake—
a gallimaufry of mistake.

In the cool of the sand-coloured Saxon church
we perch on pews. You almost comment
'It's nice here', or something similar—
it doesn't really matter what you said,
just that you tried to say it.

*We stay staring at the vacant altar*
*instead of scraping down to the crypt.*

Out in the shrinking light, we watch
the cloudy shallows lap the walkway—
the boundary between land & sea
bruising more with each tidal mark—
I picture Canute with warding hand
failing to halt the crawling waters
as your coursing thoughts wash in & out
fizzling off on a sandy vagueness.

*Canute wasn't here in historical fact,*
*& you come & go with the tides.*

## MERMAIDS' END

In the pea-green nursing home
a future shadowed the wall:
all leads to this dead-end—
life, then death, that's all;
nothing to come afterwards,
no haloed reward, no welcoming
from a dumb other side—only this:

thrown into an unfamiliar armchair
scented with other people,
fragrances of impersonal sprays
characterless as the dead—
the kitsch serge of seats without souls
bleached & sanitised parade
stuffing-knocked ragged dolls.

*She's having one of her bad days*
understates the cloth-faced nurse
her tone in-tune with gaudy décor,
mannerly flowers on drab wallpaper.

Dead verbs drop like watered-down
doses of medicine falling useless
in brine-dark tonic ebbing from
the coiled old lady's tearless eyes
shielded by tissue-crumpled hand
craned against her egg-shell brow;
knotted in a chair, varicose shins
ending in green slippers beached like a clump
of seaweed on the sandy carpet,
splayed as a mermaid's tail.

So it is: the upholstered dead-end,
final insult to the spirit's immortal
fancies, tall-tail stories that talked us
into staying, only to take
away hereafters after waiting's pain.
It all ends here with washed-up laughter,
tears, desires, ambitions, dreams,
loves, hates, album-memories—
into the cul-de-sac of wrinkled scales,
sagging fins & tightening gills.

*The insipid painting of boiled green seas*
*against an impossible cornflower sky*
*salvaged on the hallway wall—*
*nothing like the choppy grey that beats nearby.*

## NOW BARABBAS...

What did you have for lunch today?

*—I don't know*

You had roast chicken, didn't you?
& treacle pudding & custard.
What's the day today?

*—I don't know*

It's the same as any other day.
What did you do yesterday?

*—I... saw my sons*

No, that was the day before, wasn't it?
What did you eat yesterday?

*—I don't know*

We had salad.

Who was Jesus crucified in place of?

*—Barabbas...?*

## SAINT VITUS DANCE

Once she was able to say Yes—
could mouth life's affirmation without
a quiver of doubt—
now she spills just *Yawf, yawf, yawf*—
pale spell to reassure,
mantra for thought-cushioning—
to ward off thorny worrying;
sped up, Professor Yaffle's patter:
*Yaff, yaff, yaff*—but in sticking time's
stylus-scratch, trips out as... *Yawf*...

Sometimes this stifled Yes is paired
with *Yawfit, yawbit, bawfit, boffit*—
Tolkien-fangled tongue, as if to say
*Stop it—That's it—Hoppit—Hobbit*...
Half-swallowed vowels go down the wrong way,
gristly verbiage sticks in her throat;
face crowds out with twitches,
empties with clenches:
jaw clamped in bruxism's vise.

My mind flashes to cold photos of cavities
unambiguously black, vital grey membranes
eaten away, the irreplaceable grapes
of the basal ganglia going slowly sour;
brain ravaged to rotten cauliflower.

Teeth & tongue trip elocution
that schooled her Eliza Doolittle
groomed from Manor House council stables
to treading the boards, a yawning age ago.
Now she's tutored in smudged speech seeded
in dud genes' dominos; a slur
of lines, rehearsed parlance for clunking
curtain call, retched theatrical;
her gait, no more days' gone adagio,
now locked in Saint Vitus jolting dance.


[*bruxism*: clenching and grinding of teeth].

## THE SUNSETTERS

Remarking a translucent peach sky ahead,
a Turner-scape traced by the hesitating sun,
we reflected on mum's receptiveness that visit.

At one amber moment, my eyes caught hers
glowing with nostalgic vigour, a glint
goldening her brown pupil, so long fogged

by mood-clouding pills; now, for one moment
she shone through the dark, warmly smiling.
Then the glint dimmed back to chalky vague.

Gone, that moment, that one sunny break
in a cloud of blunted brow. Back to
the blank mask pattered invisibly

by anxiety's muffled batteries;
wheezes like Heaven's artilleries.
No traceable signs. Nerves shattered by

a silencer. Shapeless shrapnel lodged
like lead in the eyes. But, sure enough,
vestiges of her abeyant fire

flared back at Graylingwell—the daily
last stand of her feistier-self;
a sign, we clutched, she might re-emerge...

I built up my hopes as we, the sunsetters,
rode back admiring dusk's deepening peach;
blushes of rouge behind clawing trees.

*Yes, it's beautiful but not a good sign*
sighed dad at the wheel, a thrum of thunder
catching in his throat. Beyond the orange glow
grey was bruising in. *Bodes storms tomorrow.*

# WAX LIKE FRAGILE DAYLIGHT

*Sunlight was discouraged: it fades the draperies.*
—Bill Turner, 'Homely Accommodation, Suit Gent'

*i.*
To always want to be somewhere else,
anywhere but wherever here is—
eyes' each yolky albumen
developing a special lens
grasping in transparency
of grainy unreality
displaced as moments' crockery
shaking in the tap-dripped sink.

Lights make movements, shadows morph
to people, shadow people who
morph back to shadows, theatrical
tricks of chilling chiaroscuro...

How to know day from night,
light from dark, when never quite
asleep or awake? Always trapped
in a drowsy dream-belt...

Is someone outside in the broken eggshell light
of the net-curtains' fracturing?
Is that one of your shadow sons visiting? Leaving?
(Are people simply memories
Frankensteined in time's stitching?).

See Time for the trickster It is:
tack & inanimate
faking painted happiness—
things are laughing at us.

*ii.*
You suspect we're ghosts orbiting
your only mind, unsettling
solipsism sinks in the missing settee...
Only you are left behind
haunted by paper-traced impostors—
you see through us all; at times, even doubt

your own foggy contours.
Wrung from mourning others—
a cat, two dogs, your cancer-faced friend—
scraps left to anticipate something
future past, safer pre-bereaved.
Funerary years haven't been kind,
threaten to trip again any moment;
lampshade Harpies grabbing at
gradually granulating darlings.

Better interpret all as already
absent, so no more loss to fear.
The toll of the phone might as well be a sign
from the other side as the end of a line.

Harold of the chorea—feather in trilby—
chair-bound Beryl, Aunties Doff
& Olive, Uncles Sid & Ernie,
all late, sat in this lounge with leaden
stares; shades from your pencilled-in mind
easily smudged, rubbed out.


*iii.*

When Dad's out you miss his duck-egg grey
freckled haunting, fear even his ghost
may fade, wax like fragile daylight
then wane to pale assurances—
a chip-toothed Cheshire Cat leaving
the trace of a crumbling grin.
Brief relief to the hum of his car
hovering into the drive. For seconds,
spared from yourself. A wax hand peels
the curtain, then sinks feather-light
back to its time-warped perch:
shiver of lace on a faded chair-arm.

# TRACING THE PATTERN

*...when you follow the lame uncertain curves for a little distance they suddenly commit suicide -- plunge off at outrageous angles, destroy themselves in unheard of contradictions*

—Charlotte Perkins Gilman, *The Yellow Wallpaper* (1899)

1.

She inhabits a dark night of the sole
in fuggy corridors of Graylingwell
carpeted to soften thought—
tripping in dull-thudding dark
absented in haze, past, present glazed,
haunted by nun-habits, convent school shades.
Should she resign from the nursing home
        she left strung years ago?
Still haunted by lifting & handling,
stoning chores that frayed her flint
in auxiliary past, blunting it.
It's too uncanny—this clotted detour.
& isn't Richmond the Avenue
they ambulanced from to treat her here?
It must have been.

2

This time: the patient, shuttered in
with slipper-wearing wraiths
for cross-symptoms of Huntington's:
no fitting limbo to billet this
        memory evacuee,
so improvise through postcode bingo;
        label lottery.
She goes outside, but supervised.
Her skipping feet know off by heart
each dip & rise of their daybeat.

*Only the fag-yellowed Miss Havisham*
*cobwebbed in smoke & dandelion-clocks*
*—who squawks like a parakeet—is forgotten*
*among the lilies & forget-me-nots.*

3.
Twig-fragile on the crackling phone
Trappist-silent ruminations
tap spine-chills. Spectral breath
prickles the nape of my neck:
telepathic cross-correspondence,
plunge of the gut, tug of the soul
to the breathily whispered dread—
made real if spoken, like a spell;
empathy trembles in postponed
            thanatophobia...
*They're dead. They're really ghosts. I think*
*I've already died. No point in visiting.*
*I'll have to resign...*


4.
I grasp her sharper past mind-tight
but the grains spill into misted vague
            snapshots of personality
now wallpapered up, trapped in tapering
sulphur-yellow patterns, shapes,
            curlicued suicides,
tasteless arabesques turning the stomach,
scraping the fabric of sanity...


5.
If only we'd read the signs: Swandean
            sapping her appetite,
difficulties swallowing for apple-core thoughts
lodging in her swan-down throat;
phobias slippery as tallow soap;
sponge-nerves, insights in disguise
too mighty to be extinguished by talk.


6.
Easy to trace the pattern once formed—
            then no unravelling.
Hindsight's a burdensome thing:
late knowledge of Huntington's
honeycombing her brain—
            the bee's tail-sting.
Time waits for her thoughts to bed down.

Too late for stripping the wallpaper,
       its pattern's long set in.
Her grasp of the real now shaved paper-thin.
But then in time they'll try untangling
the coiled springs of her thinking.


7.
At least she's in the safest place
to look for herself again.

*The photographed doctor in clouds & khakis*
*stares out on his wards beatifically.*


## THE MOTH & THE SONG THRUSH

When mother shot into my bedroom
In the inky early hours, night-blind,
Confused as to where she was, as I,
It reminded me of that cottage morning
I'd woken in rickety summer to spy
A huge shape flapping across my room
& out onto the landing—a moth,
I'd thought, of abnormal scale, as I
Slammed my bedroom door shut till
It settled leaf-like to shiver on a wall...

But it turned out to be a song thrush morphed
Through the bars of my sleep-blurred eyes.
Natural things can, when trapped in a room,
Seem an unnatural size.

# IN                              CARNATIONS

I walked with her,            talked with her
without being there          just one of my
faint incarnations'          soothing words
echoing her head             round ghostly grounds
of crematorium-quiet         Graylingwell

on half-suggested paths      by emptying meadows
pastel-brick labyrinths      boarded-up stucco
Georgian wards               white-gravel drives
dream-scattered annexes      Austenian pilasters
thought-pausing porticos     waiting, waiting

for ghosts to come haunt     with old pillow hopes
thought long ago gone        but all this time hidden
just round the bend          by sand lawns, hydrangeas,
carnations, paused plants    slipper-parted grasses

from Richmond Avenue         to Richmond Ward...
*Has it all been a dream...?*   *Has it...in the end?*
Peace stilled in absence     of needling questions
no weeding need              for stitching answers
softly detouring             calm, in carnations.

## RAGING GRAINS

*for Simon Jenner*

Dust-deep, lime-curtained, labyrinthed in
blanched prints & sun-published spines,
hobbit of the cubby-holes & foxed metaphors
inspecting your perfect-bound regiments drilled
in dark kitchen cupboards glued to attention
for tunic inspection. You introduced me
to future-thumbed numbers of posthumous lodged
in your stucco pad's book-wombed spare room.

Got to know broke John, whose thirty bob a week
barely kept him dapper in his dog-eared flaps,
just scraping by to share a shilling's worth
of rhotic ectoplasm trailing like lime-scale
in the kettle crusted with greening litotes.

Shook hands with Harold, a dour sottish cove,
whose none-too-silent pool of lonely observations
dosed us high on dipsomania; choked
crimson with glottal hiccoughing for
his bottlestopped catamite tendencies.

You corked a rosé, poured three glasses when
Bernard, Muse-commuter, missed his train.
Thought we'd make a night of it therefore
& toasted his de-railed posterity.
Apparently they found him stretched on the rails
in Vienna—a faulty carriage door?
PINSTRIPED MYSTERY... & tumbled Alun,
heaped by his pluming revolver in Burma.

Shame I missed short-notice Clifford drop by—
he was gone at the first flash of day—but I
picked through the scraps he left, straight or curly.
Struck lucky that time khaki Keith unpacked
his kit-bag of sand grains & aphorisms
still yet to be simplified, now he was dead.
How 'Drummond' rolled from your tongue like a tick
or nostalgic tattoo of rosed admiration.

*All this time Sidney K jangled keys on the stairs.*

Can't repay these chance introductions
to such sub-tenanting literati
immaculately jacketed in time-scale rinse.
Spiders sent crawling across the page
ink-scratch incantations in their names;
nib-tributes to faded cream-papered Fabers'
cover-flapped staple. Onion-skinned shades
indelibly Brailled on raging grains.

[Key to poets: 'broke John' Davidson; 'Harold' Monro; 'Bernard' Spencer; 'Tumbled Alun' Lewis; 'short-notice Clifford' Dyment; 'Sidney K' (Keyes); 'khaki Keith' Douglas; ''Drummond'' Allison].

## THE VULNERABLE STAG

*i.m. John Davidson* (1857-1909)

Jago poet, twitching pen-hand on the pulse
Of poverty; scribbled nerve unswerving,
Hacking out a coughing crust. *Mal de moderne*,
Neurasthenia, his rummiest Testament.

Dragger of dromedaries, trappings of family,
Asthmatic stag caparisoned with lions.
Vulnerable to rubs; prickly to critics;
Irascible antlers snagged by every barb.
Drubbed balladeer in a hump. Rag wage
Snatched by lightning rent for rooms like travel trunks.
O for the fire of Blake to raze these grubby slums.
No cure for hypochondria, cancer or Penzance.

[*rummiest*: of or like rum; some phrases in this poem allude to Davidson's famous ballad, 'Thirty Bob A Week']

## MISTER ASPIDISTRA
*i.m. Harold Monro* (1879-1932)

Hobo of broadsides, goblin contradiction
Among sunning Georgians. Absence-in-
Residence: poet & shopkeeper. An
Obiter dictum in the blasting storm; gloom-
Lyrics aslant the lightning rain. Foxed &
Dog-eared, my copy of his orange volume.

Moon-eyed, mustachioed, souped in lapels; an
Oaky vintage with hint of manila &
Nicotine on his tongue's bitter sanctuary.
Reclusive chaperone of shop-curtains, smiling
Out with stiff soldierly bows, a slight wave.

## HAY BAILS & SHORT STRAWS
*i.m. Thomas Hardy* (1840–1928)

Time's amanuensis, savant of the Fates,
Hay-bailed to Nature's Tantalus ways;
Oracular badger brindled by bait's
Moon-beamed betrayal in the henge's rigged rays;
Architect of rustic myth, arbitrary traits
Scattered like dandelion-clocks on rocked days.

Hubris-blunter for hutched pariahs
Aspirant in class-traps; scribe of short straws
Ravelling Shalt Knots round Christminster spires;
Digger of tragedies. Heart nabbed by paws—
Yoked to frumenty in a cat's snatching jaws.

[*frumenty*: a dish of hulled wheat boiled in milk and seasoned with sugar, cinnamon,
and raisins. Michael Henchard in Hardy's *The Mayor of Casterbridge* laced his
frumenty with scrumpy, with tragic results].

# TRAMPLER IN THE PATCHWORK
*i.m. Gerrard Winstanley* (1609-76)

Grown from the common soil, crop-haired, green
Egalitarian, made of clod & light,
Rainbow-sown. A trampler in the patchwork:
Raking the scrublands only God the One True
Absentee Landlord could snatch from our hearts.
Recalcitrant in tracts, your flat-crowned, felt-shaded
Diggers set to work to till the natural law.

Withstanding the dirt of labour's nagged brow,
Impeachments of coin-palmed Parliaments,
Nettling barbs of vigilantes' abuse—your
Spade-handed disciples disbanded,
Threw down their shovels on a chapter versed
Against the grain of transplanted times:
New tyrannies travelled on trade winds. True
Leveller, tripping your ungrounded age,
Elevated above the hedges, those berries
You reached for are ripening on the page.


[*Rainbow* is also an allusion to radical Thomas Rainborow, or Rainsborough, whose name
varied in spelling.]

## JACK OF THE BEAN-STRAW

*i.m. John 'Free Born' Lilburne* (1615-1657)

Jack-in-the-Pulpit of political cloth, pumped
Out Puritan agitprop—lashed at a cart-tail:
He'd know the allegations in his mother tongue,
No trumpery in pope-speak for Free Born John.

Labelled agitator by parliaments of owls;
Inflammatory tracts & pamphlets, pettifogged.
Levellers, so-called, petitioned in his name;
Bonny Besses in sea-green dresses slinging hail-shot
Under Roundheads' squibs. Root & branch ripped out.
Radicals dispatched at churchyards. Ribbons banned.
Nothing for it but a trade, burn of kelp & bean-straw:
England's Birthright scrubbed by a soap-boiler's hands.

[*pettifogged*: an old word for quibbling or chicanery. Note: last line alludes to Lilburne
turning to the trade of soap-boiling (making soap), though he later resumed his radical
pamphleteering, ending his days in and out of prison].

## LIGHT SHINING IN LANARKSHIRE

*i.m. Keir Hardie* (1856–1915)

Knock, knock! The baker's boy, sharp as clocks back,
Ear to the pithead's cogs—upturned prams spun
In puddles. By ten, melts in with cobbled ranks'
Resurfacing day-shadows clogging home to tubs.

His pit-lamp halos pin-scratched Pitman in lit
Anticlines. Cage-clattered up strata on a carbon
Ribbon to paper & Party. —In the after-
Damp of Parliament's scalds, he signs off under
Inked portcullis; packs up his kit, books & cough;
Ebbs back to shadow. But his shadow casts a light.

[Mining terminology: *anticlines* arches or folds in layers of rock shaped like crests
of waves; *cage* conveyance used to transport men and equipment in a shaft;
*afterdamp* a toxic mixture of gasses left in a mine following an explosion].

## RAGGED ROB

*i.m. Robert (Noonan) Tressell (1870–1911)*
author of *The Ragged Trousered Philanthropists* (1914)


Robert who? Croker? Noonan? Tressell? Alter-ego
Owen? Journeyman between midstairs & downstairs.
Blacklisted decorator of camouflaged class. Self-
Evicted from kin-in-kind to a landlord's absent shadow.
Rough tobacco & adulterated tea: his tub-thumped
Turps-tin epithets.       —O for a *Sholes & Gidden*:

Tortuous long-hand manuscripts rejected, unread.
Ragged trails of scribbled drafts trousering his bed to
Edited ends. Mugsborough mug, tached & trilby'd in
Sixpence ha'penny suit, bannered on tubercular red.
Shabby genteel, rung-skidder anti-Kipps-wise, but
Earned a dying: signwriter turned writer of the times.
Labour's landslide, '45: owed to his bold novel?
Laid to rest, not the less, with twelve tramps, in Liverpool.


[Note: Tressell lived for a time in South Africa, where he had a manservant of whom he was very fond, whom he called 'Sixpence'. *Turps*: abbreviation for turpentine. *Sholes & Gidden* was an early make of typewriter.]

## RAVELLING WILLIAMS
*i.m. Ralph Vaughan Williams* (1872–1958)

Rapt in his green-sleeved valleys, cascading
Arcadias of choral walls—*O Clap Your Hands!*—
Largos, galloping folk songs, fantasias,
Pastorals khaki—*Bonny Boy* Albion regained:
His vistas of gavotting verdant strides.

Variations on a theme of blasted times
Amplified in brasses, peace's soft-pedalled
Uncertainties—swagger cane bartered for baton
Grasped to gather quivered wheat of flailing song
Harvested with barleycorn; steep falling away
& rising like waving dales. Shelled ruins in
No-man's-land: his coral landscape flared at dusk.

Wader in the green demi-paradise old Gaunt
Idealised; Hardy patch-worked with the Fates.
Light & leaden eyes of pale pencilled grey
Like our plunging skies, rough blustery seas
Incarnated in symphonies travelling from
Abroad: Ravel's vantage carved an island voice.
Magical, his craggy gryphon face vast-scaled as
Sweeping spells conducted by his ravelling wand.

## ASGILL TRANSLATED

*To my ancestor, John 'Translated' Asgill* (1659–1738)

Tell me, maverick ancestor, were you snatched in
Rapture at the end? Did you finally translate
According to the Covenant you cited in your
Notorious tract, burnt by the hangman? Just the
Salient points of your impeached pamphlet that
Led arraigning Parliaments to expel you: an
Argument divine fusion happens in a flash, a
Translation to the immortal world 'without the
Experience of death' once one thinks like the in-
Dwelling spirit of God. We can depart before death.

Alas, this vague descendant's inherited a less
Scholastic take on death, more a morbid itch to
Grasp at any scraps that might bar it. So *if* there
Is an escape clause from the mortal cul-de-sac,
Like a cloud with a porter to transport him, do
Let him know the protocol as soon as you can.

[Note: the subject of this poem and some lines herein are drawn from John 'Translated'
Asgill's 1770 pamphlet: *Argument proving that, according to the Covenant of Eternal
Life revealed in the Scripture, Man may be translated from hence into that Eternal Life
without passing through Death*—for which he was expelled from both the English and
Irish Parliaments].

# THE LION OF PONTRHYDYFEN
*i.m. Richard Burton* (1925–1984)

*...to obviate the idea of the richness and extraordinary beauty of the world,
I thought it was best to leave it...*
—Richard Burton, *Parkinson* 1974

Roman bust on barrow shoulders,
marble-sculpted mouth & brow,
leonine; stabbing blue-fire stare—
two Satanic labradorites.

Alexander's face reincarnate
as a pitted Co-Op pulpit boy
into a flinty mining village
choked in pits & damp-steamed hills.

Voice awash of ash & granite
splashing anger, rasping rage—
now vanquished angel's caterwaul—
now hounded scowling howl—
now stone-intoning chapel roll
grafted on the thumping page.

Flame blazed out like *Zanzibar...*
*Cormorant...* on his scorched tongue
singed by tar & brackishness;
a barstool bard of verbalese
in drink's slow, slurring suicide
*to obviate the richness...*

Visage, vodka-ravaged to
cratered moonscape, wasted cast
quarried out of rakish fame's
encrusted spine, harsh fags;
roar tamed to a smoky growl...
pockmarked god with white-licked sides;
a lion snarling its last gasped drags.

# HARE

Spring-limbed sprinter of Lepus
be born fur-coated, lozenges open—
saccadic ebons trapped
in stark-staring ambers;
hind legs bucked, sprung catapults.
Sharp-listening twitcher in the thickets,
taciturn watcher in prating nature
—shy as the skies, un-graspable in grass,
skimming the swaying vision-field.
Be fast as racing waters, fast
as definition's flicking lash—
ready to rear up for sporting box
mitts fisted in March fracas, balm-raving,
braced for opportunity's knocks:
razor-whiskered competition,
nose-knitting, teeth-smiting, staring-out games.
No shelter from nature's laissez faire;
no safety in numbers, only in pairs,
or opt-out solitaire;
no place to rest save an ill-hid nest
or shallow hollow. Skimp, scrape, scamp,
moonlight or borrow, scarper your share;
never late, always sharp, daylight may wait;
never still; no time to pay, save, hate;
only the flitting shimmer of sun
chases your sprint, harassed Hare;
darting all your days till time-light
whitens your buff-brown coat,
nibbles down your tall dapper ears
to split-end sheaves, twine-bandaged as
Tenniel's caricature.      Then, brittle-
limbed, bow out brave quarreller with Time,
lay down your wicker-light skull
bound liberated into the unthreading
of those stitched-on amber eyes.

[Note: John Tenniel (1820–1914): illustrator of Lewis Carroll's *Alice* stories]

## AT AMBLESIDE

*Hartley Coleridge to Branwell Brontë*


Dear *Branwell*

That day at Ambleside my friend
where we both laid our failures,
unassailable ambitions,
like feathers onto water
to drift invisibly forever,
was as well for me a small warm summer
in the Titan stride of winter—
we have shared, I feel, an interlude
of kindred respite, a meeting &
intermingling of minds,
a mirroring of moments,
a marriage of reflections.
Know thyself, the philosophers say,
& by knowing you for only hours
I find for the first time I am nearer
to knowing that life-shy inner-me
that least of all I ever see—
as for my aspect, I suspect
that was, in all its curiousness
(I mean my prematurely white
old man's mane, autumnal gait
& jittery disposition), something of a disappointing sight.
It's also one that contradicts,
as if by inverse caricature,
my juvenile green heart:
yes you may laugh at this, but I
still believe I cannot die—
an infantile immortal sense
I know the want of pains your soul
for what choice have you but to know
your time is limited, shall stop,
with graves crowding your window?
But I can tell you life is more
unbearable without an end
in sight; it's like an endless day
un-punctuated by the dark
that multiplies abundantly.
& so that's why my hair grows white

while I'm still fairly young:
because it's not had any nights,
nor has been spared of sun.
Well, my fellow Halfling friend,
my red-maned kin-diminutive,
it seems we both are as thin-skinned
as crinkled apples felled by wind—
I'll ask for last that you forgive
the letter I will never send.

*Hartley*

P.S. —your 'marbled skies',
I truly loved your 'marbled skies'.

## THE GHOSTS OF HAWORTH

*'Let's see if one tree won't grow as crooked as another, with the same wind to twist it'.*

—Heathcliff in *Wuthering Heights* by Emily Brontë

I.
*Storming thoughts*
*no stones unturned*
*mice-feet pace*
*the ringing table*
*tossing minute-*
*scripted stories*
*to Lilliputians*
*in the country of Wainscot—*
*rustle of hems*
*shingle of hemp*
*hissing the parsonage floor—*
*Banshees of Haworth*
*casting small shadows*
*green to pen spells*
*dashing a quarry*
*in sheets' sweat & writhing.*

II.

*Anne.* We once had a brother called Branwell, I'm sure.
*Emily.* Our variable brother Branwell.
*Charlotte.* Variable even down to his hands,
     each gifted its own prehensile will:
*Anne.* ...to draw with the right, & write with the left
*Emily.* ...the scratch of the pencil, the crack of the quill
*Charlotte.* ...our ambidextrous brother...
*Emily.* ...a double-tasking marmoset...
*Anne.* ...a triple-headed prodigy...
*Charlotte.* In his place now seethes a ramshackle ghost
     trapped between limbo & this cold shattered place.
*Anne.* We warned him not to fall between four stalls.
*Emily.* But he showed not the same fleet-feet as when
     he'd scamp over the gravestones.
*Charlotte*: His sweat's all a-chill beading the rims
     of his wire eyes
*Anne.* —Hush! He might catch our whispers upstairs
     & think them Banshees' wassailing hushabyes...
*Charlotte.* He doesn't know whether he haunts
*Emily.* ...or is haunted...
*Anne.* ...as the wind knows not whether
*Emily.* ...it blows or is blown.
*Charlotte.* The word *infernal* is branded on his brow,
     its letters patterned from the pox.
*Anne.* He who is no longer who he was born.
*Emily.* Thrown back to thunder from where he was torn.
*Anne.* Poor, poor Branwell.
*All.* Infernal... Eternal...
*Anne.* ...tangled in bracken like a stag snagged by darkness
*Emily.* ...on the winnowing moor...
     [*Nine 'o' clock rap on the door*:]
*Patrick.* Good night my children—don't stay up too late...


III.

Taciturn Patrick
paternal jackdaw
breaks the silence of his beak
with habitual caw
muffled behind his neckerchief,
its inching swaddling of his chin
the tidal mark his miniature daughters
use to tell the shored-up years
moaning through the dolls' house rafters...

Haloed in candle-glow
up the wooden hill
the myopic Parson follows the shadow
of a giant crow.

The ragged stairs creak,
the banisters groan—
boughs of a dark wood.
*Don't stay up too late—*
incantation to grate
at the insatiable chirruping
of paper creations.


IV.
Too late for the family's Chatterton
cliffed upstairs, impatient for
failure—the artist's thrall—
knowing his shadow will cast no further
than the lamp-dabbed wall,
no trace of his gifts to out-trace him;
paints himself out from among his kin;
a ghost in the cracks on the canvas.

*Charlotte.* Trampled by scattering talent
*Emily.* ...too wilful, too fiery, too green
*Anne.* ...nerves too rickety, under-ripe,
          to take the strain of waiting—
*Charlotte.* scampering over the blunted causeway
          of Parsonage headstones
*Anne.* ...his stepping stones
*Emily.* ...fire-feet knowing off by heart
*All.* ...each dip & rise & mumbling gap
*Emily.* ...between the leaning graves...

Satanic chapel-goer, fox-haired
disciple of Byron, de Quincy,
opium-puffed, burnt out to cinders
in the hot squall of needling sweat
clumping his curls to knotted thorns—
soon he'll gulp his bellyful
from Lethe's dark bowl;
a full tot of broth from the Ferryman's hands
bleached bone-white as his marble brow;
parching soup for insuperable soul.

[*cliffed*: a Cornish expression for 'cast aside' or 'thrown away']

V.
*In no time his sisters will follow.*

First Emily; her paling dress-rehearsal
at Branwell's chapping funeral
swift as a swallow, stubborn as a thrush,
granite-willed till the end, staggering downstairs
the day she slips with the sprig of heather
from her limp hand on the tattered chaise lounge,
Keeper by her side (the dog she loved
so much she beat him)—crutching her lungs
till the moment she'd known would always come
effortless as the harebells' thrum.
    Anne, only a season on, abroad
at Scarborough's sighing sands.
    Lastly, Charlotte, spared a tiny
lifetime to taste posterity on her tongue...

...the Parson outlasted his progeny,
ringed as a tree, a furniture part,
a hollow-sounding heirloom, now
snowy-plumed as an old barn owl
mummified in his neckerchief...
*Goodnight my children—won't stay up too late...*

VI.
*The raised grave of the Parsonage*
*stares out the bitter wuthering,*
*the crooked headstones of the crags,*
*the darkening brow of tumbled moor.*

*Four stunted furs battered & bowed*
*by bashing winds, bark Atlases,*
*ballast the sky with tensing boughs—*
*as in seclusion's servitude*
*their minds, besieged, withstood the storms*
*& wore them on embattled brows.*

# WHISPERS FROM THE PALIMPSEST

## I. INTRODUCTIONS

Holistic sanctuary: a plush pause of room
daubed hint-of-lilac—inspiriting change
from the brush-off grey of the counsellor's broom
which can only tidy, drug or rearrange
my thoughts' spilt toy-box. A coin-palmed guide
gifts me gossip from the other side...

## II. LILY & JOHN

First Lily shines through to smile at my urge
to dig up her ceded ideas, ripe
fibres she pitted in napkin serge
for marital trappings' colic tripe;
fears of sheer impulses leaping the edge
to a green repeating end...

                              (The ledge
between tangible & invisible
precarious as our scalloping lobes:
spectres receptive—even visible
in Victorian mediums' mucusy
ectoplasmic robes—to ghost-
Morse tapped by needling clairvoyants
unstitching the distich of existence,
tracing the Braille of the ravelled thread
on table-cloths laced with after-trace;
translating spirits, eavesdropping the dead)...

Present, correct, in khaki carapace,
grandfather John, chuffed at my interest
in those I only knew through a palimpsest
of rsclist hiss. No scrape of his smoked tone
this time, just the tight-breathed intermission
of a metacarpal gramophone
cranking sound-waves to crackly transmission
(tracings of passed characters, so they say,
can be taped at a certain time of day)...

### III. BERYL & HAROLD

Next Beryl, my Uganda-raised grandma—
truncated as her elephant-foot gamp-
stand, yeasty & round, armchair rum baba,
shins like blotched sausages, blimpish with cramp—
vents through to précis on my present spell
of trumped luck: I must toughen up my shell,
pincer on through life's snagging rock-pool
braced in crustacean—apple of her eye
as a halo-haired boy; gold in the buhl
of her tortoiseshell specs... True as a die,
her under-the-thumb husband Harold,
now demobbed in the other world:
in their lino & woodchip hereafter
I'm told they communicate far better
than in stilted life: brake mustard laughter,
since Beryl still seems the tempo-setter,
at least, according to a strained reprise
from the medium's ear-trumpet expertise—
(Psychic? Or bogus reader of vibes?
Pickpocket telepath palming my thoughts?
Or truly inspired in what he transcribes?
He could tap in any time without rapport;
throw me to his circle of thimbled knitters
for their tapestry of absent sitters)...

### IV. TIME'S UP

The hour out, his palm clams up... The clock
ticks back: Time's teacherly realigning...
The palimpsest's wiped over on the crock
of coppery chrome—life's tactful self-erasing...
But traces, spectral patinas, remain;
Repeated listens raise them from the grain...

### V. TRACES

Cassette in hand I drift home with the boon
of ghost companions, an amplified sense
of those passed on but who listen in; spoon
my replication brushed by their absence—
I'm not as out of synch as I often feel
but a variation scratching reel-to-reel...

from

*THE TALL SKIES*

(2013)

## SKAVSTA ARRIVAL

Arrival at Skavsta, eight pm, Swedish time,
Swedish time, a slower pace, a smoother atmosphere.
A syrupy August balm assuages Anglo-Saxon angst.
Dulled sublime, numbed by small vanilla Valiums

For lighter flight. The airstrip has the subtle bounce
Of the spongy mosses of softer forests, Nordic
Coniferous cathedrals of thin-pillared light—
Tall swaying spires of pine rooted to the spot

Of imperceptible departures... Ambrosial
Fragrances wafting in boreal hemispheres.
That vivid Scandinavian sky, so vast, so vast,
Azure, surely azure—Atlas of Valhalla;

Vaulted pavilions arcing high—this is the tall sky,
Stalking far above, unscalable, the thorough blue
Of poster paints sploshed with fat brushes by
British children wishing Swedish summers onto

The Turner washes of misty island canvases—
Their disenchanted parents marred by adult glance
Adulterated, tea-strained, their irides no more
Blue-believing. Chalky daubs are banished now;

Vanished in this Swedish dusk streaked with rose
& striating molten orange. Circadian
Rhythms hum demulcent currents woozing bumpy
Nerves to travelled verse; rubbery limbs succumb

To tranquilising evening vibes—tight island skin
Elasticises; Englishness releases itself from its
Knots & tensions—now long-agos, those dingy pistachio
Seas obsessing back & forth on inconsolable shores;

Now seashell hisses whispering away to fainter distances,
Ground out in grim nostalgic groynes; fortresses
Of brittle cliffs; those cussed, traumatic coastlines,
Now cast away for ten days of tall shades &

Lengthening light... An hour's drive from Skavsta,
The calming views slip on the eyes like comfort-clothes:
Every level yellow field, every wind-shielded hayrick
Sealed in glistening white like moist pinches of Mozzarella,

Each tiny timber Swedish homestead of Falu-red,
Pale yellow, pine green, Robin egg-blue, icinged in
Curves of white stucco sidings, & every single
Countless pine, quietly welcoming this Woden-child.

Norrköping by night: its yellow-plaster symmetries
Ocherous in the honeyed darkness. Indoors, shoes off,
Socks slide polished wood in insulated clement heat,
Warmly sealed in Swedish domesticity. Black trumpets

Drying on a kitchen-cloth on a stool in the willowy
Hallway: spoils of an afternoon's mushroom-picking.
Fatigued after travel, my mind still thinks outside,
In the dark, across the night time park, past the cold

Gravestones intermingled by craggy physiognomies
Of ancient menhirs, solid as anything can ever be;
Up to the anthracite church perched like a chary cat,
Its Munsell blue iron conical spire: a giant witch's hat.


[*svenska*: Swedish (in Swedish). *Falu*; pr. *fah-loo*. *Woden*: Anglo-Saxon version of
Nordic god *Odin*].

# THE TALL SKIES

Saxon *scop*, don't be afraid to walk under the tall skies—
Leave the anger & the sadness of that ragtag land behind;
Take in this crisper air; cherish whispers of unprejudiced pines;
Let all those fears, formulas, resentful anthems, damp rhymes
Of that unhappy island fall away—lift your face up to the tall skies:
There's nothing to distrust here, no ulterior designs,
No smoke & mirrors, recriminations, falseness, smiling lies,
No class conspiracies or espionage of petit bourgeois minds
(In spite of a Moderate government's attempts to privatise
The amalgamated mead of *lagom* no one should monopolise;
Trace capitalist star charts after decades of *demokratisk* design,
Cemented hegemonies of comradeship, egalitarian ties,
The novelties trailed by pilots of self-interest trip a thin disguise)
This sprawling land's no truck with strata—*statarna* had its time,
As the shadow of the ash tree, *samförstånd* is the Swedish twine
That weaves the commonweal of hearts together in a line
Straight as the angle of conversation—most made with the eyes;
No room for small talk in the long country of runic signs;
Opprobrium is soberly apportioned to those stars that rise
Too showily for public stomachs—no appetite to fetishise
Vain individuals' arrogated talents: none should advertise
Advantages—the lumberjack cuts every tree down to one size;
All's crystal clear & classless as the lake-reflected skies,
The stalking skies, azure fields of Fólkvangr stacked with white
Hayricks flamed with amber brilliances, Brísingamen-bright;
Palatial vaults of immeasurable blue, sun-striated cumuli,
Giant sails of stratospheric longships launched antrorse across the nebulae,
The skyward sea, the incandescent firmamental archetype
Of our island's watercolour welkin reproduction—atlas of light,
Staggering map of Gylfaginning, Asgard's pillared heights,
The indomitable distances that failed to circumscribe
The ancient *wicing*, scourge of our wincing race in Widsith's time—
Saxon *scop*, don't be scared of vaster scale, the Skaldic cries
That carry on sharp boreal winds where the sociable plover flies—
The tall skies will take you in, shake the clouds from your grey eyes...


[*Scop*: poet (Anglo-Saxon). *lagom*: "just the right amount", "moderation".
*demokratisk*: democratic. *statarna*: pre-1940s Swedish system of agricultural serfdom.
*samförstånd* [pr. *sam-fur-stond*]: 'mutual understanding'. *wicing*: old Anglo-Saxon for
*Viking*. *Skaldic*: from Viking *skald* (poet)].

## THE DALA HORSES

Dalecarlians—the folk of Dalarna, the Swedish dales—
Hand-carve their wooden Dala Horses in flat-planed curvatures;
No two are the same; each dipped in primer: black, white, yellow,

Blue, green or emblematic red; harnesses hand-painted
In ripple patterns of *kurbits*: pumpkins of biblical legend
With luscious gourds of scrolling foliage—then varnished:

Souvenirs individually carved in whittlers' rustic
Carpentries practised for three centuries, since the first was
Sculpted from pine as a toy tribute to eight-legged Sleipnir,

Odin's steed depicted in Icelandic *Edda* & Snorri
Sturluson's *Gylfaginning*; though the Dala Horse has four legs,
In some lights their shadows make them eight. Shapes & sizes

Vary, from the stout Nusnäs to the stately Rättvik hooves;
Every Swedish house has its Dala Horse stood on
A mantelshelf or windowsill—as, at Yule, Swedish windows

Grow their seven-branched candelabra & Stars of David.
&, at winter solstice, all Swedes celebrate Sankta
Lucia with tinselled Angel maids & white-robed Star boys.

Swedish rural houses are carved of wood, painted in
Primrose yellow, pale green, periwinkle or traditional
Falu-red. Each Swede is equal to the next; all are addressed

By first names, no matter ages—no titles here: this is one
Nation as a family: all are welcomed, for all sprang from
The same ancestral Ash Tree. Excess, frowned-upon: *lagom*.

Hands link in commonality. Few are as contented in
Their places as the Swedes; as free, for their humility.
Snow coats the bone-creaking antlers of the elk & he

Shakes it off like dust from a mantelshelf... At first glance this
Folkloric kingdom might appear a nation of sameness,
Flat-carved character—but look closer: each Swede is

Painstakingly sculpted with distinctive character,
Painted in startling patterns catching on straying stares
Alert to shades no camera captures: the calm mystiques

Of uncomplaining smiles; watchful sagas of mist-blue eyes,
Like sapphires in isinglass—keeping steep vigils over
Rangier distances of taller faces; guarded angers

As crags under hushed rapids—gimleted fragilities
Gradually unfurling flags to more haggard insignias
Than creaseless symmetries misinterpreted by English eyes

As congruence, but something more sublimely binding;
Unspoken scalloping of minds: Togetherness that can't be
Lassoed & broken in with stirrups of Class, nor gripped with

Wrangling saddles of ermined deference: anathemas
To the Swedish—as rhetoric which pays *samförstånd* wished
Lip-service, while stoking its own *folkhem* with kindling

Resentments; rhubarb libertarians see uniformity
In one homologous tribe—so opt for two or three:
Shopkeepers hoodwinked into thinking replicated tins

Prettified with different labels hold different things:
Conformity by margins. Carved variations sharpen if
Framed in the wider lens... Younger Swedes may nurse cravings

For individuating, but these flare brief as winter daylights
Pinched between velvet gloves of ever-lengthening evenings—
Artificial lights lure some to greener grasses, but Swedish

Stables brim with brighter straws: transmigration of the self
To the greater need, carves out the Swede... You can adjust
To appreciate the nuances of enchanted Dalecarlian crafts,

Charismatic magics, craftsmanly charms; bite the bits
Of hubris to trace the subtle curlicues of the *kurbits*;
Throw off the harnesses of false appearances & statuses—

Stride into the unimpeded pastures of the Dala Horses...

## DALECARLIAN CARPENTRY

There's a shop window in Stockholm lit late into the evening,
Filled with a miniature population of wood-carved figures,
Mostly proletarian characters, farmers, fishermen,
Housewives in flowery blouses & aprons, & some
Caricatures of famous political figures—Winston
Churchill with cigar, Stalin in scarlet *kosovorotka*,
& a khaki Fidel Castro, belt-tightening—no doubt
To feed more cosmopolitan appetites with satirical
Flourishes: anthropomorphic specimens of Swedish
Flat-plane woodcarving, similar to that applied by
Dalecarlians to their colourfully painted wooden horses
Of the flat-plane county; such skills have passed down
Through hobbies of old country folk, cottage industries
To factory productions—& this strange shop
That never sleeps yet always seems closed is testament
To continuing demand for such rustic handicrafts...
This is a shop & workshop: wood-shavings speckling
A smooth citron tile floor like sprinklings of candy-peel
On a butterscotch tart; a desk-light beaming from
The back through a doorway gap, where, partly visible
By his shirt-creased elbow, the nocturnal woodcarver
Cranes, painting his figures deep into the night—
Demonstrably a flat-plane apostle of the pioneering
Craft of the Tryggs, a family who moved from out in
The sticks to Stockholm with their little nation of wood-
Carved citizens; then, later, emigrated to Canada
To widen their trade, by then, one of rich returns...

It had all started with Carl Johan Trygg, one of nine
Children of a poor family from Närke who left home
At twelve to earn a living—first as a clockmaker,
Then shoemaker, laundry boy, & hand in a logging mill,
Where, in his spare time, he carved rough-hewn figures
From basswood & pine, likenesses of his acquaintances,
But mostly of hobos, his signatures—by eighteen
He was exhibiting his wood folk in stoney Stockholm,
& thereafter the figurines grew valuably collectable...
Later, his sons, Nils, Lars, Carl Olaf, & a female
Relative, Ellen, all took up the trade, having inherited
Carl Johan's gift: the almost-mystical ability
To transform blocks of wood into uncannily expressive
Miniature characters with florid faces in vibrant paints,
Apparelled in robust patterns of rural plaid;

A wood-carved *statare* mounted on plinths of wooden blocks,
Signed underneath—Trygg's was a magical artistry
Akin to the Lokian ilk of Dalecarlian carpentry
& handicrafts: to sculpt himself & his whittled kin
From their shapeless agricultural caste into individuals,
Inspirited with rough-hewn personalities, using only
The flat-planed sculpting knife of his wits & imaginative
Industry; & home-made paints pestled from crushed berries:
Nature was his studio, where he breathed his brethren into life:
Scooped souls for them from gouged wounds of basswood,
Planed their gnarly textures to smoother finishes
Varnished into bucolic curios for rich collectors
Sprung among the landowners, makers of their yokes
As thralls displaced by the partitions, now the speculators
Of the products crafted with their liberated tools...

[*kosovorotka*: Russian skewed-collared shirt. *statare* [pr: *sta-ta-reh*]: 'estate workers';
the agricultural serfs who were paid 'in kind' under the *statare* system].

## BITTER ALMONDS
*i.m. Daniel "Dan" Andersson* (1888–1920)

Dalecarlian-carved; a *säckpipa* of hoofed stilts glistened in pink
Afterbirth; cast apart, casualty of witchcraft; cotton-spun through
Nuptial thralls: the slash & burn of forest Finns on his father's side

& the iron-forging rumour of a Walloon shadowing thrown
Notions of his hoisted eyes; frowning mouth soured by the bit
Digging into his tongue, but no harness could restrain this
Equid chomping poems to apple-sharp frumenty—Blåbandist
Rubric: toured with Forest Flower at fourteen, proselytising
Sobriety from Gothenburg to Grimsby... Baptised with the
Sobriquet *"Black Jim"* —First / last books: *Piston Beware* // *He Left*—
Odic coincidence? Runic code? Went to sleep at Hotel Hellman
Not noticing a prussic scent: the brain's bouquet of bitter almonds.

[*säckpipa* [pr. *sek-pee-pa*]: bagpipes. *Blåbandist* [pr. *Blaw-bundist*]: a Swedish sect
of teetotal evangelical Christians].

## POSTCARD FROM NORRKÖPING

In Östergötland by the chill of the slaty Baltic sea
Span crops of Mikado yellow almond houses with chocolate beams:
The old symmetrical textile town of Norrköping,
Its industrious sobriquet, *"Sweden's Manchester"*,
Or more exotically, *"Sweden's Peking"*—but in its
Harsher industrial past it was colloquially nicknamed
By its exploited textile workers, *"Surbullestan"*,
Meaning *"Town of the Sour Bun"*... Today, at a distance:
A cardboard cut-out, faultlessly folded on scored lines,
Seamlessly glued together—a pop-up postcard;
Its sprung dimensions flat-packed at close of day,
Shut up in a children's book, then opened up again
By the gentle fingers of crisp Swedish mornings;
A labyrinth of recycled paper mills applauded by rapids
Where salmon used to leap, before the hipped-roof cotton
Refineries grew & conical beige-bricked chimneys
Sprouted up to spume plumes of smoke like blowholes...
They say this town was always as it is today (though
Doubtless once dirtier for industry in motion):
The tall straight buildings & flat-faced wharfs were always
Yellow-washed, repainted periodically through centuries...

So, today, these mustard-tinctured rectangular obelisks
Of bitumen & plaster thrust up authentically
From archipelagos curling across the rustling Motala ström,
Wrought with iron walkways, winding paths & riverside
Loins of grass sprinkled with benches wherefrom
One might sit & gaze across the sky-reflecting silver tray
Of water towards Grytstorget & its solid silhouette
Of the statue of Moa Martinson, defiant-faced,
Head held high, robustly poised in cast-iron tunic,
Long skirt & thick clogs—an anthropomorphic
Weathervane; a crow-like spectre of oil-slicked plumage;
A petrified ghost in widow's weeds planted amid black
Reeds of metal railings, a revenant only clairvoyants
& neurotics can perceive (as prim Miss Giddens,
Anguishing governess, the spectre of Miss Jessel in
*The Innocents*, whom no one else believes)... Chalky
Paths are punctuated by small wooden, ownerless
Yellow kiosks, or coffee rooms, gazebos (*"I shall gaze"*),
Tiny Italianate rotundas with white pilasters
Carved at each octagonal angle (which the English
Might compare to summerhouses, or Edwardian

Children's miniature garden follies), always empty
When we peep inside them; pausing spaces housing
Unoccupied tables & chairs (rooms for Goldilocks
In the absence of the three bears); perfect enclosed
Spots for picnics of open sandwiches & nourishing
Swedish coffee during sudden downpours, small Romanic
Cubicles adorned with pastel murals framed by painted
Ionic columns—portals to Nordic Wonderlands; quaint
Receptacles accessible to publics—sharing spaces:
Swedes share civic spaces, both the pleasure & upkeep;
Hold municipalities in common (for this land of vast
Distances extends its hand of *samförstånd—mutual*
*Understanding*—so its scattered clans, from carpentering
Dalecarlians to the curled-shoed Sami of Lapland,
Have stamina to withstand the isolating snowdrifts
Of winter); nature & urbanity are both to share;
No one's better than anyone else—*lagom*: tacit dictum
Of a classless race (& though some Swedes might
Sometimes chafe at how this dampens ambition,
Vitiates acquisitiveness—the plastic aspiration
Of the American Dream's their anathema, nightmare);
Commonality's the mortar that binds the bricks of Norrköping,
An artisan town architected from collective effort,
Built from the labours of an heroic working class
In harsher days of *statare*, almshouses, chimney sweeps,
Factory proletariat—all banished with the Swedish
Welfare State, *folkhemmet* (*The people's home*—as
Opposed to *scrapheap* as it's perceived in England)
& green egalitarian energies released through
*Demokratisk* design (in the Thirties & Forties)...

Now salmon twilight inks to sighing night, soporific
Whispers from Motala ström soothe me into sleepiness
As I sip sweet nocturnal rosehip soup of night on
A darkening balcony; so I will close, for now; sign this
Postcard from Norrköping to figments of my Englishing,
With inkless pen, wishing we were here... O when
Will we ever be... again that gentler England—
Haunted nostalgically in Sweden's simpler *kin*-dom
Where social democracy has been left to blossom
Beyond its British abortion at the Seventies' end—when
Will we be more than an occluding body in its antumbra...?

[Pr. Norrköping: *Nur-sherping*. Grytstorget: *Groots-toryet*. Östergötland: *Urster-yurtland*. ström: *strum*].

169

## *from* STRYKJÄRNET

### I. THE FLAT IRON

*Strykjärnet*, the *"flat iron"*, mustard-coloured Arbetets
Museum (of Work)—but nothing so atomist or
Utilitarian as its name might suggest to scorched ears
Of tourists from The Country of the Grind where
The red-top headline's king (Woden's Workfare State)—
Temple of mutual effort, a celebration of the dignity
Of labour, the nobleness of hand & brain beating
Time & metal together to Bragi's Skaldic metre,
Thor's proletarian hammer striking Viking anvil
With each tock of the common metronome; Folke Bensow's
Giant dolls house of industry: heptagonal edifice built
To fit the shape of the craggy outcrop of Laxholmen,
In Holmbrogränd; its basement, subterranean,
Welded deep into the submerged rock of this serendipitous
Island (called Strykbrädan: the *"ironing board"*):
It appears to sit on the mirroring surface of Motala ström,
Chimneys launched from the water: phallic outposts
Of sprung production; hardy antennae of artisanship;
Unfinished pillars, cropped fulcrum falling fathoms short
Of propping cotton-spun clouds, truncated, hollowed-out
To spout posthumous smoke, throw mechanical echoes
Of phantom machinery, invisible belching billows
From a poltergeist factory haunted by echoes of tools
Of the defunct textile trade, & clinks & clanks
Of paper manufacturing... According to the brochure,
The purpose of this industrial reliquary is '*Not to
Collect things but to preserve them*': this is implicit in
Immaculately life-like mummifications of man-made items,
Authentic in makers & operators' absences;
Cryptic equipment bereft of hands' manual translations...

[Pr. Arbetets: *Arr-beart-ets*. Strykjärnet: *Strook-yair-net*. Holmbrogränd: *Holm-broo-grend*. Strykbrädan: *Strook-brair-dan*. Next pages: ångest: *un-gest*. Aftonbladet: *Af-ton-blar-det*].

## II. THE MOOMIN FLOOR

Not all in this industrial Aladdin's Cave is hinged on trade:
Take the lift just one floor up & the visitor is spirited
Into the curious magical world of the polemical Moomins:
Stout white little trolls who look like hippopotamuses,
Dreamt up by pinched-nosed Tove Jansson, immigrant
Finn from Helsinki, as satirical animations for
Nordic children, infant travellers well-versed early in
The nervous swerves of parents' mental adventures,
Introspective violences, interspersed with the light relief
Of Einar Nerman's postcards in bold poster colours,
& his blazes of cover jackets for storybooks by Selma
Lagerlöf—Fauvist spectrums tutored by Matisse;
The Moomins, mooning bohemians who loved nature
& diversity, yet were depicted forever on the verge
Of melancholy; Moominvalley adumbrated by
The hill-shaped Groke, an amorphous mound of Nordic
Gloom with glowing ember eyes, who froze the ground
Wherever it moved, while everything that touched it
Expired; the conformist Hemulens who liked to boss
Everyone around; the introverted Snork who changed
Colour according to mood; the mushroom-like
Hattifatteners who roamed in groups & turned electric
When struck by lightning; The Muddler, an anxious
Button collector who lived with his wife, Fuzzy,
In a coffee-tin; Snufkin, an itinerant philosopher
Who believed in travelling light so not to complicate things;
& Little My whose mouth formed aphorisms:
"*Possession means worries & luggage bags one has to*
*Drag along*"—food for a race of philosophical children
Hypnotised by the hurdy-gurdy of Jansson's Finnish burr;
Wiser Little Times brought up to tropes of obsessional trolls;
Imaginatively traumatised with best intentions
Through animated inoculations to future bruises,
Neurotic cartoons, Kierkegaardian sketches guarding
Against adult *ångest* (angst), steered away from intolerance
& conformity (foundations of imprisoned consciousness);
Those Moomintrolls were grown out of Jansson's childhood
Terrors cultivated by her uncle trying to frighten her
Off pilfering from the larder at night: "*They live in*
*The kitchen & breathe cold air down the back of your neck*";
The '*Moomin*' had metamorphosed through a Hippo-line
Of grotesquer forebears: through '*Proto-Moomin*',
Back to the more abstracted '*Snork*', or '*Niisku*',

A dialectical caricature scrawled on the wall
Of the family toilet with *KANT* scratched underneath it
(After her brother's triumph in a philosophical argument),
Intended to depict the *'ugliest creature imaginable'*,
A more angularly cut ancestor with symbolically missing tail...


IV. *ARBETE*

Smoking a stout cigarette (that might have suited
A Moomin as an allegorical accessory, as it did for
Their chimneying creator), I drag a shaft of sunlight,
Then launch the butt into acid-hissing swim
In the silky waters wobbling below with yellowy
Reflections of the Arbetets Museum & its whirling
Wood-decked bridge that links its heptagonal hive
Of archiving—a co-operative run on volunteering:
The Swedish type, so, by stipend—to the mainland...
I think on how industrious Kronos took the svenska
From Varangian silver stripped during raids in
Samarkand to the minters of the krona... I'm partial
To causality; particularly when away from home,
Adrift from familiarity: it soothes my nerves to root
My thoughts from spot to spot, to find a foothold,
A firm refuge to ground me; & each place my shadow falls
Another plants itself, casts centrifugally, ever taller,
With the intensifying light—the sixth sense of anxiety
Is stimulating of second sight; perhaps a vestigial
Saxon gland once vibrated nervously, like cats' whiskers,
To alert them to propinquities of longships, now long-
Consigned to the English collective unconscious;
Low thyroids of social tolerance vented through
Shadow-projections of vicarious vices onto victims
Of administrative vandalism: the urban *"churn"*
Of tenants evicted through *'gentrification'*, all to
*"Make Work Pay"*—far cry from the Swedish
Collectivist view that a society of shared values
Makes every man & woman *want* to work, no
Blackmails necessary; boreal labour strives towards
Natural rewards of leisure, where true inspirited
*Arbete* by itself's the forge in which all citizens
Mould freedoms through fruits distributed equably—
Work doesn't make us free (except from stigma);
Freedom's no employee; it's irrepressibly self-expressive,
Like an inspired child; only creativity sets us free...

## PER BRAHE BAUER
*i.m. John Bauer* (1882–1918)

Jönköping was a matchstick city, but its phosphorous fumes were
Obfuscated by fragrances from father's charcuterie
Heaping up in our damp apartment—phantom abattoir not for faint
Nostrils… My sister Anna wasn't revived with smelling salts, but I

Brushed her back to life in paint: flaxen Princess Tuvstarr, foundling in
A nightgown, tiptoeing *grön tårta* moss of organ-piped woods; or touring
Underground grottos with gross-proboscised trolls… She grew into Esther
Ellquist; together we planted Bengt—but turbulence took us to Stockholm:
Rather than risk the train after Getå, we boarded the morrow's ghost ship,
        *Per Brahe…*

[*Jönköping*: pr. *Yun-sherp-ing. grön tårta* [pr. *grurn torta*] (green cake), or
*princesstårta* (princess cake): a traditional Swedish cake covered with marzipan
(usually green) and filled with sponge, jam, custard and cream. *Getå* [pr.*Year-taw*]: site
of the worst train crash in Swedish history on 1st October 1918. *Per Brahe:* a steamer
shipwrecked on 20th October, 1918].

## KNOPARMOJ
[pr. *kanoop-arr-moi*]

Soot ghosts of Norrköping's industrial past:
A photograph of charred-faced Swedish chimney sweeps
Circa 1900s, begrimed & brow-beaten by poverty,
Insolent-eyed with that special acrid proletarian pride
So challenging to those who have never had to forge
Their own dogged egos through the grind of growth-
Eroding labour; barefoot in rags, cramped bags of bone
& bloody-minded industry; undernourished blond-
Haired shadows, scrubbed up with coal tar soap;
Grubby water babies, resuscitated into industrious
Life with pumps of smoke, weaned on char-black spit;
Prone to rickets & consumption for want of milk
& calcium; black-lunged soot-nosed helpers
Of Mímir; fire-licked refuseniks of Loki's fickle gifts;

Sweepers of the dampers used to trap & harness
Its sacred properties of light & warmth;
To keep the soot from clogging up the chimneys
& throwing smoke back into shuttered rooms;
To halt the restless flames—ever attempting
Escape from the grate, hampered & torn at by
Norns of muscular Nordic winds—from stoking
Themselves into berserker frenzies, spreading
Raging amber tongues through slumbering houses...

So up the sooty pitch-black shafts those spluttering
Children climbed, grip to grip, up the sheer brick
Mountainsides, blind; the unluckiest among them
Trapped until they starved, then thinned, slid down
In a cloud of soot, black-plumed crows, all feathers
& bones; so to most this daily workplace was
A charnel house in waiting; a dormant cremation
Chamber, a sepulchre out from which sweeps
Sometimes had to be hacked by psychopomp employers;
Wily pallbearers scraping pennies from boy-corpses' eyes...

From the Sixteenth century on, small, nimble troll-
Children of lumpenproles were apprenticed to sweeps
At eight years old; moulded in moleskin shirts
& trousers with leather patches at the knees
& on the seats, to protect them from the heat—
The balls of their bare un-pumiced feet, so thick
With hard-skin they needed no such protection—
& baggy caps to keep their straw hair from catching,
Or blackening with soot; as for their faces, arms & legs,
They rarely washed them: proudly wore their dirty
Skins as trophies of their chores; this sacred trade's
Sacramental tools: lead line, sweep-broom, scraper...

By about eighteen, those who'd survived into adulthood
Were promoted to journeymen: Viking-whiskered,
Angular-visaged with tall white stares & black mouths
Where butter turned to mud, all food smoked before
Washed down; but their oiled tongues inherited
A slangy Glossolalia indigenous to their trade—
Language of the ravens, untranslatable to other mortals,
Understood only by them, morphemes of the psychopomp
In floppy blue-grey hat & cloak: Odin, the Thought-God
(Shaper of Wyrd, Bender of Orlog, who hanged himself
From the Great Ash Tree Yggdrasil to gain the wisdom

& omnipotence of the runes); a *"working language"*,
Complicated, occlusive, occulting, even kept locked
To their families, like Masonic ceremonies (though
A sample was smuggled into poetry by Alf Ragnar
"Sten" Henrikson in his *Anacka*) —they called it
*"Knoparmoj"*, a *'sociolect'*, workers' Skaldic dialect,
Spoken in the Swedish sweepers' soot-togged brogue
Punctuated with glottal stops of black sputum;
A tongue, no doubt, with equivalents throughout
The industrialised globe, but now long lost
With phantom trades—apart from driftwood
Salvaged for the marketing game: *pants* & *sneakers*,
Forgotten by the world's labourers unburdened
By trumped struggles, invalidated dialectics
Of tub-thumped pasts, verbal barriers once raised,
Now lowered to whispers of deference, or quaint
Scrapings caught in echoes of empty museums...

It no more matters: now Lotto can immortalise
Any random aspirant, amber any ambition,
Arrest any extravagance, avarice or tragic glance
Of graspless Midas suicides in celebrity aspic,
Or glossy isinglass of gossip magazines;
Ever since Loki the Trickster let the misanthropic
& self-interested harness fire for furnace,
Forge & foundry, wield molten hammer on lava-
Avid anvil, to meld iron & steel, make armouries
While stripping labour of dignity—*This* they called
*"Progress"... Knoparmoj* succumbed to a humbled
Dumbness among brainwashed human commodities
Indoctrinated by dialectics electrically
Conducted through idiots' lanterns; Bakelite
& plastic gadgets rinsing brains in intrusive
Ultraviolet rays, reducing all to blue-overalled
Lotus-eating wage-slaves, aphasic camels happy
To carry cans for *kapitalists'* gains—they pawned
Their sacred *knoparmoj* for caravans, humps & grains...

## PAPER WRAPS BONE

The printers' ink-fumed studio is lined with wooden work-desks,
Boxes full with clumps of pulp spoilage, one displaying flyleaf
Paper with swirling grey marbling, as cambric moire—
Faintly chafing against my automatic comparison
To one of the Dutchman's roiling skies, if he'd worked
In blue inks, instead of discovering paints & colour
(& never recovering again); metal cups dripped with
Spilt paints: multicoloured teas; a cluster of brushes
& abstruse tools laid out: the wooden vice clamping-
In glued leather binding of a speckled-fronted book
That's been drying for a century or more; a gnarled oak
Contraption with iron hooks hanging down from it
(Almost a miniature torture instrument), looping strings
For accordion stitching of a sandwich of browning pages;
A vintage bookbinder, intricate as all mistakenly
Phrased *'primitive'* things—lettered tiles lining it,
Like Ouija tablets; leathery peelings of casts once used
To print infinities of frontispieces, wrought in decorative
Curlicues around elegant typographies, curling
Like autumn leaves; glass display cabinets inhabited
By splayed hardboard books: reclining, spreadeagled
Moths with pale paper under-wings scrawled in frantic
Handwriting (cramped strings of prices), the thick-piled
Page-edges calendered with a curvy effect like half-moon
Icing on a marble cake, buckling—two bowing strips
Of aging marzipan; assortments of buckram-bound
Heterocera with industrially adapted melanins,
Shut-winged: a Rare Marble resembling a slab
Of mouldy Gorgonzola; a Ragged Russet; a Gold-
Lustred Red *Folksagor* (*Folk Tales*); Brown *Läder*
(*Leather*); other cabinets displaying creamy insides,
Minutely scripted, with plates, etchings, architectural
Illustrations of scrolling pillar capitals & ionic
Column mouldings; naturalist studies of static
Amphibians shaded in obsessions of inked lines by
Innumerable densities of nib: labyrinthine
Thumbprints; two warped fat Lutheran Bibles,
Thick chunks of tissue-paper-thin calliper, trimmed
Edges tinged in variegations of grey, branded with
Gothic fonts; rough-edged, numbered, smooth-faced
Slabs riddled in print-impressions, spidery writing—
Graffiti of another life; calligraphic baroque; gnarled
Wood-engraving tiles for xylographical application,

Blind-embossed in pencil-grey negative *bas relief*;
A chestnut-coloured chair-shaped paper-slicer,
Ferocious as an antique Inquisition apparatus,
Or an over-complicated animal-trap; a beetle-grey iron
Printing press—a Vorticist sculpture: a metallic affair
Of rollers, clamps, pedal & bicycle-sized wheel bolted
To its side, crouched cryptically by a wooden chest
Of drawers where the types are kept: each slide-out
Department containing tiny mounted tablets of runic
Characters: detritus of typesetters; curved clusters
Like miniscule pencil shavings, minute hinges or
Baby nails, stored in alphabetical cubbies under
Glass partition in this moribund Composition Room
Of once well-greased knuckle-joint & platen presses...

Something presses in the gammy machine of my head,
Clamps my mind in its vice till it bruises slowly,
Blotting to Rorschach moth-wings (such a balancing-
Act to think in contradictions—a tensing of my skin:
Skull-stretched creamwove hairline-cracking,
Colour of milk curdling—I'm an Anglo-Saxon phantom
Touring (or scouring) this museum of distraction
From abstraction & intrusive visiting; a crumbling
Edginess of indecipherable anti-feeling;
Chalky primrose like the microscopic pill-cut cliff
Of a halved Valium (am I vitamin-deficient? No: lacking
Serotonin; still unacclimatised to the quotidian)—
My tar-starved tongue itching for a cigarette's acidy vim,
A fillip to pacify my magical thinking—*Magical!*
No such thing: more grotesque; hope-stripping—
My marble slab of brow blind-embossed with obsessions'
Morbid pitting only perceptible to probing thumbs
Fumbling for pause-switches of nerve-points—
I'll not succumb, but drift on through this therapeutic
Exhibition, sublimely numbing ambivalent
Inhibitions; no psychical menace in inanimate things,
Old objects, blunt contraptions; the unflappably
Practical—though now & then impulses well within,
Whirlpools, churning waves measured in stomach-knots,
& little twitching currents, limbering reflexes
Prising themselves from the swelling oak-beam
Of my head—I'm tempted to let go, jump into
The moment, be a lightning Luddite, clench
The nearest cudgel of agitating thought, & launch
Into phantasmal spasms of machine-breaking...

# FLIGHT OF THE ALBATROSS

*i.m. Harry Martinson* (1904–1978)

How can a flower grow without a root? Look to the autodidact:
Abruptly thrust from school at just thirteen, but who continues
Reading, eating literature, to feed an appetite for paper
Raptures, the addictive ink-fumed mysticism of print; book curds
Yellowed with knowledge, sap-dripped in maple of aged glue...

Malmö salvaged him after jumping phantom ships, ill-starred
*Aniaras* of *Härskare Jim*: arrested vagrant at twenty-one,
Rootless as a chugging tramp, nomadic amid mosquitoes,
Tugged by sails of malarial imagination incubated
In tubercle blood... He wrote himself to Gothenburg—where he made a
Name, in *Brand* magazine, then pledged it to Moa... At Johannesdal,
Sank anchors for a decade—one which rooted neurotic blooms:
Obsessions' *Nässlorna blomma* bruised him into absence... His
Nobel of dotage, an albatross, Seppukued with a pair of scissors.

[*Härskare* [pr. *Hash-ka-reh*]: *Lord*, hence allusion to the novel *Lord Jim* by Joseph
Conrad. *Nässlorna blomma: Flowering Nettles*, the title of Martinson's debut novel
of 1935. *Seppuku*: Japanese *hari-kari* (ritualistic suicide)].

## *from* MOA—THE LONE CROW OF NORRKÖPING
*i.m. Moa Martinson (née Helga Maria Swarts; 1890–1964)*


### I. MOA THE CROW

Crows flock across the Brandeis blue August sky
Of Norrköping cawing over the vast pavilions
Of Skaldic cloud, a stalking sky which should be called
Something like *skaallaa*, as it scales away so spaciously...
But one particular crow flies separate from the rest,
Always alone, though not in thought or sentiment;
A solitary bird of high solidarity... Sometimes
One crow must scout ahead of its murder to chance
New views; climb more difficult distances to cultivate
Less accessible perspectives; evaluate the vaulting
Of collective architectures; individuate the lava-
Scalding forge of the heart; touch the molten coals
That hiss & smoulder in the soul; grasp the hot
Red embers until they scorch no more—then fly
With greater winged ignition... A stray Valkyrie
Scavenging for long-sequestered privileges of the pen;
Scratches of the tethered quill on parchments of the skin,
Robed in inky black, the char of authenticity...

The lone crow flies here still, an avian surveying
The freshly painted refineries, the yellow-plaster
Cotton mills, the sumptuous peach & coffee-coloured
Cake-slice houses decorated in rococo stucco icings,
Delectable baroque; porticos, basilicas, arcades,
Oases Romanesque among the glowering Lutheran
Spires of copper-clad mould-blue that caused many
A snagging of her once-grounded thoughts: the thorns
Among the stones... All that grimy industry, now so
Remote, yet paid tribute by respectful replication
In architectures past her time, & magical lights
Of moonlit waters, calmly rippling, or rushing;
Aquatic illustrations in lassitudes of light...

—It was her, *Moa,* Moa the Crow, whose courage wrought
This bold design: this sensitively sculpted panorama
Of human flourishing, of myriad flower blossoms,
Gardens & springs, all this has grown out from
Her iron courage, this town, this Norrköping...

The lone crow rests awhile, perches on the sculpted
Shoulder of what she thought when high above was
A giant member of her species (perhaps the Crow-god?),
Though strangely grounded, never in flight, unmoving;
Thick black legs implacably planted; wings crooked
& bowed in against its sturdy body; its raised
Head ever-staring up to the sky—but why? Only now
She understood this object was moulded to an
Anthropomorphic shape, an enigmatic figure faintly
Familiar to her birding eye, similar to the human
Uniform she'd once worn in a former incarnation...

That one born into a lowly station & glooming
Life of dingy slums cramped tight in the town's
Out-swept peasant cheap-side, barely separated
By narrow tortured little alleys of Falu-red earth
Fractured with jagged flagstone paths, rags for togs
Clothespegged on makeshift washing-lines;
Grubby babies clutched by frowning-browed mothers
Clasped in threadbare shawls, with thickly drooping
Skirts that seemed to anchor them to the ground;
Mothers who nourished themselves on cold sandwiches
& fended off biting Swedish winters with coffee
Briefly hot from the hob; these hard-bitten women
Spilt back into the lone crow's mind, with spluttering
Paraffin lamps, cracked candles she held in her
Wax-scalded hand for the absent father she
Would later fictionalise, idolise, demonise...


## II. KRISTINA THE CROW-MOTHER

Only a muddy image of the grandfather who reared her
Until he died, but a sharper picture carves itself out
From the dark of hardship—*Kris-ti-na*, Kristina,
Her workhorse-mother, who took her back & packed
Them both to Norrköping where she scraped a vague living,
The long-spun hours—strung out in knots of hunger pangs—
At the wool mill, spinning cotton, abysmally waged;
An endurance of sunless days, winters of wedged
Daylight cramped between dark & dark... What was
The crow's name when she was human? *Hel-ga*, yes,
Helga... Swarts... Still some years short of menstruation
When, after barely ripening to matriculation
At a finishing school of her unfinished education,

She was made apprentice to a baker, worked as a bread girl;
Years of kneading dough, but doughty, stout-hearted,
Strong-willed, she'd count her stone resentments
With every step to the bakery each dismal lightless day...

Aged fifteen, she absconded to the archipelagos
& onion domes of Stockholm, where she laboured as
A smorgasbord manageress (a Duchess of Jute Street),
But was abruptly stripped of her independence through
The onset of the Swedish Depression... She returned
To her old stalking haunts in Norrköping, the yellow
Plaster textile town of Baltic-cut factory outcrops
Clustered on soul-torn Motala ström: that same churning
Canal into which Ture Nerman tossed his bible,
When Moa was just thirteen, partitioned from his
Middle-class aesthetic turmoil, which cast off
Christianity in his first revolutionary act towards
Socialism, negotiated through an atheistic cul-de-sac;
Sometimes the teenaged Helga re-christened Motala ström,
*Malström*; but now its rushing waters seemed more
Inspirational, less inhibitive, to her, for having been
Away & held her head above the rapids in spite
Of obstacles; a new gleam in her eyes—a change
Had unhinged something frightening yet exhilarating
In Helga, a strengthening of fortitude, a polishing
Of conscience till its shine reflected back at her
A glinting truth, a spirit-crutch of chore-scoured
Conviction which had come through Stockholm
Metamorphosis into the working person's politics
She now sought to articulate; & she thought more,
& wrote down what she thought, & what she wrote
She wore on her pill-box brow, in her riveted eyes,
In every blueing fold of her insurmisable blouse...
Her first efforts rejected by a notary of literature,
But nothing short of having her hands tied would stop
Her nightly trying to catch the shadow of her teeming
Pen as her knotted hand trawled static surfaces
Of rag-papers, streams of words dragging across
Like tramp-tugged fishing nets... Then... she forgets...

## III. KARL AND THE CROWCHILDREN

A mist creeps like a grey cat swelling its fur into her mind,
Then a strained male face forms from its purring
Ectoplasm accompanied by an uncomfortable
Knottedness of feeling, gut-tugging, & a thump of grim
Remembrance bruising thickly like congealing haemoglobin—
*Karl*—Karl Johansson, an older soul but one she thought
A kindred, who chaperoned her through the red flag's
Unfurling, not knowing he'd slowly lose her bit by bit
To each new calling: soon she was writing causerie for
The women's page in *Arbetaren*, then *Vi kvinnor,
Arbetare-kuriren, Templar-kuriren,* & *Tidevarvet*
(Liberalistic mouthpiece where she first wrote as *'Moa'*
So as not to arouse suspicions in anarchic circles she skirted),
Causing ripples by arguing for equal pay for women...
But the seed of what drew her to Karl had swelled inside her,
Weighed her down with its indigestible bread, leaden as
A stone but far from dead, ready to rise, grow out from
Her head... After their drift to Johannesdal she gave
Birth to Olof, first of many children... All the while,
Her mind racing knots, Karl's stagnating, drinking,
Sinking, but Moa had to keep their home afloat for Olof,
Helga, Tore, Erik, Manfred, Knut—not even little Knut
Could hold the tides back for Karl, the castaway father,
& after that youngest vanished in a lake with Manfred,
Karl distanced further; he'd thought marriage would
Save him from himself but putting down roots tugged
Him under... After her brief absence in Gothenburg—
Where she first met that hobo-poet... *Harry*... Martinson,
A leading light of *Brand* & *Arbetare-kuriren*—
Moa found Karl in the depths of a *"nervous disorder"*,
Something beyond fathoming, whirlpooling within him,
He couldn't eat or sleep, adrift on seas of hallucination
Until he struck the reef of shattered sentience: dashed
Himself that winter with dynamite, widowing Moa...
O Johannesdal, painful landscape, Johannesdal, home
To her husband's undoing—& her guilt for having
Left him so many times in the projected stills of her mind
(Morbid superstition: had she somehow subconsciously
Willed his demise?)... But now she was too rooted here
To ever move from the Falu-red torp where she'd planted
Apple trees from afterbirths of branching ambitions...

[Pr. *Arbetare-kuriren*: *Arr-beart-a-reh-koo-reer-en*. *Tidevarvet*: *Tee-de-varvet*. Näxö:
*Nex-ur*].

182

## IV. KRISTINA'S ROOST

Moa's pen progressed slowly; the wrangling Yggdrasil
Of her mother's dishrag tongue always nagging at the back
Of her mind: *"Those critics won't understand this—Why*
*Would you want to put our poverty into print? I'd be*
*Ashamed! & anyway, who on earth would want to read it?"*
Moa knew the Swedes, especially those of her obscure
Strata, saw only meaninglessness in fame, a thing
Unearned, & only worthlessness in words—the stumped
Tenets in the rule-book of her rule-of-thumb upbringing:
*'To receive something for nothing was as embarrassing*
*As seeing your name in newspapers'*; only manual work
Meant anything; *"Work for keep"* was all the advice
Given her ever since she could remember... & who
Was she to think herself so special as to be the first
Swedish working-class woman to write a book; the first
Female proletarian author...? Such airs! A baker's girl!
Hardly the right start for such highfalutin ambition...
But in spite of this, her pen scraped on, her cramping hand,
A blazing tumbrel of thumb & fingers, she had to try
& empty her teeming brain, but the more she wrote,
The more the questions heaped up on the paper, as if
To fill the space of absent answers: *'Always working,*
*Yet hungry...'* The answers never came... So she wrote on...
Of Kristina: *'She had the knowledge & expertise*
*That could never be taught in school or university,*
*Only through life in its direst form...'* O, Moa railed on,
Self-sculpted scribe, her choppy prose, chipped but hypnotic,
Impelled itself forward; its compelling motion pulling
In public opinion with its whirlpooling polemic:
*'I'll go to the grave with the indignation &*
*Disappointment left in me... that academic education...*
*Didn't forge more open-mindedness & compassion*
*With the larger number of citizens who fought... on life's*
*Outmost edge...'*; but she resurfaced, triumphantly:
*'It was all the more difficult for me compared to my*
*Mother because I was aware this was Hell: I knew*
*The injustice done to us all, & our powerlessness...'...*
Her ragged cry against unconverted critics: *'Maybe*
*You'll get an inkling of how necessary a fight is*
*When [it] is for real values—mainly to stay alive...?'*

[Södertälje: *Ser-der-tell-yeh.* Äppleträd: *Ep-le-tred.* Saltsjöbaden: *Sallt-shur-bah-den.*
*Den osynlige älskaren*: *Den oo-soon-li-geh elsk-aren* (*The Invisible Lover*)].

## V. FLASH HARRY

Summer of 1928: that literary acquaintance she'd made
During her sojourn in Gothenburg, Harry Martinson,
Came to stay at Johannesdal—to write, but soon found
Himself romancing Moa, to her reciprocation,
Fourteen years his senior (echoing George Eliot
& John Cross, less so, George Sand & Chopin)...
So their rocky nuptial course was ominously in session,
After her marital baptism as 'Moa Martinson';
Their union seemed troubled from the beginning:
Moa was hospitalised at Södertälje for depression,
& soon after, the first eruptions of Harry's
Consumption, which nearly devastated her; & all
This grimness in the shabby surrounds of genteel
Poverty—O so bohemian, but numbing! So she
Wrote for loaves throughout the Thirties, having
Found a publisher, Tor Bonnier: her first book,
*Kvinnor och Äppleträd* (*Women & Apple Trees*)
Received wide circulation & the kind of circumspect
Attention accorded *"proletarians"*; her prose,
Judiciously slipped into the newfangled rubric
Of *'Modernism'*... Then the shadow of neurosis crept
Up on Harry—first Karl, now *him*! Was she a curse?
Was her cussed feminism a thorny hem with which she
Unwittingly entrapped, then ruined, sensitive men?
No: most likely, as Karl before him, Harry's symptoms
Surfaced from turbulence of anchoring in one place
For any length of time: his nomadic nature
Unaccustomed to the rootedness of Johannesdal's
Dim-lit cottage life; its long branching shadows thrown
Upon him insurmountably, where from he launched
His *Phantom Ships*—but soon their sails seized up,
Heaped into depression... With royalties from handsome
Sales of her debut in print, Moa rented them a plush
Apartment in salubrious Saltsjöbaden, nestled by
The Baltic, for Harry to take his cure, & for them
To prune the Hydra heads of their cropped coupling...
But after this respite, Harry started disappearing,
Seeing other women; one, called Karin, proved the most
Habit-forming of many mistresses of his phantom
Paramour persona; sometimes he'd disappear for days,
Or weeks; elope with Karin, then return, tall tale between
His legs; other times he'd hide out at a literary
Friend's primrose-panelled apartment peeping out

Across Stockholm spires—a writer's voyeuristic view:
Bookish bachelor pad of Ivar Lo-Johansson, his fellow
*"Proletarian"* scribe whose prolificness was strictly for
The printing press; no doubt a part of each of them
Envied that part absent in themselves—their stillbirth
Children—but abundant in the other: Ivar Lo,
Harry's amorousness / Harry, Ivar Lo's freedom—
But freedom had its obstacles, unexpected stones
Cropping up on paths of lone shadows, collecting
Into albatrosses weighing in the head; no lack
Of disappointments for those who claim they expect
Nothing from other people: those tugging ghosts
Of uprootedness... When Moa rang Ivar Lo to ask if
Harry was there, as he invariably was, sipping coffee
& smoking out his primrose refuge, choked from
Flowering nettles of their thorny relationship,
Ivar Lo would heed the smoke signals from his puffing
Guest, his revenant visitor, & put her off the scent...


## VI. MOA THE MOTHER OF THE SWEDISH

After Harry's discharge from Södertälje (the same
Hospital Moa had adumbrated him, & would later
Return to have hailstones removed from her appendix)
Where he'd spent a convalescing spring in 1939
Following another nervous crisis, Harry never
Returned to Moa or Johannesdal again; & so
Their marriage withered into wintering... In spite
Of their permanent separation, Moa kept his surname,
Under which she wrote on, so stout-hearted, indomitable,
Without men, until reacquainted with another Karl...
Gunnarsson, now a fellow writer—a chance meeting
Which rekindled memories of her embattled youth,
& led her into *Den Osynlige älskaren* (*The Invisible
Lover*)... Then she moved publishing houses from
Bonnier to Tidens for her polemical poems, *Motsols*;
Soon she won the moniker of *"mother of the people of Sweden"*—
Though her heart was always strung to hungry women
Of unemployed men; & though her reputation dwindled
Into twilight of critical distancing, Moa never crowed
For worms of comfort, or at least made sure it never showed:
She'd worn her words in every crease of her worsted
Human clothes, so many prickles on the skin; so many
Apples on the tree rotted past ripening... She never

Expected to match Kristina's innings, but then she
Only missed it by a score: three scores & ten—& four;
She'd documented every flagstone step, accounted for
Her time through a storm of furious writing—that first
Spark in the bakery dark that lit the fuse of her firebrand pen,
Still glinted in the sunken sockets of her septuagenarian
Eyes, & the fading leopard hide of her liver-spotted skin,
No solar lentigo but a great cat's rare markings:
A stealthy panther prowling from the dark of charred backstreets;
Her trampled class's answer to Kata Dalström,
But scrubbed up from spit & grist, the spirit of a striking
Matchgirl but one in no need of an Annie Besant
To champion her cause, nor clipped patronages
Of bluestockinged Pankhursts in her fight for female suffrage,
Employment rights & equal pay—more a Nordic
Storm Jameson, twilit with her tousling torch of freedom,
Her ash-stumped vestigial fifth finger smouldering
Defiantly in that last sepia picture when, no doubt,
Her soul started to count back those steps to Helga Swarts,
& drudgery; stretch the floury dough of that doughty
Clay out for the rolling-pin & kneading of another
Incarnation—how about a lone sky-stalking crow,
Scorched black as that baker's oven in which she rose
From apron-floured slums of platted girlhood to toughened
Crusts of more authentic pastries latticed with yolk-brushed
Paths she chose—her broom of womanhood thrown down,
She poured out the shadows that she'd swept into
Violent blooms of pounding prose... Now Moa knows:
Out from the cryptic prison of the body's arbitrary sex,
The sempiternal neuter of true personality grows...

# NOW, IVAR WAS A TRAVELLER...

*i.m. Ivar Lo-Johansson* (1901–1990)

*In kind*—paltry payment for the unwaged *statare* whom
Valkyries of *kapitalism* picked off to work grabbed lands;
Agricultural slaves, beetroot-eaters, viewed as the lowest
Rung of Swede; who ploughed the long shadows before *folkhemmet*

Lifted the fogs of serfdom from the iced fields. Up to then,
Odin lingered on, eyes bloodshot with tears like lingonberries

Jewelled in dew, for how his world's sorrows rose, flowered from
Open wounds to words of a hobo-boy from Ösmo; bicycling
Hawker of wares whose green evening verses vented spleen
Against settled folk, those rooted to the spot like standing stones,
Never venturing out of their valleys to travel, even though those
Soils were carpeted with thistles. He'd grow into the stonemason's
Skaldic wisdom, to know it was the stone that drove the blow
Of the tool: a Christ he sculpted on a fount refused to frown,
No chisel could chip its smile, no valley could carve out Ivar Lo.

[Ösmo: pr. *Ers-mor*].

## ORO

'No Grand Inquisitor has in readiness such terrible tortures as has anxiety'

—Søren Kierkegaard, *The Concept of Anxiety*

The sorrow of the cold Norrköping crow spoke more to me this time
Than the sugared-almond houses & marzipan confectioneries
Of yellow-plaster warehouses trickling along the wharfsides;
Or the early autumn trees still camouflaged in late summer fatigues—
It was as if my groundless thoughts had launched themselves,
Not into flight, but anticipation of flight, suspended somewhere
Vaguely in the atmosphere, glaring down at my improvising body
Anchored by weights; moving, speaking, conducting itself routinely,
But on automatic pilot; neurotic trajectory motored by
Atrophied thoughts...
      I thought: if only that lonely crow could
Know of my weightless state below—out-of-body, stony, remote—
As it stole off on its wings, black gloves grasping at white sky...
Could its own notion of sorrow compass anything so
Fundamentally dismantling as anxiety? Its excruciating
Scrape of tectonic plates of sense & nerve? Flightless vertigo;
Knife-grinding edge; knotting of hollow-cawing stomach
Stripped of appetite yet craving something nourishing to fill it...?

What could the crow know of a stomach's self-imposed emptiness?
Of the worry of tomorrow's horrors re-grown all over again
From the twisting root in the gut to wrangling stems
Crawling away from the light to shoot out blooms of obsessions
In wakeful darkness; unshakeable shadows in which they
Blossom from unanswered correspondences of futilely
Resisting thoughts? The gut-plunge that inevitably debuts
At uneatable breakfasts after churned rehearsals from chilly
Hinterlands of pillows; the emptiness; nausea that courses
Through the bone like a poisonous serum from the tip
Of the nail-bitten finger, as the gooseberry green
Of a burgeoning whitlow; sensitising every nerve
Essential to surviving, but which, once activated,
Agitates against its own mechanics; twists & stutters
Towards an uninstructed function, tapped to panic,
The maladaptive aim of arrival before departure
(Much in us is sacrificed to survival)... We always crave
Vaguest inklings that something of us, *spirit*, survives
Bodily death—but then there are those living, or thinking

They are living, who wonder if the spirit can last *as far*
As death... Anxiety: the tipping spirit-level of trapped
Adrenalin, mingling into itself, percolating in a test tube
Sealed in a figure of eight clamped in a vice caramelising
Over a simmering Bunsen—only cooling down once *mind*
Accepts its sour tonic... Midwinter Swedes have long
Compiled a lexicon of words for it, & one of them is
*Oro*, which rings the truest in its sound like *sorrow*—
*Hollow*—*horror*—*hole*; in its slow roll, its ghostly echo
Round the vaults of the mouth... The skalds sang of angst;
The Intimists laid lyric wreaths on rag-paper altars
Of anguish; the second Dane, Søren Kierkegaard,
Biblicised it in *Begrebet Angest* (*The Concept of Angst,
Anxiety*, or *Dread*, depending on translation)—
(The first Dane, Hamlet, adumbrated it): Kierkegaard
Described *ångest* as the *"dizziness of freedom"*;
An aftershock of ancestral trauma; a tremor
Recapitulating the ancient thunder of Original Sin,
That first tingling anticipation of the Fruit, distilled
Through millennia to a petrified fuse of guilt at an
Apple already bitten, which might be bit again... But
The crow throws the call of *oro, oro, oro*—so do all
Those vigilant wingless legions trudging through
The heaping snows, encircling themselves, doubling
Back on looping footprints sinking in inscrutable
Drifts of snow; soldiers stooped to tramping thralls,
Self-besiegers, head-berserkers, ambushing themselves;
Carrion of their own preoccupations; raptors
Of the passing brutal thought primed to swoop & seize it;
Pick its threads apart; store them in its throat for future
Ruminations; bones that can't be swallowed; days
That aren't digestible; stringed gristly hours—
& the chilly promise of tom*orro*w haunting
The night before with faint tattoos of thought-taboos
On the stretched drum-skin of the prickling scalp:
Already drilled for the early dread of rosy-fingered
Trepanning; the dredging plough of the chewed-up gut's
Ritualised fasting; the trawl of wakening anxieties;
The anguished march of another dawn patrol...

# STRINDBERG'S MIDNIGHT SWEDEN: RED ON GREEN

Among a universe of things, Strindberg said the Swedish flag
Shouldn't have been a gold cross on blue but a red cross on green:
The Falu-red of the typical Swedish log house against
The pine-green of the forests—this, for Strindberg,
Would have been the more representative colouristic banner
Of his country... But most Swedes associate the gold
Of the cross (that shape, a quaint but obsolete token
Of a distant Christian ancestry—Sweden, all but secular
For decades) as symbolic of the sharp Scandinavian sun,
& in the blue the deep pure azure of the Swedish sky
At Midsummer—or the spring blue of the Baltic sea
That magnetised the Vikings' compass onto far-flung
Voyages of new discoveries in longships of curvaceous
Lapstrake (overlapping planks) culminating end to end
In wood-carved figureheads, invariably dragons,
Timber serpents with dorsal sails swept along by
The wind's bawling Valkyries... But in Strindberg's
Colour vocabulary, his own vexillology (the very
Association of which has as its flag a yellow-gold
Sheetbend knot platted on Palatinate blue), the true
Flag of Sweden, the one he nightly unfurled in the red room
Of his soul, his nation's authentic colours, at least, at
Midnight, were definitively Falu-red against pine-green...
This might ring true for all those not so prone to typical
Spasms of patriotism (not commonality or togetherness,
Just rootless hysterias, street parties, bunting &
Buttered bread, margarine gregariousness); underneath,
Each of us has our own distinctive view of what our
Country means to us, what it represents, what it is,
What it was, or what it might have been—nations are
Unsatisfied fantasies, demotic compromises between
Legion incompatible utopias... But for my part I'd
Much prefer my native land to have some of Sweden's
*Samförstånd (mutual understanding)*, more than
A tinct of socialism, & respect for nature; Strindberg's
Alternative Swedish flag would suit the British banner
Of my wishing: red Nordic cross—not centred, but
Shifted to the hoist side (*Left*)—against Forest green,
Sherwood Forest green, Lincoln green, anything to
The Cambridge blue gonfalons of our dismal island sea...

## *from* THE QUIET IMMENSITIES
After Harry Martinson's *Aniara* (1956)


*'I could go on describing this story about Aniara*
*But to wander the same road that you once poeticised*
*Is too perilous. For that, others see better than*
*The poet who has only acted as the medium & reporter*
*For his or her own time...'* Thus translated Matilda,
As I found I was too slow to save a wasp from drowning
In her coffee... The wasp curled lifeless on the serviette,
Its wings glued together in one gelatinous teardrop;
Its body ambered in a lethal sweetness—strange feckless
Insects dissembled in the manna of deadly addictions;
Globules formed from their own greed... But we pitied
This particular wasp, this little black-striped yellowjacket,
Caparisoned in colours of typical Swedish townhouses...

*Aniara, Aniara*, a name without a past, or future,
Its floating, drifting cadence, a phantom invocation
That haunts the fevered breath of an amorous youth
Pining after an indifferent beauty who perpetually
Turns away on her untouchable pedestal; a name, fluid
With longing; more lyrical than Dante's Beatrice,
Keats's *La Belle Dame*..., or Poe's Annabelle Lee—
& like that doomed object of a boy's desire, *Aniara*
Plays eternity; airy, incantatory, a verbal spell,
An aural charm; a terrible lullaby sung by The Mima:
A gestalt of semi-mystical machinery on board
The eponymous spaceship adrift in the pitch-black
Wastes of uncharted space; driven off course & flung
Off orbit, destined to travel forever among the stars,
Cut off from the port of its departure, the city
Of Dorisburg, long ago atomised along with Earth;
The stranded crew condemned to endless odyssey
Perpetually voyaging an eternal intergalactic saga,
A Flying Dutchman destinationless... On board, a culture
With no history, no hope, only sordidness of boredom,
Despair, decadence & desperate distractions;
Empty entertainments; a Saturnalia of ennui
& acedia adrift in Andromeda's uncharted galaxy...
The Mima, faintly naïve, hard-wired with Nordic angst—
A Romantic dream-machine, or nightmare agleam—
Ultimately destroys itself, having lost its faith in
Circuitry, after witnessing the terrible melting

Of Dorisburg by its psychopathic cousin, the phototurb,
In a spectacular eruption of *'white granite tears'*—
A sight too much for The Mima to bear in Her memory banks;
Then, only emptiness, without end or return,
Both outside in the oceanic blackness & inside
The soulless bodies of the stranded eight thousand human
Passengers (would-be Martian colonists)—emptiness
Is their only remaining reality; the psychical salvages
Of the *'quiet immensities'**; the *'immeasurable sadness'**
Of objectless sentimentalities; hence the name,
*Aniara* (an almost-anagram of C.S. Lewis's
Contemporaneous Narnia): the meaning under its
Aural aria of mystification: ανιαρός *(aniaros)*,
Ancient Greek for s*ad, despairing, tiresome, boring,*
*Cloying*, as well as harnessing the sound of *a*,
Which had a mystical resonance for its wanderlust author,
Autodidact proletarian poet, Harry Martinson...

Of what was Martinson's eerie futuristic lamentation
In one hundred & three cantos warning..? Cults
Of critics have dissected it canto by canto since
Its first appearance on the Thirteenth of October
Nineteen Fifty-Six; the year of the violent Soviet
Oppression of the student-led Hungarian Revolution,
Stamped out with boots & bullets by the troops
Of the Politburo—that bloodbath in Budapest
Had stamped itself on Martinson's macro-conscience;
They say he dictated *Aniara* after a disturbing dream
(As Samuel Taylor Coleridge had similarly drawn his
*Rime of the Ancient Mariner* from a phantasmagoria
Relayed by a friend), at a time when Swedes were
Troubled by Russo-rumours & Midgarðsormr
Sightings of periscopes surfacing from Russian
Submarines in the Baltic; & despatches of Soviet
Incursions into Finland; *Aniara* was, apparently,
Martinson's warning against the rise of technocratic
Tentacles; of totalitarianisms of all kinds,
But, by the mood of the time, mostly those from behind
The Iron Curtain—this was the Cold War, a period
Of red deliriums; of starfall fantasias, blinding
Lights of green meteors, Triffids & body snatchers
Marshalling strange invasions after lulling humanity
Into routine cohabitations; bathyspheres
& submersibles plumbing popular paranoias...

Martinson, self-educated poet from Blekinge County—
Near the Baltic tip of Sweden's flaccid phallus—was always
Sensitive to atmospherics; statics; so his fictive
Feelers prickled with trepidations sufficient to build
A poetic tension bristling beneath the surface of his
Stark imagination; which, by the lancing of his pen,
Launched into the epic flight of *Aniara*—*a review of man*
*In space & time*; gilted with semantic mystifications,
Glossaries of neologisms, phantom nouns, portmanteaus,
Strange projected jargons of future days—possibly,
In part, shadow-plays on perceived Swedish Newspeak
Germinating in the long golden teething stage
Of the first decade of *folkhemmet,* the Swedish
Welfare state: emancipator of a generation's
Agricultural *statare*, the hitherto inescapable
Caste from which Martinson himself had been rescued,
Along with the rest of the legislatively salvaged...
For it was the fashion of those early days of socialist-
Administered altruism, for the inheritors
Of the bourgeois literati to poeticise their scepticism,
Enshrine the term *welfare* as a motif of cultural
Defloweration (though it was the belated social
Fructification of Swedish Grace—simple yet elegant
Egalitarian design in furniture & architecture);
Some cryptic threat to their unaltered individuation;
A bureaucratic crèche; a nursery of memes to net
Personal responsibility to make moral decisions,
To *choose*—that is, for their own propertied class
&, as always, at the expense of others' freedoms,
From *statarna* to the factory drudges & urban
Colonies of slum-dwellers... But Martinson's polemical
Space poem chills in this new century: reads more as
A proleptic metaphor for capitalist atomisation
Of moral standards: an aimless tailspin of nations
Into the hurtling nullities of hedonism, division,
Material greed; valueless, morally anarchic, but
Always pretending to please—a pilotless culture
Of astral tsars; existential *statarna* of the stars...

As I sit gazing at the wasp in its amorphous capsule
Of aspic, its bubble of absolute self-absorption, I
Think of Martinson's microscopic analogy—ventriloquised
Through *Aniara*'s fatalistic astronomer—in conjuring
The imperceptible movement of an air-bubble trapped
In an untouched glass, which '*moves interminably*

*Slowly to a new position in the body'* of the sand-
Melted vessel: a journey it completes *'after gradual*
*Millennia'*... Then Martinson pulls the rug from under us:
*'The same way in interminable space/ abyss within*
*Abyss ... around the bubble Aniara is...'* (—*Nautilus*
To Martinson's neurotic Nemo)... So merciless, so final,
So immaculately sealed within this claustrophobic
Aphorism, inimitably his—the spaceship a moving
Tomb, a cruising sarcophagus; the thirteenth Canto
Magnifies this image, keeping it lingeringly in mind,
An intrusive leitmotiv that can't be banished through
Any effort of will: if seen *'against the depths of space'*
*Aniara*'s pace parallels the air-bubble moving
Invisibly in the glass...
                                    We leave our café seats,
Matilda gently embalming the drowned wasp in
The sodden napkin, & placing it under some shrubbery,
Where it might eventually disintegrate with dignity...
Or resurrect? If only my hand had been quicker, lighter,
In fishing out the immersing wasp before it drowned—
But then, no matter how stealthily I performed this,
The coffeespoon scooped up a pool with the wasp;
& during those brief seconds I conveyed it to
The serviette, futilely, & carefully tipped out
The saturated wasp onto the fluid-absorbing fabric,
Was, from the wasp's concept of time, far longer
Than it seemed to mine (a saga—millennia in transit!)
& more than enough for it to fully drown to the dying
Insect-scream of *Aniaaa-raaa:* inaudible to us,
Iced in its glassy cubicle, its quiet immensities...


[*phrases from Theodore Sturgeon's review of the 1964 American edition of *Aniara*
(originally published in Swedish in 1956). *Midgarðsormr*: the Midgard serpent of
Norse mythology.]

## THE COLOURS OF STOCKHOLM

This is a country unafraid of colour, a nation of all spectrums,
Pigments, tones, ocular harmonics; in its towns & cities,
No street unturned without its confident tinctures noticed
& noted in the sample-book of neutrally toned interiors;
Neoclassical chamfered frontages of coral orange or
Primrose-yellow with cream or tan entablature; rococo
Townhouses decorated with ochre scrolling or coffee cornicing,
Delectable to the eye, Italianate gâteaus; stucco
Nordic baroque; Swedish National Romantic (protégé
Of its piloting English cousin Arts & Crafts Movement)...
But no provincial Swedish town is as robust in its use
Of colour as Stockholm—a ragout of onion domes
& Romanesque basilicas; Gothic ball flowers & bossage;
Conical or pyramidal copper-clad shingled spires of worship
In teal, mantis & mint, thrusting up from char-black
Lutheran Churches sparring with classical porticos
& columns; Stockholm City Hall: illustrious statement
Of National Romanticism, its lustrous Blå Hallen
(Blue Hall), venue for auspicious Nobel ceremonies—
& home to the vastest organ in all Scandinavia:
Ten thousand two hundred & seventy pipes; the Hall,
Illuminated at night to a stunning silhouette: its lantern-
Shaped belfry penetrating the retina with luscious
Ice-fired turquoise—an enchanted citadel thrusting up
Above the glinting waters on Riddarfjärden's shores...
So many architectural contradictions jostling in cropped
Propinquities of steep-stacked archipelagos; Palmstedt's
Peach-coloured rococo Stock Exchange, now housing
The Nobel Museum in Gamla Stan's Stortorget (Great
Square): a melting-pot trapezium of different styles—
Basilica lantern cupolas loom harmonically above
A classical pediment triangulating planted pillars;
Hans Bremer's Germanic blue-grey Grill House, circa
1640s, still with its original cross vaults, ornamented
Since with rococo portal & cloverleaf gables,
Now home to the City Mission & its *"Bun Church"*
For homeless sandwich-eaters; an 18th century
Tall-house in asparagus green built on medieval foundations;
The House of Bo Ribbing, Falu-red with eighty-two
White slabs of brick for every Swedish head decapitated
By Christian II of Denmark in the Stockholm Bloodbath
Of 1520; the three-hundred-year-old Raven Pharmacy:
Coral-pink frontage with taupe sculptural *bas relief*

Enframed in friezes; & the Square's water-haunted well
(Dried up since 1856), a baroque affair of shrubbing
Ball flowers & stone-sculpted foliage... O Stockholm,
Such a harmony of colours: from cylindrical pink-brick,
White & pistachio-coned *"secret houses"* (outside toilets)
Resembling giant Neapolitan ice-creams, to your
Acrylic basilicas, bold splashes of pilasters & capitals,
Rainbow-coloured houses, leaping turquoise spires—
O Stockholm, you surpass the rustic Stoicism of your
Worsted etymology: *'Log Islet'*; it's not the Baltic
Slate of Lake Mälaren that you nestle on, but the wine-
Coloured mouth of an iron Tiber even Roman eagles
Couldn't conquer: jewel of Sweden—the Nordic Rome...

[Pr. Blå Hallen: *Blaw Hall-en.* Riddarfjärden: *Rid-ar-fyare-den.* Järntorget: *Yairn-tor-yet.* Målaren: *Maw-laren.* Änglamark: *Engla-mark.* Mälaren: *Mare-la-ren*].

# INFRACTIONS OF A CAMERA'S EYE
*i.m. Ingmar Bergman* (1918–2007)

*"Infractions"*—his father's coinage for transgressions hewn from
Nomenclature to sculpt aural neurotics out of Christians;
Guilt-gripped trophies of Lutheran patriarchs... But the *Laterna
Magica* of Ingmar's imagination was his infant antidote to
Antinomianism: it danced in carved dark of punishment closets;
Religious grotesque, moral phantasmagorias, graven anguishing—

Bursting with potential for Rembrandtian treatments; brooding
Expositions of blasted skerries; billowing sands by Baltic seas;
*Rauks* of craggy Fårö; swishing pines in angsting summers;
Gables of marble-beaten brows: the crag-carved visage of von Sydow's
Menhiric face; the dark molasses of Ingrid Thulin's eyes... Through
A glass, starkly in Fischer & Nykvist's brutalist black & white;
No sympathetic tones, just nerves rubbed raw in bone-bleached light.

[*Antinomianism*: the Protestant-Calvanist belief that moral law need not apply to an *elect* predestined to salvation through *Grace* or 'faith alone'. *Rauks* [pr. *rowks*]: rocks, or crags. Pr. Fårö: *Faw-reh*].

## *from* AUTUMN CLOUDBERRIES

I.

Golden-yellow gems of the boreal climes; gamboge
Blackberries; amber raspberries; small drupelets of sunset;
Known as *"knotberries"* by British borderers, but as
Cloudberries by the Swedes who pulp them into jams
To bejewel white tundras of ice-cream or pancaked
Landscapes... Cloudberries can grow in wet meadows,
Marshes, bogs, even in the arctic wastes where few
Other shrubs can withstand the icy blasts; berries best
Appreciated by twilight; little beacons of trapped flame
Aglow against the angst of autumn amblers, rumbled by
September chills; psychically braced for the cold
Oncoming spell, the interminable, tenebrous blackness
Of boreal winter... It will be then, in that darkness,
Memories of cloudberries will lodge in minds as autumn
Mementoes of hibernating vibrance; arboreal beads
For the unstrung rosaries of dwindling twilights;
Inimitable glimpses of warmth & light which seem
So distant in the grip of black Februaries; they will
Keep cloudberries in mind all through the lightless days
& moonless nights, when the soul is snowed under
Drifts of piling white; & the wolves of thought are
Howling for lost endorphins of light; & fire-glowed
Nostalgias hug green flames—they will remember
Cloudberries' golden tinges, & their adumbrations
In pale pink assemblages: amaranth & cerise tints
Before the amber ripening in sun-bashed pastures
Of summers' phantasmagorias... Some inoculate
Themselves against the long dark night of winter,
By turning from the light before it turns from them;
Burying their eyes in snows of human blight; immersing
In psychic winters in the midst of visceral summers;
Inverting violences of colour; spinning cottons
Of *thanatos* in their souls to black floss of funeral plumes;
They are the pilots of anxieties; the pallbearers of our
Agitated bodies, nerves & steep depressions,
& they light beacons of cloudberries in the unlikeliest
Of regions: East, into the unmapped tundra of the right-
Hand hemisphere, the darkest recesses of our souls,
Where even trolls refuse to delve; under the marble mantles
Of impenetrable temples inscribed by inscrutable
Runic characters; through a glass, darkly; through blue
Windows of the Swedish lens; the turquoise mosques

Of Nordic eyes—pupils of lapis lazuli—to the Baltic
Slate beneath; grey of anguishing; the turmoil
Of undercurrents simmering to tight-lipped maelstroms,
Into the dark soul of the Skald; the inner storms
Traversed by silent Vikings voyaging angst sagas,
Wracked by Valkyries & stalking Kierkegaards...


II.

Those silent rushes of the soul, amorphous dreamscapes
Of replayed traumas captured in ambers of memory's
Glutinous isinglass; roseship soup of the mind
That traps the past in its gooey aspic; the albumen
That brines the Swedenborg gland—the pituitary pea:
Not a part of the brain but embedded in the mind—
The soul, maybe; what else to do with these
Abstracted phantasms but channel them through
Mercuries of consciousness; browning ambrotype,
Tinctured with afterglows of amber halos—
Like cloudberries... So much of life is painted
In autumnal hues, amid stark winter chiaroscuro;
Tonal inwardness; while spring & summer are
Lurid hallucinatory episodes awash with unreal
Colours isolated from one another; spectrums
Of self-contained tensions: blood reds, sulphur
Yellows, galvanic greens; phantasmagorical
Acrylics of neurotic dreams; the deep red plush
Of the invertebrate tongue, boneless mollusc in
Its cavernous shell, recoiling with cries & whispers;
Black-soaked tissues of monochrome consumptions
Mopped up in moments' churning silences;
& doubts that coat our scopes, becloud our brows;
Plunge us into glooms of muddy winter light...


III.

Bergman, Nykvist, sons of Lutheran patriarchs—
Bridged by artist sailor Fischer—would take oaths
Of atheism while young & porous to outside influences;
Throw off hoary dogmas; gather up the mystified strands
Of hair-shirt faith & sacrifice; harness religious
Anguishes, brocaded mortifications & flagellated
Tapestries of inhibitions, & make an art from angst;
A visual literature of arrested catharses; motion-
Paintings of shade & light; chiaroscuro landscapes

Of magnified faces: shadow-cast sundials of daily stages;
Momentary seasonal changes; elliptical penumbras
Of human pages clouding with obscure moods & subtle
Surface creases at turbulence assembling beneath,
Bubbles from mind-submersibles, inner turmoils
Of the only animal embattled by its own thought—
Trumped by the impotent promise of speech; existence
As a coming to terms, an attempt to compass
The incomprehensible: the mounting improbability
Of an immortal soul; the terror of nothingness
That adumbrates barren terrain of the perishing brain—
Only rivalled by dread of world without end;
Strapped in quixotic armour of rusting mortal coil,
We face out savage gods; resist urges to swing
Ourselves from tangled Yggdrasils of staggered days;
Navigate the snagging branches as winter winds us
Into darkness; we suicidal playthings; topophilic
Human salmon; cloudy vessels of distilled anxieties;
Death-instincts; incorrigible addicts to gremlins
Of oppugnant existence; our ruptured spirits papered
In politesse, mute composures; raw materials for
Swedish Sartres to set alight the kindling of human
Kind & illuminate magic lanterns of startled eyes:
All rings & harrowed shadows ruthlessly scrutinised
In merciless close-ups; sentient statues holding poise
In impossible insights; plaster brows sculpted from
Millstones of ruminations darkly alchemised
To throbbing obsessions; stringless dolls in Freudian
Puppet theatres; sometimes interrupted in tortured
Etudes by barbaric gasps of laughter—each, a tragic
Clown, a schizophrenic Scaramouch whittled down
By faintly tapped taboos, forbidden desires rising
Into nettled throats, expelled by mute screams or sobs
Of mood-ventriloquists; occasionally breaking out
To caterwauls, then collapsing back to hissing silences...
Yet, in the midst of this blistering, there is a glinting
String of light, an energy triggered by the knife-edged
Surge of emotional metallurgy; an electric current
Travelling the nervous verge that lights up everything;
Scars constellations of cathartic stars across dark skies—
Countless cloudberries stabbing ambers into night...

IV.

Vikings of passive civilisation cast out strident oars
Into uncharted silver waters—cutting-room conquistadors
Of the Nordic unconscious, splicing moments up in jump-cuts;
Muffled tocks from hand-less clocks in pre-dawn autumn light
Of a phantasmagorical Gamla Stan tapped by nostalgic
Agnostics; dream-dabblers; affirmations of wild strawberry
Patches of frittered youth; grimacing emissaries of being's
Terrible celebrations that reverberate in the magic
Figure of eight—age Ingmar lost his faith—looping back
To the painful rip of birth; nihilism committed to film;
The rationalist's irrational; spools of existential poetry...
Some critics might say: psychological pornography;
Exploitation of despair; vivisection of the soul;
Dismantlement of personality framed in a camera's
Callused lens... Viewers have vacillated: some have been
Avowed voyeurs of private minds held captive in public-
Glare asylums; others have had nervous aversions;
Many have vilified these feverish films as morbid,
Interminably bleak—see aspects of themselves reflected
In coruscating landscapes bleached in sepia: public
Charades peeled away in the palmist's lamplight, dissected
Under cinematic microscope... Bergman's unabashed
Strindbergian surgeries of godless modern souls are
Avoided by many a wary Swede, aghast at such angst
Displayed against the backdrop of a placid country
Attuned to natural harmony; strangers in the grains
Of Ingmar's ravaged Angstland: Kierkegaardian dreamscape
Jump-cut into portmanteaus of psychotropic photography:
Fischer's expressionist overexposure; Nykvist's gothic
Shadow & needling light—or his Munchian wash
Of neurotic colours, intense tinctures, luridly unreal;
Patinas of Bergman's soul-scouring communions
In celluloid, tapping back into *"fashionable anguish"*
Of the literature of his Forties' youth: Lindegren,
Vennberg, Aspenström, Grave—all of whom would have approved—
Adumbrated by Gunnar Ekelöf's poetry of *'many egos'*...
Still back, further, to Artur Lundkvist; Harry Martinson
& *Aniara*'s haunting post-atomic trip into
Interplanetary inner-space; past satellites of vitalism
To D.H. Lawrence's crusade in fiction against Cartesian
Dualism; deeper still, down into Sigmund's *'abysmal*
*Vegetation of the subconscious'* (as Helmar Lång coined it
While writing in Helsingborg in 1981); down to
The bottom-most depths where Karin Boye submerged herself

In *'language beyond logic'*, translated T.S. Eliot's
*The Waste Land* into Swedish (while English scholars were
Still untangling its strange target language), campaigned
Against fascism in *Kallocain*, depicting a truth serum
Used by a totalitarian regime—took her own cathartic
Draught, no more to resurface after wading to 41...
At a similar age, Bergman learnt to live among outcasts
& extras on Fårö, a rocky outcrop of Gotland;
Though took offence at tax inspectors whose subterfuges
Re-sensitised his prickled nerves, prompted breakdown,
& his departure, vowing never to return to
The mainland, nor make another film there, in spite
Of pleas to repatriate his bohemian talents—one
Of them opined from the Prime Minister, Olof Palme...


V.
Bergman's strange fruit tailgate the balanced intimations
Of the modern Swede, invisibly; but the sour juices
Sometimes seep into the brain with bitter interactions:
Sap serotonins, sink links between distancing
Archipelagos of thought; tap ancestral glands of angst;
Saturate the autumnal mind to anticipatory winters—
Perhaps why those braided pilots of longships were so
Eager to leave the land behind... It's then some might
Strangely find psychic consolation in those rushes;
Filmic undercurrents; notice again cloudberries
Glowing on the leaf-greased grounds of autumn;
& in their ripened properties, brilliant medicines;
Miraculous tonics that alleviate disturbances
In mental tectonics—How so? By mining magmas
Of anxieties; spooning oils of molasses obsessions
Into silver cans; reel on reel of petrified sentience
Committed to grains; catalogued in elliptically scripted
Shadow-plays; germinal images; septic metaphors
& wrangling symbolisms of barbed & unfathomable
Feelings; ghastly charades of magic lanterns... So much
Of our conscious lives are left uncommunicated;
Only suggested in the jellies of the eyes; so much
Communication lies outside lips' amplified pronouncements;
So much is unarticulated, lost to downcast looks,
Storming stares, piercing silences—we are green novices
Of our own volitions; blind interpreters of physiognomic
Hieroglyphics—these suggest a language to us but
In incomprehensible glimpses; the fear of ourselves

Is the one last frontier for us to cross; the far ridge
Over which we've yet to catch the shadows of psychoanalysts,
Lab-coats, clapperboards, loud-hailers, directors' chairs...


VI.
Impossible to subtitle symbols of tossed consciousness,
To translate emotions between teeth & tongue,
Feelings' strange ungraspable languages, to verbalise
Obscurities of the soul, interpret the Ingvaeonic
Sing-song of Swedish's psychical dialect, or elucidate
Occulting metaphors of thought—there's only awareness
& witness; perception's clouding scope; speech is
Processed noise; echoes in the ear; phantom whispers
In the brain's byzantine labyrinth; chthonic cutaways
Of the anterior hemisphere; all we need to read:
The thrumming atmosphere; the anxious stare;
The strangled laugh; the hysteria; the claustrophobic
Sepia; the anguishing sands, the anguishing sands;
The stormy bays of Fårö—sorcerous tip of Gotland;
The eyes' bruising skies... Ingmar—magician, conjurer,
Cinematic Cagliostro—& his second light apprentice,
Sven Nykvist, whose asphyxiating photography
Seemed as if the camera was anticipating its framer's
Autumnal aphasia—that portfolio of thought-prints:
His invaluable aid to fathoming phantom mouths
Of a language-shuttered twilight; as are those harrowing
Films grainy guides in our wilting times: those months,
Hours, when nothing touches us for being too sensitised;
Nerve-strained; when everything seems unreal,
Unbearably profound, glutinously sublime;
When objects throb with symbolisms obsessing our eyes
By what our souls project into them: tortuous mouldings
We bore in their bossages—morbid memorabilia;
When every movement whittles us to stooping pallbearers;
It's then we must remember autumn cloudberries:
Glimpse them in the unprotected warmth of thawing smiles;
Peer close into their bubbled ambers; appreciate
The petrified insects, so lifelike, pinched inside;
Paralysed in aspic; captured in escape; pinned between
Fight or flight; quixotic miniatures that seem too fragile
To be alive; to withstand the weight of grotesquely large
Tagmata; yet they startle entomologists for being so perfectly
Preserved in glowing embolisms of autumn cloudberries...


[*Ingvaeonic*: North Sea Germanic languages.]

## SWEDENBORG GARDENS

*i.m. Emanuel (Swedburg) Swedenborg (1688–1772)*

Emanations of warmth & light correspond to love & wisdom.
Mariatorget has yet to forget the cast-off face his parents gave him.
Affections that ruled his heart when mortal now describe his
Numinous looks on the other side... But here, bronze eyes gaze out
Under dark arches below a brow's cropped aqueduct; teal highlights
Eagle his features, sunken cheeks & chamfered lips—at a distance he
Looks like a Gorgon, asps of hair rolled up into scrolls of a periwig...

Södermalm, home to bohemians now who avoid falseness '*the*
*Way owls avoid daylight*'. In malls they can't breathe, marble-mouthed;
Ether fails spiritual asthma. '*There is only an appearance of*
*Distance*', depending on acceptance. '*The sun the angels see is in the*
*East. Faith is second-hand belief, muddy as the light of winter.*
*North is wisdom beclouded... We are made up of pairs: eyes, ears, hands, feet;*
*Brains have two hemispheres, lungs two lobes...*' We are half-glass; we are
Our own part-reflections... The Last Judgement had already
Rumbled by in the spirit-realm, in 1757:
God had allowed Swedenborg to peep in & witness, then,

Essay it, as cross-correspondent; & he'd been privy to the
Mooted Second Coming, which came shortly after—unveiled to him
As a revelation—*within*... His *Earths in the Universe* revealed
Not only life, but an *after*life, of other planets in the solar system;
Under the influence of the music of the spheres he'd communicated
Easefully with spirits of other worlds—a catholicity spanning
Light years... In the baroque bowels of Reason, rococo calluses of

Science, he hit on immaterial Enlightenment but too late to convey to
Wesley, whose visit was scheduled after Swedenborg's predicted death day,
Exacted that March, 29th*, his rent paid up to that date... How that
Dining room in Gothenburg had smelt to him of burning churches:
Blazes at Maria kyrkan, four hundred kilometres away; that
Utterance put out the imitation flames of damp dinner chat...
Rumours spread of his unstable mind, but it was refined as Swedish
Grace—& angelic code: charity, not faith alone... Queen Ulrika

Eleonora ennobled his name from Swedburg to Swedenborg... & now
Mariatorget honours him, albeit in disguise as a peruke-wigged eagle,
Arrogated features of his mortal form that he no longer recognises—
Nor his grey & yellow gazebo at Skansen, his holidaying wood-walled sun
Umbrella... Earthly shrines are shadows in eternity, clung dingily to the sides,
Emulsified like half-fermented wine... Feted abroad, & by Blake,
London launched him back to Stockholm—regained grail of its fugue state.


[Södermalm: *Ser-der-malm*. *1772. *kyrkan* [pr. *Shure-ka*]: church. Mariatorget:
*Maria-tor-yet*].


# BASTUGATAN 21 *A SÉANCE WITH THE COMPLETE BOHEMIANS*


## I. *BLECKTORNSGRÄND*


In the brilliant white boreal winters of Södermalm's
Snowy summit, the blond children play, watched over by
The frosted head of Ivar Lo the cast-iron snowman,
Whose name has long melted into memory & common
Nomenclature—as that apportioned to Ivar Lo's Park,
Just up from the crookback cobblestone road locals call
*"The Hump"*, up through Blecktornsgränd's ochre
& chocolate-brown townhouses catching rationed
Sunlight in sharp-lit gasps; up, up, past the lantern
Chapel spires, a stone's throw from the steep cobbled
Road of Bastugatan... But it's the earth-red plaster
& stone presumption of apartments that tugs my
Pilgrimage up this hill: museum of a proletarian
Pioneer of whom I know precious little, yet to whose
Posthumous home I'm drawn—albeit by pre-
Appointment, to be shown round the bookish Pharaoh's
Tomb by a Swedish curator, friend & aficionado
Of Ivar Lo: an artist curate draped in loose-fitting
Charcoal-black clothes (the bohemian's clerical robes)—
He is one of Ivar Lo's apostles: a living, breathing

Barrel-load of his autodidactic ideals: for ordinary
Working men to graduate from hand to brain,
Fuse the anvil with the page, hammer out a mallet-thick
Portfolio of furious prose; this manual man with artisan
Hands has an artist's riveted head attached to his
Lumberjack's frame: a proletarian man of letters,
An ambassador of Arbetarnas Bildningsförbund
(The Workers' Education Organisation)
That administers an annual prize in the name of his
Late benefactor & mentor towards self-betterment...

[Pr. Arbetarnas Bildningsförbund: *Arr-beart-ar-nas Bildnings-fur-boond*. Next page.
Klarabohemerna: *Klara-boh-heem-er-na*].


## II. *KLARABOHEMERNA*

The epochal apartment of Ivar Lo is kept intact;
Alive in a way; on psychical self-support; thought-
Inhabited; mothballed by one of his protégés
As a repository of daily worship & quiet reflection—
We are cordially invited into the *art deco* catacombs
Of Bastugatan 21; across its marbled entrance hall
& into a cast-iron-fronted Otis lift, then up a couple
Of floors & out into a dim-lit corridor... The curator
Ushers us first into Ivar Lo's living room & to
The far end's makeshift kitchenette—wherein,
We're told, the writer used to breakfast on baby food—
Now a multipurpose space, improvised as a quixotic
Office with pale-blue wooden shelving & a welcoming
Clothed table displaying blazes of hardbacks:
Deciduous samples of Ivar Lo's prolific output;
Gallimaufries of print; prose outpourings protected
In strikingly illustrated jackets... I browse some
Pages from an English translation of *Peddling
My Wares*, stop at a passage where Ivar Lo recalls
His hobo childhood selling bric-a-brac as he cycled
Inexorable country roads, while he spent his nights
In washhouses versifying against all *'settled folk'*
In his first stab at epic poetry: a verse drama called
*Vale of Thistles*... I wonder what it was which stole
His thoughts from poems to prose (especially since
Poetry was the more natural proletarian
Medium due to its shorter form & inbuilt metre
Not dissimilar to the rhythm of manual labour)—
Perhaps the carthorse pull of narrative, the journeying

Of storytelling, appealed more to his peripatetic
Spirit than the moment's anchoring in lyric? Yet Ivar Lo—
& he would no doubt have pondered long on this irony—
Was demonstrably a homebird, in spite of, or due to,
His formative days of no-fixed-abode: here at Bastugatan
He'd rooted himself to the spot for over fifty years,
All the time writing of his lifelong gut-feeling
Of *'uprootedness'*; of belonging nowhere; not even among
His contemporaries, peers of the proletarian school—
Some of whose signatures were carved into the oval
Table hung on nails on the wall, like an upside-down
Wooden coracle in a fishermen's pub... So, apparently,
He sometimes had others round to chimney away
From pipes & cigarettes over perfectly pitched coffees,
Laying their hands like table-tappers as if partaking
In séances but probably comparing latest drafts
Of fiction or life writing; some drawn from the shabby
Ranks of *Klarabohemerna*, the *"Complete Bohemians"*,
Brothers of the Karla District, implicit proletarians,
Fugitives from the agricultural *statare*, southerly
Migrated Northerners gathered from Gävleborg,
Jämtland, Västernorrland, Västerbotten, Norrbotten—
Ambassadors from the lands of midnight suns where
Night skies in summer bruise rose & mauve but never darken;
While winters oppress the senses through epic nocturnes—
Seasonal polarities accounting for the restless springs
Inside the minds of hardier Northern writers;
Although always welcome to join their 'club', it wasn't
In Ivar Lo's nomadic spirit to anchor himself in any
Particular 'school' or (imperceptible) 'movement',
Just as he avoided close-knit circles of Intimism's
Anguishing fashionables; & the flower mouths
Of the *"Green Wave"*... But he at least associated with
The Karla set, & doubtless sometimes accommodated
Selected delegates: the Draculic-looking Nils Ferlin,
Poet of folksong & *Barefoot Children* (immortalised
As a shiny iron statue in Klara kyrka like an anthracite
Horus salvaged in an oil-slick, a coat-hanger-shouldered,
Pinstripe-suited troubadour perpetually trying to light
His cigarette); Helmer Grundström, the *"lumberjack poet"*;
Tor Bergner, the bucolic troubadour; Birger Vikström,
The scrawny raven-like storyteller; & melancholy
Emil Hagström; or Ivar Lo would partake in sporadic
Outings to the countryside round Stockholm: pilgrimages
To the torp of pipe-smoking Gustav Hedenvind-Eriksson—

The proletarians' pioneering guru—his Falu-red
Log-cabin in Kyrknäset, along with craggy, ravaged
Rudolph Lund, & Olof "Eyvind" Johnson, as the forest
Picnic snapshot of the quartet in dark suits & sun-
Shading fedoras, testifies... & on occasion, Ivar Lo
Was visited by Harry Martinson, whom he'd take in
To his bachelor-pad when the poet sought sanctuary
From the nettled throes of nuptial rootedness with Moa,
As much mother as lover... According to his apostle,
Ivar Lo believed one's living space should be
Completely separate to one's place of work: so he'd
Purchased a second apartment seven paces down
The corridor; in fact, next-door, where he could closet
Himself away in his rambling thoughts during the day,
Then leave at night to rest, psychically partitioned
In a wordless, leisurely space of purely physical
Repose—& sleep; only a moment's commute away,
But mentally so much further; & of so much more
Comfortable upholstered furniture: cushioned chairs,
Low-lying coral green futon bed, restful pale green
Walls punctuated with soporific oils—one by
That Norwegian magician of *angst*, Edvard Munch,
When his paintbrush captured a rare serener moment...

[Pr.Gävleborg: *Yeah-vle-bo-ree-yeh*. Jämtland: *Yemt-land* Västernorrland: *Vester-norr-
land*. Västerbotten: *Vester-botten*. Kyrknäset: *Shurk-nes-et.*]


III. THE PRIMROSE APARTMENT

Our pilgrimage turned into the other apartment:
The chamber of his labours, for which he is remembered,
& celebrated; in through a narrow hallway of panelled
Doors & walls of pale yellow, primrose possibly,
We enter the womb of Ivar Lo's prose burrow:
His writing room, austere but sparsely comforting,
One wall bedecked with a gangling wall-abridging
Waist-high shelf like a buckling launch for a longship,
Lined with mummified tomes, all leather-bound,
Baroquely ribbed & lettered spines; all, no doubt,
Interminably thumbed, but kept pressed tightly together
To protect them from warping in the dampness
Of Stockholm's archipelagos; on top of these tomb
Relics, piles of curled paperbacks & pamphlets posted
To him by legion writers, editors, admirers, numerous

Tributes signed & dedicated to him; even some
Old records in sleeves with his image on: songs sung
& recorded in his name, none of which he'd ever
Listened to for he'd no record player, &, besides,
Was too busy writing in his soundproof studio
To revolve his way through vinyls... The centrepiece—
What else but the writer's altar: a desk, broad & rangy,
Branching out from the middle of the window-ledge,
Facing an opposite wall, so its sitter wouldn't be
Distracted by the panorama of spires & basilicas:
The ever-altering architectural seasons across
The immaculate Lake Mälaren... On the desk: a neatly
Placed pile of blank paper; a dormant black metallic *Halda*
Typewriter crouched inertly like an insect husk,
Or calcified mollusc; a fountain pen; a pair of wiry
Spectacles, the kind that curl around the ears; a folded
Copy of that morning's *Arbetare* (*Worker*) newspaper
Yellowing from two decade's draughts of sun-glare
From the uncurtained window; these relics of literacy
All gathered under the drooping daffodil-shadow
Of a large brass-petalled desk-lamp; on the window-ledge,
An economical crop of ornaments, including
The sculpture of an outstaying guest whom he only met
In body briefly when starting out on the path of letters
But who had proven a formative influence, twilight idol,
As he had been for legion Swedish writers—especially
Proletarians, among whom he has since been numbered,
Though more as a progenitor than product of that school
(Like Blake to the Romantics): Dan Andersson from
Dalarna (where they carve the Dala Horses), archetypal
Proletarian poet, Orpheus of the option lands,
Peripatetic, prolific, whose hooded eyes & brooding
Handsomeness seemed to foredoom his sudden death
At only thirty-two while asleep in a hotel room
Which hadn't been aired by the valets after gassing out
The bedbugs (still filled with cyanide fumes), there he'd
Passed his last night, in Stockholm—Sweden's maturer
Chatterton; his epithet, a poem posthumously
Published: 'Now darken my path & my day's work
Is done'... Ivar Lo had kept this clay statuette, this
Anthropomorphic memento of his hero, mascot
Of the proletarian autodidact school, self-monikered
"Black Jim", by his desk of composition, a lugubrious
Figurine, head downcast, faintly Puritan, or Quaker,
One palm of a hand held open, soberly posed in

Blåbandsförbundets immobility; poet teetotal
Paralytic with temperance; petrified as effigy...

[Pr. Arbetare: *arr-beart-a-reh*. Blåbandsförbundets: *Blaw-bunds-fur-boond-ets*. Tr. Blue
Band temperance movement]


## IV. THE POSTERITY-SEEKER

Ivar Lo wrote only for posterity, so we are told,
Not for worldly fame, wealth or popularity, but for
A lasting place in the minds of those who followed;
Rooted like a standing stone, posterity was
The rootedness he longed for, the rootedness of history;
To be a part of it; for his writing to outlast him,
Be remembered, &, thereby, *he*, though not through
Gauchely posed photographs with pipe & beret—
But for what he wrote, & what he built up through
The energy & industry of his iron-wrought words...
No joiner, no team player, no natural party member;
He believed that true socialism was grown within
& expressed centrifugally through shadows of deeds;
In simple acts of compassion towards those orbiting
One's temporal hemisphere: *"In how you treated
Other people"*, I breached—*"Ja précis!"* the curator
Reciprocated with a sharp glance of recognition:
Ivar Lo's was a socialist soul, generating outwards
Through a generosity of narratives; a giving
Of allegories in the guise of a misanthropic recluse;
A solipsist inked in aspic... But his sentiments were
Philanthropic: to donate his gifts through parcels
Of rustling examples: hardbound paper packages
Published in a blaze of vibrant covers; products
Fashioned by hand & by brain: from the sweat
Of the *timberrrr*-ing lumberjack to the fastidious
Peck of the typesetter; all so others from his
Rootless class, outcasts of *statarna*, might discover
Their own voices & carve them into roving stones
Of stories, or travelling verses... Ivar Lo was
A working-class Loki: stole ambrosial fruits
Of imagination from bourgeois gods & scattered
Them among common mortals, knowing only quiet
Revolutions in the hearts of people could ever bring
Lasting transformation of the system... Many now
Honour him with the epithet of having written

*Statarna* out of existence: a lingual engineer
Who oiled the cogs of outrage at generations'
Agricultural bondage, which triggered a more
Enlightened government's abolition towards
Egalitarian Sweden, a *folkhem*, a welfare state
Where there were no masters or servants, except in
Human consciences—not only author, but social
Reformer, & well he knew the rootless worker
Must labour to forge his own roots; put down stones
To plant his shadow in the post-industrial light,
Sharper than before, a disinfectant of hearts & minds...
So Ivar Lo's fixed shadow casts its antumbra
*Väster och vänster—West & left*—across the sundial
Of diurnal lands, &, when we least expect it, throws
From its occluding body a nocturnal sundog
Of howling light; or, by day, a dark, ecliptic, bruising
Ring haloing the dayglo gauze of our westerly sun...

[Pr. väster och vänster: *vester ok venster*].

## V. IVAR LO AS STONEMASON

One carious photograph captures Ivar Lo in his days
As a stonemason, immortal in stone-dusted overalls:
His twenty-five year self staring back at the camera
With a penetrating impudence: eyes lit with ambition,
Missing nothing, drinking in everything
Like a squinting child; drinking in the sobering
Medicines of torrid labouring, one hand with a mallet,
The other sunk into the pocket of his dungarees,
Its arm bowed at the elbow, a black bough rooted end
To end to a recalcitrant trunk, stone-dust mottling
Its stump like spots of moss—there stood a stubborn
Tree where a man had been planted, & from it
Blossomed sacks of fruit, Odic fruit dangling
From a raggedy Yggdrasil, bulging with inky juices
Of imagination: Ivar Lo was an autodidact but no
Poor studious Jude obscured through the dark glass
Of class-stained academics, told to stick to his own
'*Station*' in spite of scholarly genius at teaching
Himself Greek & Latin; that he must nevertheless
Spend the rest of his days chipping away at the masonry
Of his rejectors, suspended high above the chiselled

Streets—Christminster's quixotic Quasimodo
Dangling among the spires & deafening belfries,
Flocks of mortarboards thrown upwards but still just
Out of reach to his cramping hands... It was more
Fortuitous for Ivar Lo: he was an artist, so relied
On no establishments to liberate his gifts: he would
Grow his own opportunities in the furrows of his
Notebook's line-ruled fields; he would wander among
Vagabonds, underdogs & gypsies; his wheeling
Head, a living caravan, would travel on a way only
Visible to him, discover his own villages of creative
Privileges, unpopulated by people but inhabited
By bristling ideas... & he'd gather those ideas,
All tested through experience, then place them in his
Depot of supplies: the pausing space of a primrose
Apartment, a temporal repose, so he might embark
On new inner-explorations; put down thoughts' footprints
On the sharp white distances of paper tundras—
& never stop his travels; be forever on the move,
Even though to outsiders he seemed so sedentary,
Rooted—but his was a world of soulful motion,
Camouflaged flux, too fast even for sharp-eyed
Sara Lidman to keep up, so she upped sticks in the end:
Her brief cohabitation with Ivar Lo sculpted her
Into a reclusive Miss Swamp, spinster... Only one
Prolific path for Ivar Lo to follow: the sowing of words,
Knowing he would be a terrible husband & father,
For he must always put his writing before other people,
Particularly those closest to him: like a prophet,
He could only grow by setting aside those who loved him—
Only then could he begin to help the poor, empower them;
This apothecary of prose... It seemed an obvious
Omission that no Nobel gong sounded for Ivar Lo,
But it wasn't for apples of vanity he'd stretched
His fiddler's bow... Nevertheless, he rose from
Stonemasonry to *Ordre des Arts et des Lettres*;
From dusty dungarees to a green & white ribbon
Attached to an eight-point green-enamelled gold-gilt
Asterisk, worn with an emerald rosette, resembling
A crushed carnation at an educated distance—
A wilted bloom pressed in a velvet-cushioned case...

## VI. THE ABLE CAIN

Many tall steeples of principles, compassion &
Empathy sprung up through accomplishments in
Adulthood have grown from unpromising crops
In whimsical souls of children: as a small boy Ivar Lo
Had loathed his brother, often fantasised about
Pushing him from off the *farstu* ramp onto the stony
Path that wound into un-witnessing forests
At their parents' home in Ösmo, so his brother's skull
Would crack open like a nut against a rock—& though
He relished this phantasm of Cain, it also troubled him:
Not the violent thought itself, the rising desire to
Destroy his brother somehow broken into his infant
Consciousness (no, for it felt pleasurable as prickles
Of water against the toes), but the realisation
That this murderous urge, this anticipatory tingle
Accompanied by galleries of bloodied images,
Did not, in itself, trouble him, that troubled him...
Once he'd matured through years of vicarious
Voice-throwing, fictive ventriloquism through
Mouths of his own creations, lives he'd invented,
Or embroidered, played puppeteer of the pen with,
He realised that all dark thoughts were subverted
Kindnesses, & that writers could manipulate them
Into better things through a simple pulley system
Of prevention by suspension applied with gentle
Tugs of hidden strings—those of others' hearts;
He'd not set out to capture any, nor to cast them
Ruthlessly aside, but many women had been
Smitten with him at stop-off points in his life,
& he'd come to see in them temptresses scheming
To spite his pen, pin him down to domesticity
& turpitude—& so he'd felt compelled to cast them
Off each time; even reconvene juvenile fantasies
Of evil-doing in order to be rid of them—venting one
Such femicidal daydream in his novel *Blue Lady*...

## VII. ROOTLESS SOUL

Ivar Lo could never put down roots for knowing
In his soul they would sprout into human obstacles;
So he kicked the stones from the road, wandered on,
Unencumbered, with nothing expected of him

By any other living soul—nothing except those
Plenteous epistles that poured out from him... So
Ivar Lo lived alone, & long, & to some seemed
To sleep for fifty years—the Rip Van Winkle
Of Bastugatan 21... But for each secluded year
There had grown a book; not any ordinary books,
But books for all readers, from the bourgeois gentleman
In need of glimpses into grittier trials on life's fringes
To those readers carved *from* those terrible edges;
Not normally the sort prone to thumb a book in
Their tired, limited private time, but compelled to
Plumb these books, immerse their minds; re-explore
The thorns of their own daily plights, thorns
Of unrewarding chores, thorns of thoughts &
The untoward, wrought with new textures through
Tugging undergrowths of grimoire-words grown
From the rootless mind of one of their own kind
Born under an ambitious star, who chose *"Lo"*,
A soldier's sobriquet to bridge his own two names,
To bolster them, as if to shout *"Lo! Listen to
Johansson!"* & many numbers listened; understood
To follow his example & transcend the accident
Of parental class—star-eyed *statare*—take the artist's
Path contrariwise the crow flies towards authentic
Pastures of taller grasses; a path that knows its
Obstacles stretch ever far apart after the daunting
Start is mastered—the long steep climb out from
The landless classes & the threshing of those barleys
That belong to resentful 'betters'; the threshing
Of letters between the teeth & tongue; to spit out
The bit of illiteracy, cast off the blinkers of aphasia,
Thence liberated by being able to discern the runic
Standing stones revealing boundaries of former scopes:
Now gateways, portals into other worlds of thought
As symbol, song, poem, prose, sources for spiritual
Growth—Ivar Lo knew the time would come when
Those standing stones would no more symbolise
Limits of weary bones, but mark milestones for paper
Travellers; a time when no page would be left unturned;
When books would no more throw shadows of obstacle
Across the worker's shrinking looks; when all partitions
Would tumble & the literate light nourish all...


[*farstu* [pr. *fash-tu*] a small wood ramp leading from a door to the ground].

## *from* SVENSK VÄNSTER (SEVEN RED VERSES)

II.

The Swedish Life Guard stands inside his yellow sentry box
Outside the vast but vacant royal palace on Gamla Stan,
Gripped in long grey coat, aligned with white rifle-strap,
No flash of a smile on his sedentary face for the camera,
Just the glint of his nickel-plated Pickelhaube splashed by
The sharp Baltic sun, as he faces incongruously right.

III.

In Norrköping Stadsmuseum, a left-turn takes us
Into a reliquary of Swedish labour history,
Past two crimson flags, bloodied dish-rags, or drooping
Heads of two gored swans; a portrait of doughty-faced
Kata Dalström, silver-streaked hair in a bun,
Round shoulders cropped in high-buttoned puce blouse,
Hands resting on a chair-back at the foot of a mound
Of industrial grey skirt, captured for posterity
In oils (applied deftly by Sven Persson, 1934),
Facing left, as she had in life, in spite of upper-class
Parentage—the Damascene moment struck her young:
First woman to sit on the committee of the Swedish
Social Demokratiska Party; champion of Norwegian
Independence (before even many Norwegians were)
& proletarian male suffrage (knowing, if it came,
Then votes for women would follow from its crumbs);
Then to Communism: a proselytiser for the Bolsheviks;
First female delegate at the second Comintern
In 1920 when the Soviet Union was still set on
Red intentions under eagling Lenin—but Dalström
Followed a more mystical dialectical materialism:
Felt Christianity was fusible with socialism
(Two streams towards the same shared transformation;
Flipside faiths), for which she was ostracised by
Ture Nerman, her outspoken foil, who believed only
An atheist could grasp Marxism—but to Dalström
The same was true for *kapitalism*: many self-proclaimed
Communists had swerved off course through right-
Turning straits out to contrarian rapids:
All materialisms run into materialistic traits.

IV.
It might be my idealisation of the Swedish way
To remark that even before Sweden's welfare state
An average Swedish worker's house was still a cut
Above its shabbier alternatives in England; that,
Historically, Sweden captured colour earlier for
Its labouring classes than the British—that is,
If the little wooden living-room behind museum glass
Is an authentic sample of proletarian domesticity
Of 1900s Sweden: interior walls, strips of timber
Painted a pale moss green—as if to reflect a tincture
Of nature within the home—colour of pine-forest floors,
Hugging the angles of the room like tailored clothing,
Enhancing curves with blunting undulations;
& the floor: no dust-trap carpets, but varnished
Seal-brown wooden boards; curtains bowing out
Like pairs of frilly bloomers on flowered window-sills—
In these creaky miniatures, hobbit homes, polished
Burrows, enclosed evening environments of urban
Poverties at the turn of the twentieth century,
There still appeared to be some semblance of aesthetic
Sense as well as utility; of ergonomic geometry;
Rustic chic, which caught on in the slapdash washes
Of clashing colours, tones & contours of Charleston's
*Art deco* farmhouse—home to the bohemian
Bloomsbury set; then recaptured & commercialised
By IKEA, founded 1943, by Ingvar Kamprad,
That still exports its stylish range in furniture
Of every shade of fruit—orange, lemon, lime, plum—
Distributed throughout the known & unknown worlds:
From The Netherlands' Antilles to Shanghai,
From Småland's Älmhult to the tattier trams of Croydon;
It's the irony of retro fashion when it catches
To the rich, & they crave a back-to-basics look,
Homes hewn from wholesome wood, simplicity
In rustic, rough-carved bric-a-brac; chthonic kitsch;
Then serendipities of decoratively cheap block
Ornaments, artisan tat become the new *objet d'art,*
& things which once were practically worthless,
Are now much sought after, even in some cases,
Priceless—a bit like those soul-torn oils on tattered
Canvases hawked by starving artists, sold for bites
To eat or swigs of beer to charlatan taverners
Who tossed them into attics rather than hang them
On brown walls to disorientate customers,

But which, generations on, accumulate posthumous
Worth (& profit) through glazy eyes of bow-tied
Experts who canonise the mould-mottled coats
As masterpieces, auction them for millions under
The hammer at Christie's; these priceless samples
Of impoverished authenticities outlast
Themselves (not least, their artists); collectibles
That fill the roomy landscapes of vast apartments,
Mansions, palaces, hotel receptions & plush
Corporate boardrooms dappled with insipid
Pot-plants—while their creators have long
Crumbled into piles of bones in unmarked
Graves assumed as presumptuous mole-hills.


V.
May Day, 1889, a blown-up photograph
Of the Socialist Internationale: 10,000 people
Demonstrated, their crimson banners confiscated,
But their thumping boots echoed a call for reform
Of labour conditions: *"Eight hour work days with
Wages intact"*—hardly a tall order... Then a primly
Posed snapshot: Kata Dalström, Anna Särström
& the other five of the all-women Cotton Weavers'
Union, gathered round a wooden table topped
With monolithic books; a small black mounted-stag
Paper-weight as its militant centrepiece;
Five of them seated, two stood up behind, at each end,
Framing the banner of their union in an antler formation—
A stag-head of oestrogen; wrung-out angels in
High-necked blouses, wilting in long worsted skirts
Rooted to the floor like slipped stone aprons;
Faces of chipped marble, pale as aspirins;
Alabaster brows sculpted by blunt labours & serrated
Tribulations; clothes-makers' petit manikins;
Models of the rag trade; Doll's House governesses
Risking poorly remunerated entrapments of 'positions'
By campaigning for better rights; only two among
Them remembered by individual name: posterity
Commemorates them collectively as the *"Textile Seven"*.

VI.
At the time of the English enclosures that permanently
Scarred our land in patchwork & made the commoners
Landless, doomed for all time to prostitute their labour
As mobile commodities to turn in others' profits
In return for *wages* (those pecuniary albatrosses
Paid in dribs & drabs at dates set attritively apart
To maintain workers at the verge of poverty),
The common Swedes endured their own uprooting
By land-grab: the partitions disrupted their settlements,
Disturbed their villages & distributed new poverties
Of 'progress' to those who could least resist it...
The drooping penis of Sweden was circumcised
Into municipalities, newly established rural parishes,
Merchant cities, & market towns that sprang up
Between them, each sprinkled with peasant labourers:
*Statare,* who tilled the fields of landowners, were paid
*In kind* with food & rags, & cramped wooden chalets,
Slaved their lives yoked in agricultural bondage...
In the towns & cities, the smog of rising industries
Brought with it a crossbreed of factory workers, housed
In grubby slums, labouring in chilly mills to rhythms
Of hunger-rumbles for frigid diets of cold sandwiches
& tepid coffee; employed until undone by exhaustion,
Or deemed no longer viable investments due to signs
Of consumption: sudden weight loss & the tell-tale
Chin-stain of beetroot soup or red blot on the napkin
From tubercular lungs subtly erupted; vitamin-
Deficient & weak-boned for lack of calcium—so
*'Let go of'*, of course, without compensation... Small
Wonder in Norrköping, circa 1860, a Workers' Union
Sprung with a moderate ambition: that *'the members*
*Should, through study, libraries & seminars, become*
*Equally educated as the bourgeoisie...'*... So
The Swedes' Red Flag had sprung from the ruby blood
Of consumptive tongues; unions blossomed from
Undernourished tubs, & funds were started for
The unemployed, sounding the trumpet for the long
Tramp towards abolition of *statare* under the first
Socialist Government, eighty-five years later, & its
Establishment of the Swedish Welfare State, *Folkhemmet,*
*'The people's home'*—almost in parallel to Britain's
Social transformation of the same year, 1945:
Start of the all too brief Attlean calendar... Similarly,
As there were those who believed the revival of a ragged

Novel by a Hastings signwriter among the khaki
Rankers returning to a land postponed for heroes helped
In Labour's landslide victory—in Sweden, the novels
Set in the hinterlands of the *statare* (estate workers),
Also taking in gypsies, underdogs & all underprivileged,
Pounded out by the prolific labourer's scribe, Ivar Lo-
Johansson, was thought to have led to the dismantlement
Of *statarna*—one of the mightiest achievements in
Swedish (or any other) literature, that a nation's
Social renewal should be prompted by a pen replacing
A chisel in the imaginative hand of a stonemason;
Ivar Lo personified the future welfare transformation...
O there was resistance at first: bourgeois misconceptions—
Red terrors stalked the literati: Lennart Dahl, Lars
Forssell, Björn Håkansson's *"critique of values"*;
Even among the scribes of the women's liberation
Movement—both Siv Widerberg & Sonja Åkesson
Satirised its teething deficiencies—*'welfare'* became
A pejorative leitmotiv in nettling poetics of those
Born in the Twenties, the last generation to grow up
In the shadows of *statarna,* who now feared the state
Would confiscate their better-heeled freedoms
& confectioneries of choices, but past the early
Weaning problems of providing a *"people's home"* for all,
Including those who only wished to own their own,
Even at the price of others' dispossession, this *folkhem*-
Sceptic school of Forties & Fifties' antipathetic
Poets put aside their brittle tropes of that last artistic
Gasp against egalitarian vegetation cultivated by
Proletarian interpolators whose gritty-fingered poems
First planted seeds of change among the rootless *statare*,
Empowering their ploughs through narrow furrows
Of thin-ruled moleskin journals, in days of partitions,
When future poets were still in finishing schools...


VII.
Roving through curio bookshops around Norrköping's
Salutorget Square, one wizard-bearded bookshop
Owner mutters cussedly in Swedish to Matilda:
*"The country's slowly tipping down hill now that*
*The Moderate Party's secured its second term,*
*The old social democratic spirit is waning, a new*
*Materialistic scent is starting to taint the air"*...

[Pr. Småland's Älmhult: *Smoor-land's Elm-hult*. Särström: *Sare-strum*].

218

# SWEDISH FOLK SONG SUITE

## I. PRELUDE IN ALLEMANDE

In 1846, William Thoms patented the term *'folklore'*—
After a Swede, Peter Wieselgren, had coined it in 1834;
Its musical application came via Germanic *'Volk'*
(*'The people as a whole'*) from Johann Gottfried Herder
To evoke its harmonic commonality, chiming
With Romanticism; Percy Scholes, Cecil Sharp & Bartók
Appreciated in the folkloric echoes of the countryside
Distinct from town or city: something more authentic
Than urbane baroque; Charles Seeger heard in its brisk
Fiddlers' allegros, a stout-hearted, spirited music
Of the rural underclasses—but more: something
In it tapped a primal vein, an aural fundamentality,
A strain of ancestral past uniting all under one name;
Lush adaptations sprang through florid chords of Grieg's
Norwegian sound-fjords, & gallivanting Siegfrieds
Repatriated to Norse Sigurd; old Swedish village
Waltzes & folk songs collected by Gunnar Arvid Hahn,
Recapitulated in latter day Scandinavian variations:
His vibrant *'Brudvals från Ragunda'*; the spirit-lift
Of Olof Wilhelm Peterson-Berger's *'Frösöblomster'*
(*'Frösö blossoms'*)—its sprightly refrain bristling
With sharp airs from Jämtland; the craggy Romanticism
Of Hugo Alfvén's 'Skärgårdssägen'; the *hambo*;
The Gammaldans; the Swedish *schottis* partnered dance;
Alternately spirit-lifting/wistful, verdant
Transcendental combinations of buoyant brass,
Haunting woodwind & winnowing strings—something
Of the Skaldic—even Viking—in folkloric compositions;
The rustic spirit of spontaneity; but one only just
Frustrated, skilfully, on the ever-verging edge
By corals of shivering refrains, not quite ejaculated.

[Page 73. Pr. Frösöblomster: *Fruh-sur-blom-stare*. Skärgårdssägen:
*Huar-gorge-sare-gen*].

## II. *SCANDI-COURANTE*

That captivating Scandinavian vastness carved
From stalking skies & rangy distances of crawling forests,
Jutting crags & lakes of liquid silver: part-captured
Tantalisingly just out-of-reach in the rumpled
Lilliputian hills, dwarf swards & burrowing woods
Of Woden's crinkled realm, through more wounded
Movements: mood-songs, tone-poems, Anglo-Saxon
Adaptations; folk songs rooted in Varangian wisdoms,
But blunted by an island's contrapuntal sea-winds;
Collected like cropped mushrooms by foraging
Musicologists: Sabine Baring-Gould's garlands
Of country song, meticulously excavated as
The hut-circles he & Burnard dug up in Grimspound...
Later, gathered by a craggy eagle of Gloucestershire
Seeking folk-song carrion to underscore symphonic
Landscapes: Ralph Vaughan Williams, vast-visaged
As his rangy, unhyphenated double-barrelled name;
Menhiric physiognomy: a standing stone gifted voice,
A rock troll well-travelled in ravelling vocabularies
Of Nordic syncopations, dramatic terrains evoking
Tolkien Country, sculpted from damp-warped buckram sleeves;
Wizard of the quaver, his baton a magic wand unfurling
Wings of folkloric gonfalons; the breezy spell
Of 'My Bonny Boy': a through-draft of pastoral aria
Between galvanic marches of the *English Folk Song Suite,*
Adumbrating Gunnar Hahn's bucolic pilgrimages—
'R.V.W.''s Scandinavian cravings had rubbed off on him
From a diminutive kindred spirit, Radagast to his
Gandalf, invited into his prolific musical reliquary
At Dorking, the shrunken, bespectacled Nordic son
Of an organist & choirmaster: Gustav Theodore 'von'
Holst—of part-Swedish & Latvian strains—his
Great-grandfather, an émigré from Riga, on the Baltic;
Fellow Cotswoldian & student of this great oak
Of a friend, since they both studied composition
Under Charles Villiers Stanford—together, through
Harmonic corresponding, they harvested a mutual
Magpie nostalgia for English choral, folk song, madrigals,
Church music; many misericords shuddered to organ
Chills of their convulsive reinventions... Holst wrought
His Scandinavian mark on the brittle British bark,
Wore England as easefully on his symphonic gown
As arch-magician Ralph: wound rhapsodies & cool

Woodland *rallentandos* of the *Brook Green Suite*;
The heartfelt *marcato* of *A Somerset Rhapsody,*
& the russet *pesante* of *Egdon Heath*—summoning
Clym Yeobright's dwindling-eyed returning native;
Holst's glinting optics caught starlight: astronomy
Launched his *Planets Suite*: the wistfulness of 'Venus',
The ominous prowl of 'Mars', the spur-jingling
Shingles of rustling tambourines, cascades of brass
& woodwind scales of fathomless seas in majestic
'Jupiter'—strident Nordic canter through the staves
Of Scandinavia's vast sound-country, its sprawling
Glades, high-stalking skies, craggy *allargando* heights.


## III. THAXTED SARABANDE

Yet Holst saw himself as a failure: a straw-grasper,
A galloper who made chromatic distances but only
Hit on instances, chance tintinnabulations; sparks
Of Skaldic mimicry lacking authenticity (to *his*
Ears only)—adulterated brandies of the damned
(To paraphrase a Shavian dram); this restless spirit
Flitting from theme to theme: English folk song, Hindi Sanskrit,
Flighty orreries of planetary octets; his telescopic
Soul felt rootless, though rooted routinely: most
Notably in Thaxted, where his fingers plunged the parish
Church into swells of organ grinds, under an incongruous
Red Flag beside Sinn Fein's banner of gold harp
Against Cal Poly green, & a battered Union Jack...
Aural valet of Conrad le Despenser Roden Noel,
The *"Red Vicar"*, a Catholic Trotskyite, to whom Gustav
Was the perfectly pitched parishioner: a socialist
Composer with a flinty sky-gazing stare... But in spite
Of his own deeply grown convictions, Holst bowdlerised
His own lento from 'Jupiter''s tumult, a lachrymose
*Calando*, into a hymn tune to accompany diplomat
Cecil Spring-Rice's insipidly patriotic lyric,
'*I Vow to Thee, My Country*'—Holst insulted it as
*"Thaxted"*, which he practically spat, an association
Which always chafed against his transnationalist spirit.

IV. ASTRAL GAVOTTE

A tragedy, that this vastly travelling, thought-provoking
Music of colouristic vigour couldn't convince its own
Composer of its power to convince—but even now his
Haunting strains & rousing orbits hypnotise human
Labyrinths: the cryptic percussions of 'Neptune' still
Mystify, the sympathetic magic of 'Uranus' charms,
'Mercury''s wings have yet to melt, & 'Saturn''s rings
Still spin... Holst was right in the end: there are only
Eight planets in our solar system: Pluto long demoted
To a gassy dwarf planetoid since wrongly catalogued
As a *bona fide* giant: now seen as a minor sphere
Of the Kuiper belt, no greater than Chiron with whom
It orbits the ice giant, Neptune, accompanied by
A brass section of contrapuntal moons—but Neptune's
Greatness might not have been so well-defined without
The propinquity of Pluto... No doubt by now
The spirit-Holst has composed 'Pluto, The Pretender',
&, after correspondence with the howling soul
Of Harry Martinson returning from his epic
Interstellar flight on *Aniara*, the astronomer-
Composer seeks to rediscover old folk songs from
Quixotic cultures of other planets' symphonic
Atmospherics; compose his Galactic Gammaldans:
An astral *Swedish Folk Song Suite* with gavottes
To rival the gravitas of Ralph's English triptych;
Storm a score for Martinson's pitching spaceship
Flung off course from Mars, catapulted out to endless
Drifts of tin-eared stars where reputations flare, eclipse...

from
*BLAZE A VANISHING*
(2013)

## MAGE OF THE GAMMALDANS
*i.m. Gustav Holst* (1874–1934)

Gammaldans augmented in his mind's stringendo ground
Under pounding metronomes of Baltic stone: seven-eighths
Swedish, via Riga, Latvia—the rest, English as Cheltenham
Tearooms. Asthma & an arm's neuritis withered with vast
Ambition. A schoolboy Symphony in C Major, along with organ
Voluntaries. Unworldly choirmaster of the Cotswolds swept to

Halls of scholarship, poring over composition. Pulled into the
Orbit of an Ampney giant, a towering Wordsworth to his
Languishing Coleridge—a fellow traveller through folkloric
Scores he'd thrust to heights to trumpet Jupiter! Then thump down to
Thaxted's uprooted lento: his poison soup for the patriotic.

## T.E.'S MATCH TRICK

He'd strike a match & watch it light,
Mesmerise with the flame,
Then pinch it out between his fingers,
Not flinching from the pain.

Fellow officers would scoff at him:
*"Lawrence, old man, what's the trick?"*
But he'd just smile madly back at them
& lick the burnt-out matchstick.

## BROOMFLOWER

Where have I heard that voice before? Those brusque Northern *aft*-s
That hatch abruptly; catch as matches in the air;
Ruffle the southerner's softer ear with the brush of rough bark;
Wood shavings from bluntly carpentered tongues; swung hafts
Of gnarled aural cudgels; hatchets of starker articulation:
Not more severe, simply flintier—this particular sample:
A phlegm-rumbled Northumberland thrum gathering from bracken
At the back of the throat; a guttural pipe-smoker's brogue
Underscored by tobacco-pouch rustlings of rookish wisdom—
Something almost Nordic in its steeply pitched tones:
The weathered drag of the tongue tip's drogue—& the ends
Of words chafed to sharp *f*-s & *v*-s on the windswept cliff-
Edge of the teeth; a skald's sageness scraped underneath...

Was it the reedy timbres of distant grainy poets
Bassooning croups of tropes into trumpet-eared gramophones
Which sparked comparisons in this carved voice's classless
Finish cultivated in cavalry stables, drilled with verbal
Bits to batteries of brassy artilleries...? Or was it
Tolkien's Entish inflections? Treebeard's straggled
Gradualist growl? Or how we imagined Gandalf
Might have spoken: with a craggy Icelandic burr?
Or was it Roald Dahl's gravelled Norwegian prowl?
Or Wystan Auden's chalk-&-silk locution?
Or Ralph Vaughan Williams' *white shoes-why choose*
Costwolds fricatives? Or the tufted enunciation
Of Richard Murdoch's wispy narration for *The Moomins*?

No: I remembered where I'd heard it before: on the same
Hissy *Arsclist* catch as that I listened to now,
Transfixed as I was that first time as a boy when my
Father clicked the time-switch of the tape-player
& those carious reels unwound their hoary bandages
Of ghost recordings to the spools' sperming looms...
My grandfather, John, discussing Scottish folk song
Over tea & scones at Rock, Somerset, late Fifties—
'Gordon' to those closest to him, who'd passed over
Some years before I'd sprung, his stone-cut features,
Hook nose, stormed eyes gazing out under khaki cap
From a photograph's gun-fog: such definite features
That seemed so remote to our milkier entablature—
Crackled back to life as his crockery voice broke
Its silence from the other side: wistful yet stern,

Fern-edged, willowy but stoic; a brush-scrape
Of heather & granite; smooth-thorny as furze;
Rough-soft as *broomflower* sounds on the through-draft
Of the mouth... & the older & smokier I grow,
The more I hear his tone in my own: a thorniness
Of intonation; a tarry, tobacco-coated brogue...

Our voices are transmitted salvages of ancestors'
Thicketed whispers; oral aggregates of homecoming ghosts,
& though our thoughts & choices of words might be our own,
Our elocutions are honeycombed in echoes thrown
Through revenant ventriloquists: our mouths blossom
With broomflowers, our throats boom with tombstones.


## AFTER HARVEST

Before I puff to bed, I roll some fags,
As night imbibes its last dark drags.

Tipping with light into ashtray-dawn:
Ochre stubs to shocks of razed corn.


## SILVER & GOLD

Five days a week to earn silver & sweat;
Two days a week to drink gold & forget.


## HEART SPECTACULAR

The heart can erupt into volcanic upsets—
But from it we get some spectacular sunsets.

## THE SPHINX & THE HARPY

*i.m. John & Lily*

I got to know the ghosts of my grandparents through
Crematorium recollections, & old recordings:
John's tobaccoy tones snagging on hissy tapes; Lily's
Light hands stacking kitchen plates... I pictured her
Scrubbing the stone floors at Rock, dishcloth
Suffragette to chores' chained railings. Groomed by
A charitable father who'd dine alone, throwing scraps
To the poor—she took his socialisms with a spiritual
Tonic of Baptist altruism; tripe for colic. A plaster
Keir Hardie lit her heart's rose grotto under
The Sphinxed Asgills' scrolling motto: '*Sui oblitus
Commodi*': '*Regardless of one's own interest*'...

*"Our country right or wrong"* smoked from the khaki
Tongue of her patriotic husband, unsaddled hussar
Of an armchair's Northumberland. She soldiered on
Under a Damocles of nerves jolted by doodlebugs—
But no outbursts, just cobwebs obsessing the nooks
Of her thoughts; harassments of mirrors missing out
Her nose; she saw herself leaping off shelf-edges...
Nothing so tropical for her end: cancer—prosaic
Macro-noun: nester in cells scoured by its
Uncancellable shadow... *That* harpy had already
Ambushed John in its fast-advancing pincer—
More than a match for all the snatching Madsens
At Passchendaele that couldn't catch him:
Humiliations of the guts' artilleries: stools like silkworms,
Albino grubs—piss, black as Lapsang Souchong.

For Lily—teetotal, only occasional smoker for months
Of a Twenties' bloom—the mustardy crawl across
Her lungs was an ill-starred scarring of abstinent tissue
For lotteries of nostalgic tar... A doe shivered by
Delirium, she mistook my father for the ghost of her
Own as he broached her dank tomb, betraying no
Tears in his elliptic eyes... She cradled her youngest
Grandson in twig-arms, hushabying under thundering
Breath decibel by decibel distancing its pitch
To the other side of the room's partition...

## WILFRED'S RIFLE

*i.m. Wilfred Salter Owen* (18 March 1893–4 November 1918)

Who killed Cock Robin? —"*Not I*", wept the kettledrum sky,
"*I only rattled him with my artilleries of rat-a-tat rain*
*Lashing down on mud dugouts of conscripts caped in raglan wings,*
*Flightless as rats...*" Wilfred's rifle jolts to pity's whistling
Ricochet, packs up to scrap. At Craiglockhart, he enlists to
Edit *The Hydra*—fumes of its polycephalous paper crop
Drowsing odourless corridors; souls re-grown from wounds of song...

Siegfried swore he'd stab him in his leg if he returned to those
Amphibious fields; dark Shropshires of cloth-clad Pickelhaube spires;
Lucifer flares hissing fuses of soggy dog-ends, spluttering
To acid-sips of oil-black tar; khaki killer-milk weaned from
Empress sows of tobacco'd nostalgias—1st Btn. Artists Rifles—
Rigged on cigarette cards, Cartophily's tarot... Sambre-Oise,

One week to armistice: a ducking mudlark picked off in aspic,
Wings of barbwire, stiff serge tunic, palls for quail-egg grey
Eurydice—his singing head bobs downstream to Oswestry...
No crosshairs sought Cock Robin, just the stray bullet of poetry.

[*Polycephalous*: 'many-headed'. *Pickelhaube* ('Pickle-helm'): Germanic spiked helmet.
*Cartophily*: the collecting of cigarette cards].

# CHARLOTTE IN A DIFFERENT LIGHT
*i.m. Charlotte Perkins Gilman* (1860–1935)


*Crie de Coeur?* The choice was chloroform or cancer: an easy or
Horrid death—put so elementarily, there was little room for
Argument against suicidal dialectics; in any case,
Reason was a meme for androcentric academics taking
Liberties with gender accidence: '*The brain is not an organ
Of sex*'... Much more to her neurosis than an Elektra Complex:
'*Ties by this dread disease*' that made her thorny literature seem
To '*contain deadly peril*' for those whose living narratives had
Entered '*mental derangement*'—were these crinkled men projecting

Penis envy into scalloped groins of aggressive suffragettes,
Emigrés of gerrymandered oestrogen skirting virile
Rotten boroughs with grooved incursions of pelvic valleys?
Katherine's birth had stirred that which tobacco-whiskered doctors
Invested in her as "*postpartum psychosis*"—proscriptive rest cure:
'*Never touch pen, brush or pencil as long you live*', instructed Dr
S. Weir Mitchell. But words were her escape: *they* left her husband,

Stetson, made her Gilman again; *they* sent her daughter west
To live with him & his new wife, her closest friend, Grace
Ellery Channing—happy for the more compatible pair,
Thinking Grace would be a better mother, for her's had only
Shown her affection when she thought she was asleep; iced
Out her access to close friendships, & fiction. So Charlotte ate
Natural philosophy; a tomboy student neutered by correspondence,

Not cut out for scholarship, she cut her own cloth from mental
Embroideries; illustrated trade cards; took to design, painting;
Evolved from a 'nervous' being into a creative vessel—ideas

Germinating to vines crawling on yellow wallpaper trapped
In sealed hymens of her mind—she had to strip it; follow those
'*Lame uncertain curves*' to where they '*plunge off at outrageous angles*';
Mutations that emasculate themselves; that musty '*yellow smell*',
Acrid as azane-stained linen, that clung to everything she'd write;
Nettled patterns of neuter letters cast Charlotte in a different light.

## HIS BITTEN SMILE

*i.m. Thomas Stearns Eliot* (1888–1965)

*'to have bitten off the matter with a smile'*

—'The Love Song of J. Alfred Prufrock', T.S. Eliot

Thomas the doubter—but in doubting, so convincing:
Hoarse oracle scrubbed through Doric columns of bombed crockery;
Orator of wasps in beehive archives —Heart, a derelict
Monastery: emotional teetotal of the nervous remote;
Augustine startled among the preening nightingales;
Sipper of ambrosial poisons through a gramophone's throat

Sweeping out prosodic cobwebs with his scribbling besom;
Tsar of modern macro-conscience; ventriloquists' thrown
Echoes: Davidson, Bysshe Vanolis, Calvin... Self-described
Anglican & Royalist, antimacassar Carlist—deemed
Richard, his cat-sitter, fur-balled by Fabian aboulia;
No sops from this purring expatriate. Dark honeyed pupils'
Slick-blacks: a pair of melting weepers on pallbearers' heads...

Ear-twitched March Hare; a tiffin-griffin smitten with
*La Falange...* Poor Prufrock, a worry-bead gingerly rubbed
Into baldness & rolled trouser-ends, pinned to celluloid
On blue amberol to the quale of his quavering shellac voice:
To have mattered, but so bitterly, in spite of his bitten smile.

## THE MARK

'Here you come to the real secret of class distinctions in the West—the real reason why
a European of bourgeois upbringing, even when he calls himself a Communist, cannot
without a hard effort think of a working man as his equal. It is summed up in four
frightful words which people nowadays are chary of uttering, but which were bandied
about quite freely in my childhood. The words were: The lower classes smell.'

—Chapter 8, *The Road to Wigan Pier* by George Orwell

It wasn't the Odour Bohème of dusty cushions, mould-
Mottled throws on shapeless futons & stained anarchies
Of kitchen carpets—the shabby-chic musk of 'opt-out'
Brighton Enderby-maisonettes, kitsch hutches for
Gordon Comstock pendulum-dowsers of elliptical
DWP prose... No, it was a more chronic, danker odour,
A stain on the air sustained through generational agents
Of degradation; the historied tradition of 'have not-s'—
That thinner, paler species that coexists, at a distance,
Alongside us; ghosts of our gains; cast-offs of our
Material imagoes; *'the poor relations'*; refuseniks
Of social securities; refugees regenerated through
Germs of *"respectable greed"*—& the strange mangy
Osmagogue that gathers among them: the Gog & Magog
Of indigence; the contrapuntal scent to the sickly
*Eau de roses* of acceptable decadence; rank fragrance
Of gentrified negligence; the minty halitosis
That congregates around today's alfresco kitchens...

I remember it well, the subliminal smell that undermined
The 'Devil-may-care' clown act of vitamin-rinsed Mark,
Bony council house kid I'd knock about with at school:
Luminously pale, all freckles & uncombed ginger hair;
I'd been inside his gloomy mole-home, regularly plunged
In daytime darkness for an electricity meter's
Weekly Lent—a musty fume clung to scant furniture,
Clutched at everything with the hircine mark of phantom
Bailiff hands reclaiming higher purchase settees;
That smell of arrested developments; cabbaged decay,
Artificially grafted in fragrant sprays of disingenuous
Deodorants; decomposition postponed for time being—
Time being what it is: not a passage but a static thing,
Which, but for us, doesn't exist: a check-point for those
Without passports to anything but Knock Down Ginger,
School expulsions, shoplifting, borstal, dole, dead-end jobs,

Prison, or conscription, clinched by glossy recruitment
Campaigns; earmarked for social services while still embryos—
Presupposed *"scroungers"* of unemployed wombs;
Prepackaged ill-preparedly as repeat episodes
Of bollarded parental roads... Eyes scrubbed to school sores,
Dazed brains left out to graze through glacial educations
(*'Must try harder to concentrate'*—deep-stained as
Malnourishment)... Carted from damp cradles to hasty graves;
Waifish thins buried in fat foolscap case loads; marks
Of council house Cains—inheritors of vicarious sins
That can't be rinsed; stains no washing powders can remove
With biodegradable ablutions of olfactory forgiveness;
Stains ingrained in fibres of Mark's grease-glazed Sta Press
Paling from charcoal to dingy grey, cloudy as poorly rubbed
Blackboards; clung with the osphretic stigma of stale reeking
Urine; & when he spoke too close, O that sour, ironless
Breath of unregulated hunger spiced with class traces...

Years later, I bumped into Mark again, but didn't
Recognise him: he'd filled out, & shot up several
Inches taller than the brachyskelic rake I'd known at school,
Finally grown in to his skin; well-fed through wholesome
Army catering; brought up by his bootstraps to a strapping
Specimen—a manifest statement of resilience
& redemption after a lengthy sentence for teenage arson;
The only thing still paying testament to his years cheated
Of nutrition: a carious grin of irregular yellowing merlons...

Eric Blair (George Orwell), eloper from polite society,
Tried describing poverty's distinct odour: a scent
Like betrayal, redolent of the nasal tyranny of Class;
An ammoniac fume of damp pram that ripped through
Potpourris of upper-class misconceptions, & well-
Intentioned Mass Observations: he uttered the rumoured
Truth only his borderline *'shabby-genteel'* breed—
*'The shock-absorbers of the bourgeoisie'*—would dare to breach,
But which the better-heeled disguised in petunia seclusions,
Partitions to that *'impassable barrier'* of plum-mouths:
*'The lower classes smell'*... Snobbery was biblicised
Into unadvertised behaviour but, like sex, never mentioned;
Nor admitted to, beyond innuendo, vague adumbrations,
Copulative charades mystified behind pious screens;
The elephants in other rooms—but the clammy acts
That make us facts; the 'unhygienic procedures'
Of procreation—we are all made in the same slovenly way,

But after that, develop at different rates, depending
On resources we're born into: some are weaned on weaker
Lactations, thin milks for thirsty mamelons, lacking
In calcium, nutrients, vitamins... Growth can be truncated,
Surreptitiously; curtailed through malnutrition;
High birth often architects tallness—recall, historically,
Longshanked kings stretching to six feet two inches
As far back as the thirteenth century: in history
It was an opposite play of scents: the rich rarely bathed,
Stale sweat & natural filth were fragrant status symbols
Of the rich, while the offensive whiff of cheap soap tended
To be the scented betrayer of manual workers forced
To wash routinely lest they reek of the agents of their trades—
The once taboo bouquet of labour; the graveolent
Stigma of a mythical moral karma that predestined
'Corrupt souls' to work for the endless leisure of rich
Elects revived with smelling salts from status faints
Caused by their presences... Those moschate concentrates
Have long since been camouflaged in chemicals
Of sweeter smells among new perfumer classes...

Scent: transparent measurement of social difference;
Of Class (more than accents, patois or appearance);
Of poverty in the misty surrounds of others' plenty—
Smell being the most potent of the senses, the most
Mnemonic, evocative—an odiferous embarrassment
Rubbed off on those whose powerlessness is hung with
Its blameless musk; who keep away from the rest of us...
An almost-myth in partitioning minds who claim they
Are no longer *"always with us"*, as the rich—but they
Are still a part of our neglectful fabric, even if they
Tend to stick to their own stations, allocated colonies
Of incubations, self-conscious of the aromatic mark
Of their (contagious?) material disadvantages &
*"Limited aspirations"*; they shrink in their reservations
In sink estates & out-of-town doughnut districts
Where even private landlords fear to let; still uninitiated
Into *"national purpose"*; the secret people who slowly
Grow from mushroom glooms in the shadows
Of the guilty privileged; rarely admitted into the light
Of dialectic for they bruise the sensibilities of social
Engineers; dog the egos of 'progressives'; sully
Reputations of pinkish planners; taint their primrose
Fumes with cowslip pheromones, *"feral"* essences
That offend yet oil the scentless & senseless

Distinctions that keep English noses resolutely
In the air... At the twenty-first century's stilted turn,
The existence of class distinctions was sniffed at as
The acquired aftershave of quixotic Marxists,
But in the main, was electively undetected by noses
Of anosmatic academics, circumspect commentators
& focus groups—poverty was the guilty secret
Of casual tsars (tasked to damage-limit it; beak about
In proscriptive prosopons, play down statistics) &
Apocrypha of social workers' avalanching clip-binders;
Privation was no longer polemically permissible;
Damped out at the perfume counter of mainstream discourse;
Stigmatised as the miasma of *"moral failure"*
In *"maladaptive"* individuals—recidivists, drug addicts,
Alcoholics, *"scroungers"*, *chava*, travellers, gypsies, *Roma*,
& the *"voluntarily homeless"* (shadows of misnomer)...

So too were certain scents in contradistinction to
The graded samples of mass affluence, reconstructed
As stains of Cain, & fumigated like the plague...
Though now, in this Fugitive Decade, austerity
& the welfare hate are spreading contagions of stigmas,
Fertilising future generations with resentful taints,
Essences of decaying states; shiftless stains on stale airs
Too potent to be contained in ring-fenced doughnut ghettoes,
Outlands generated by metropolitan "gentrification",
The scentless cleansing of rental tenants by a breed
Of Buy-To-Bet Dorian Grays—the new alfresco musk
That hums around food banks & wheelie bins will
Germinate & spread; cause olfactory offence
To retrenching protectorates of vested scents—
The Mark will come to reclaim its place as sacrificial stench
Perfected & projected by this anosmic island race...

## LAPSED ANGLICAN

Racketing in quixotic Volkswagen past
Vast avenues of interminably detached
Mock Tudor follies & pillared McMansions
With imposing porches, groaning bay-windows,
Immaculately gravelled private drives—
We anchorites gazed disapprovingly
From our monastic car, & all its trappings:
Poverty-beige with ripped roof linings—
Our driver, a lapsed Anglican, observing
These palatial retreats from under the brim
Of his waxy tweed cap, intoning through
Tarred ochre teeth his hard-gravelled song:
*"Makes you wonder what they've all done wrong"*...

## VIOLIN DISORDER

There it was, cradled between the scorched instruments:
A counterfeit Stradivarius varnished & shining,
Washed up on a glass shore of sands redistributed;
His fractured reflection, no rioter's, no fractious
Raskolnikov's, but a music lover's, an admirer
Of unaffordable craftsmanship: the womanly waist
Of lacquered Gum Arabic hourglass, curvaceous
Spruce hips & shoulders, slender maple neck,
Grain of honey & egg-white—its dimly vibrating
Strings tantalising him to salivating music-envy—
This stringless musician. There it sat rocking slightly,
Unspoilt apart from part-scorching on the lower loin
(A serendipitous sunset burnish), waiting
To be handled, to be played, to impart its liberties.
He seized the instrument with the moment—at last
Owner of a violin in near-pristine condition;
Willow-light to hold, hollow as morals echoed back
At him in a tone-deaf court: *"SIX MONTHS IN PRISON"*.

# TERPSICHOREAN RHAPSODY

*i.m. Vaslav (Vatslav) Nijinsky (1899–1950)*

*for Jeremy Reed*

They say—& we only have what they say—Vaslav
Nijinsky defied gravity in his self-propelling leaps;
Avian of the balisage; flaming cockerel of tulpa-plumage;
Indisputably, in death, & after, defier of posterity:
Nothing would frame his mythical artistry: no recordings
Exist of his balletic sorcery, only old eerie
Photographs of his uplifted beatific face made up
Into terpsichorean prosopons: the melancholy clown;
The supple Scaramouch; the diamond-sleeved Harlequin;
The sensual faun—Nijinsky! Therianthrope
Of tulip-opening pineal eye; springing spectre
Of the yet-living—immortal through others' memories,
Recollections, & his own scribbled records that mapped
Out his mind's metamorphosis into something
Sprite-like; unclutchable tropic—an exotic bird
In shouts of violent colours... His adoring Romola,
Who ever found him, never left him, a soul-mate in thrall
To his ribboning shadow—she claimed an x-ray
Of Vaslav's feet revealed chimerical structure,
Somewhere skeletally between man & avian—
*"No wonder he can fly; he is a human bird"*, piped
Dr Abbé, pinching the wing of the illuminated plate
Against the light... His feet, that tripped the air so
Effortlessly, spring-light, prehensile; tapering down
To elongated toes that could grasp rope or bar
Like a bird on a perch... Athlete, acrobat, artiste,
Aesthete, mystic, stringless marionette; bounding
Leveret; tightrope walker of elevated spirit;
Zarathustra of the trapeze... Sometimes a tumbler
To the spin of Diaghilev's voodoo; the unscrupulous
Conjuring of those white magician's gloves:
Abracadabra & his terpsichorean protégé's
Halo rattled to the stage; his fragile ego congealed
To darkness; his unearthly gift melt away at an instant—
His identity spilt like salt... The patron & manipulator
Knew Nijinsky's Achilles' heel; had only to snip those
Sampsonic puppet-strings with a spell from his cruel lips
For Vaslav to collapse in a heap of parts—such was
Diaghilev's legerdemain, but the bow-tied pederast
Had grown to fear the powers of this rangy Ganymede

Whom the impresario could not possess: once the music
Irrupted in Vaslav no earthly force could arrest it...
Pipes, strings, reeds, flutes, brass—all collided
Within him in contrapuntal trance... Those feet
Would swell, split the seams of the kid glove leather
Ballet shoes: pair by pair replaced mid-scenes,
Sole after sole scuffed in powdered rosin... Each
Movement: osmotic, lithe, lyrical, muscularly cryptic,
Breathless, elliptic—no conjuring tricks: just tendons
& hamstrings hereditarily dipped in Stygian
Gene pools of obscure lineage; his pulse pumped
With pirouetting troupes of peasant hummingbirds
Of the Caucasus & Crimean mountains:
Generations of gymnastic Gopak jumps to cimbaloms
Charged his song-sprung haemoglobin; his conspicuous
Cheekbones & vast brown Zaporozhian eyes,
Spoke of Ukrainian steppes; Tartar ancestries
& Slavic Kiev; his thick neck propped the vital
Purpose of his sculpted head: a nimble bust; clipped
Torso poised on muscle-bowing thighs, balanced by
Long arms' trunk-like wings... Each performance
An epiphany, a revelation, miraculous, magical,
Almost supernatural, no need for highfaluting
Diaghilev's hyperbole for here *was* Pan, Apollo,
Bacchus—Rasputin of the greasepaint; scintillating
Tsar of the dance; high-priest of poise & posture
To roses & sores, bouquets of jonquils, cut tulips,
All flowers of rioting blooms & rapturous applause....
But, surely, not applause for *him?* This medium
Of the Steppes? This wide-faced Ukranian with
A labourer's biceps? Not applause for poor Nijinsky:
For poor Nijinsky didn't actually exist! He was a figment!
Simply a funnel through which all this refulgence crept;
A flesh-&-bone conductor for celestial effect—
But nothing, *a nothing*, as all human ciphers;
An empty vessel sometimes filled with ambrosial blood
Pumped by the Bacchanalian wine-skin of the heart—
That globed bulb buried in clay, nothing but a beetroot
Dug up from peasant earth to nourish rushing blood;
Succoured on unconsciousness, he'd no identity,
No grounding ego, no sense of self, only a sense
Of oblivion in movement; to spin fast as planets,
The spiralling rings of Saturn—the scale, the vast
Dark of racing galaxies; stage-lights, waxing stars
Obscuring gasping galleries... The stars are us,

We are stars, atoms, splinters of God—he knew this,
Felt this, grasped this as he spun, & it was the only
Thing he grasped—the whirling Dervish of Kiev
Knew he was nothing & everything in one, as every
Man, woman, child, bird, fish, fowl & familiar:
All as one, under one spell, one fragmentary trance
Of light, colour, colour-echo, colour-sound, colour-smell;
A propulsion of the soul propelled him from the ground—
But his were the witnesses' wings: his leaps, sprung
Anticipations of the body politic... All was change
To Vaslav: motion, flux, limbo, fandango; all was
Without him, whirled around him; surface things,
Materialisms: temporal seams & sequins of hubris's ball—
& he was the thing which channelled them,
Symbiotically... He was not Vaslav, or Vatslav,
He was the dance, he was its vassal, he was its
Whip-lashed slave, he was anything but Vatslav;
His essence was not invented as his name; he was
Nijinsky, never Vatslav—a visitor at his own vaunted grave;
Invalidated by valve or vein; invalided by living;
Reinvented by velocity: now convivial Faun;
Now frowning clown with tear-drop-painted cheek;
Now sailing swan; now strutting Harlequin;
Vaunted by the venerable, bourgeois & powdered-
Nosed patricians—but no one's property (not even
His own): no Armide's slave of Diaghilev's or
Stravinsky's—though he served his *Rite of Spring*
Devoutly: recoiled his toes like a brass monkey
At the chill of its rambunctious reception; stamped his
Stick to keep the dancers up to tempo through
The howls of outraged laughter; mockery; abusive
Chants pelted like rotten cabbages at the stage
Till a riot erupted in the thumping boards... But still
The music crashed & dashed its brash cacophony,
Desperately, euphorically; all the while Nijinsky
Clapped his dancers beat by beat, stood on a stool
In the wings, heart-flayed with splintered feet;
He clapped them on in their jolting choreography
Of chorea—ugly angular spasms of frantic radical dance!

Nijinsky resisted temptations of Chaplin's to brine
His sublime alchemy of motion in cinematic can—
Perhaps he sensed a hyperkulturemia in himself
Could erupt if exposed to his own performances;
No footage exists of his swift footing, only the ghosts

Of those who shadowed his dances with gushing lines
In besotted biographies can give glimpses of his
Energetic genius—he alone knew the magic was
In the mystery, & the mystery was in the fling
Of the moment's *gigue*, confined only to the mystique
Of memory, its filtered mystification... He knew we
Were all only atoms, star-splinters sparking apart
For seconds in time, then shooting up to the vast,
Everlasting commonality of dark—but O that hypnotic
Self-propulsion, sprung muscular limbs, sinuous
Giraffe-neck, feet of avian skeleton (so some
Mythologised); & those leaps & bounds; the jump
Which catapulted him impossibly high from the ground,
& the sorcery of his slower gliding down—enchanted
Peter Pan, Magus of the stage, Cagliostro
Of choreography, Houdini of terpsichorean escape,
Almost seeming to levitate, elasticate: an elongating
Dunglas Home of the *Ballet Russe*... How tragic, then,
That the meteoric flight that propelled him so high
Spun into schizophrenia's triple *tours en l'air*;
Launched him into its maelstrom—no slower landing
As he once could perform at will with invisibling
Hummingbird wings: its dissipation brought him down
Into the sulphur pit... So Nijinsky denied himself
The immortalisation of film, the capturing
Of his flights of wingless tapering arms; somehow
He seemed to know the *mythos* was the show,
The moment everything, & nothing, its banishing
To rapt spotlights of memory: means to mystifying
His miracle of movement; for that brief tripping
Time he spread his tulpa-plumage, a puppet without
Strings; he *was* the Harlequin—the chameleon
Who danced himself out of his own identity;
A force of nature; a sped-up projection of the living;
Who could only find his sense of stillness in
The vertigo of spinning spinning spinning...


[*hyperkulturemia* (or Stendhal's Syndrome): a severe form of vertigo (panic,
(dizziness, fainting etc.) when exposed to a plethora of exotic art. *gigue*: jig].

## THE AUDEN SAGA

*i.m. Wystan Hugh (W.H.) Auden* (1907–1973)

*for Norman Buller*


What a saga! From fourteen anxious windows at 54 Bootham,
York, to scrolls of Miltonic sonnets & walnut-puckered skin—via
Solihull; Oxford's hoary dorms; a night train through the neurasthenic
Thirties: taking in Iceland's black Gabbro dales & basalt crags—
Ancestral landscape of Skaldic fancies—to dusty Spanish pastures that
Nuanced your political tempo: ambulance driver/ contra-Franco

Haw-Haw for a wired Republic stormed by rumours in uniforms;
Under Sino-Japanese seas; then, periscope up at Manhattan's
Giant's causeway of skyscrapers, moored grampus, spouting out of blowholes,
Harpoon-proof in a chunky ashtray *Nautilus*... Wystan! Where was your

*"Auden Country"*? Was it Rookhope, your *"sacred landscape"*, somewhere
Under a Pennine rainbow? Or underwater? Can we raise its Atlantis—
Drain its anthems into silos for emergencies? Your ectopic *Edda*
Ebbs in the pulse of Northern heirlooms, but its malpositioned mouth
Needs urgent restoration: has a way of detouring, a South.



## SNAGS & RAPIDS

*i.m. Alun Lewis* (1915–1944)

'He saith among the trumpets, Ha, ha; & he smelleth the battle afar
off the thunder of the captains, & the shouting'

*—Job 39:25*


Among the trumpets, ha, ha, you smelt battles before the brass crashed
Like thrashing branches, strapless faradised arms ungrasped...
Under bleak Welsh skies you grew out from the shadow of Aberdare...
Nonconformist... Socialist... Your soul was public but your heart was

Let to private nettles... War wrenched you from snags & rapids of thorny
Entanglements: you enlisted into tropics *'seeking less & less of the
World'*, but found *more*... Slippery acceptances in clammy fingers
Insinuating triggers; smudged pages' greased onion-skins —Time,
Sun & inky jungle insisting on *'a thing so long delayed...'*.

## MEETING MR. BELL

*i.m. Martin Bell* (1918–78)

*for Barry Tebb*

*Maudit!* Blasted out the day before your grant
Arrived... We too missed each other by a slant:
Reading, Ninety-Seven, posthumous *Reverdy*
*Translations* appears through Whiteknights' tweedy
Imprint/ I sip a pint, browned off in a pub\*,
Numbed by a Third, the aspiring poet's rub.

By chance, years later, I stumble on your haunt;
Empties for eyes, face see-through, green-steeped, gaunt,
Luggage at your feet, you croak, *"Is this Hell, or*
*Leeds? I could never tell the difference for sure...".*

[\* taken from Bell's poem 'Unsumcasane as Poet Maudit']

## THE NEIGHBOURING VOID

*i.m. Sylvia Plath* (1932–1963)

*'...the utter exposure and defencelessness of the frontiers of human existence against*
*the neighbouring void'*

—Erich Heller, *The Disinherited Mind*

How everything conspired that cryptic winter—
The pipes that froze, the telephone that wasn't there—
To snow-in her susceptible thoughts in a sparse, icy flat,
Gloomy & cold as an igloo. That shadeless light-bulb:
A throbbing white goddess above her in the lunging hallway.
How the scene was starkly set, too temptingly prepared
To pass up as if a blip in atmospherics. For one brief
Moment she fancied it might all be ameliorated
By a fillip, a pill, a sensory clipping. But, still,
The woozy hypnotism persisted, felt more permanent
This time... Even if Al Alvarez had perceived,
In retrospect, more of a dress-rehearsal compared
To her ultimate attempt as a child—his Savage Goddess

In dressing-gown; mothing Snow White of silent carpets...
The shadows wore her solitudes while she slipped
Into their robes, tripped in slippers into the pale paint
Of impassable walls; a mere Shade—Domestic Dido
Mourning her phantom lover of the overworld:
The torrid Trojan from Mytholmroyd, eloper with her
Future gas-apostle, Assia Wevill... Efforts towards
Oblivion were purely incidental tropes in a long
& somnolent monologue winding to its close;
A narrative in which she was the absent party,
Going through the motions, disembodied, alienated
From her own movements as if a ghost already,
Dissociated, pure spirit lifted weightlessly from
Her milky body... The scene was set, implicitly:
The patient furniture, the once-happy sofa, the resentful rugs—
How hollow-souled her human bowl, a liberal lobby of bones,
Yet she felt boneless; luminous; unassailable as an x-ray;
Emptied of immanence... How *being*, to her, had always
Been a nervous dizziness, a terror of freedom,
Some kind of chilly consciousness ever combing
The skirting-boards to a neighbouring void... & how
Could anyone simply carry on, knowing oblivion was
Just next door? That all-attracting vortex;
That centrifugal negative energy that always beat back her
Frail attempts at becoming something other than
A thought-filled superfluity of refrigerated flesh,
& corpuscles only responsive to panic, a turretless
Fortress prowled by pawed exposures... & now
She couldn't tell if she'd already slipped next door,
Her body so cold, icy, the house dipped in unworldly
Whiteness... Now she groped from room to room,
Shapelessly, a spectral understudy on the stage after
The audience has left, their empty chairs, sealed lips
Between two jaw-clamped armrests... Phantosmia
Of greasepaint... Then the view of the empty stage,
Where she was supposed to be, now stood in the wine-dark aisle,
A solitary usherette with plastic-coated confectioneries,
Bitter sherbet lemons—this was no intermission,
This was the empty premiere: absence anticipated her.
A chill of fingers tied her hair. Wet towels & cloths were
Her willing accomplices; conspirators against the air—
They'd insulate her from the through-draught that brushed itself
Like a guilty cat retracing the bare wall under the stairs...

## OBLIVION ON DEVONSHIRE STREET

*i.m. Harold Monro, poet & publisher* (1879–1916)


Harold of rag Argonauts, hinged orange in amaranth gatefold trimmed
Against grains of anthologised Georgians, clothbound Colchians
Raised with Aeëtes' sewn teeth—but no embalmer could burnisb
Oblivion's bruise, clotting to black catafalques cradling glue-
Ligatured signatures. Flyleaves like pinto tomb-lids brushing
Deckle-edged nerves at Devonshire Street's nicotined frontispiece

Marbled with Bloomsbury-mould; foxed flophouse & posthumous shop
Of mummified spines like dust-bloomed pupae, or hatched buckram moths.
Nipping stems poems' decomposition in card sarcophagi: scrolled
Relics of consciousness: curse of aphasic pharaoh-souls... We outgrow
Our nerve-verged shelves: our bandages unpeel; our words throw shadow...


[*Colchians*: of Colchis, home to the Golden Fleece possessed by King Aeëtes—
'Colchians' are today called 'Georgians': Colchis is a province in Western Georgia.
*burnisb.* to smooth and seal by rubbing. *signatures*: sheets of printed pages. *deckle-edged*: feathered edge on specially-made paper. *buckram*: stiff cloth of cotton. *nipping.* pressing sheets to expel air at the sewing stage].

from

*SHADOWS WALTZ HALTINGLY*

(2015)

## STAFFORDSHIRE FLATBACKS

Will we ever know our full authentic selves?
Can we even picture them, assemble their dimensions
From the flat packs of our half-assembled minds?
Or are we to remain for the rest of our natural lives
As Staffordshire Flatbacks pretending on shelves?
Pretending three dimensions through moulded frontages
Drip-painted in naïve rainbow vibrancies,
Or flambé glaze bravados to mimic numinous gleams,
Boasting sophisticated facets in robust bas-relief,
Seemingly real, but all the time pretending,
Deceiving the eyes of beholders with our bossed façades,
When all the while we are our own deceivers
Concealing the plaster flatness behind us,
The mere adumbration of being, the sculpted
Blankness only the blank wall is canny to,
Pressed in on its own cream darkness, fitted for
Purpose of superimposition (Supermen in two
Dimensions); ornamental fixtures mystifying
Featureless voids above mantelshelves which—but for
Battlements of *objet d'art*—would swallow us
In sightless, soulless glares—so we clutter up
These plinths, furnish them as shrines of self-
Forgetfulness; here we daily worship at altars
Of possessions which don't recognise us, nor owe us
Allegiances, but spurn our ownerships, rebuff us
With indifferences, circumscribe our presences,
Resist us, obstruct us in their insolent protests—
Mute resistentialisms; we worship as pitches
Spilt in spite of ourselves; pictures pull the strings
Of English astringencies, slip at their own wills,
As plaster flakes away from traumatised fractures,
Unhinging the nails... We are half-fake Frankensteins
Whose beautiful monsters are inanimate miniatures,
Petrified figurines, that incubate our souls
In borrowed shadows—prestige Easter Island
Midget effigies sipping precipices, buried up
To their chins in thin wooden ledges with nothing
Underneath them, at least, to our split-perceptions
Tricked by light's magic crystal sawing—we might
As well be worshipping empty mantelpieces
Instead of these steep displays of chipped simulacrums:
Our highly prised replicas, sought-after familiars,
Curiosity-value avatars waiting graven, crazed
& glazed-eyed, to be authenticated, then certified...

## CHATTERTON'S SCRAPS

*i.m. Thomas Chatterton* (1752-1770)

Twentieth of my Composition was Pride—the rest, Imagination &
Humour—a practical joker; I learnt my alphabet from capitals
On old music folios & elephantine Bible-print. Rowley,
My made-up monk, dusted himself from musty parchments
At Canynge's Redcliffe, in the muniment room upon the porch;
School at Bluecoat Colston was a bore, so I spiced things up a bit:

Canynge taught me how to counterfeit illuminated manuscripts—
Heaven to a scrivener's apprentice! Kersley's *Dictionarium
Anglo-Britannicum* versed me in mediaeval diction; port-spoilt
Tories gormandised on my finds for their thirsty periodicals—
Those milking editors drank my talents & tipped me into penury;
Expurgated my forgeries to sculpt out profits! But scrolling
Rowley poured a poison posset to glaciate the garret glooms:
Tipple enough to leave me heaped like a crumpled string-puppet
On an attic bed, one knuckle rooted to the floorboards—a wax
Nocturnal Icarus, wing-singed, pinched out by an arsenic nightcap.

## MARIGOLDS TO DISTRACTION

*i.m. Emily Dickinson* (1830-1886)

*Eyes like Sherry in the Glass the Guest leaves —*
My mind is too near itself — cannot see Unclouded —
Indian Knots Stitch my Heart — *Hair like Chestnut Bur —*
Leave me to see into myself — transparently —
Youth Clouds my Mousy Brow — Yellow Buttery.

Death, my Shadow Correspondent — can't Un-think me —
I'll not invite Him in again — He shan't irrupt in my
Churchyard sleep — with his Wainscotting Knock — Bone-
Knuckles — grind to Cheese-Rind on my grating Door —
*I'm not in!* I squeak — this dispels His purpose — for now —
*Not in — Out today —* out in crowded Garden's worsted
Shawl — a Blaze of Blooms — & *Marigolds to Distraction —*
O — They call me Recluse — but I'm in Bliss of it —
Nerve-ends nestle into me — Stings back into Bee.

## REFLECTIONS IN THE TWO-WAY MIRROR

Who observes? Who sits beyond that glass?
I stared back at my pale reflected face scarcely half-made
But already made up by scrupulous shadows under
Startled slate greys, phantom mascara, or smudges
Of plumbago shaped like upturned timberwolf rainbows...

Who were those screen-obscured observers
Partitioned off like mute priests behind tinted glass?
I knew my confessions weren't meant for deaf ears,
But if they absolved me, I was blind to their blessings...

What bodies, what minds, what demiurge scribes
Watched me from behind my untelling reflection
In that bird-blinding hide? What beak doctors roosted on
Its fogged other side? Were they grooming mushrooms
In the shadows of my thumbed obsessions? Sometimes
I chanced darting glances to catch suggestions of heads,
Human-shaped shadows, crouched silhouettes
Of thought-ornithologists spotting & jotting
Unconscious nuances to tones of my plumage,
Each muscle-sprung rumple & shimmer of feather...

Would they ever emerge to illuminate me
As to which weird species of fluttering Furies
Was filling my head with blasphemous phantasms,
Flashes of dark acts uncommitted,
Repellent pictures on permanent repeat
Mesmerising me into presuming I was guilty
Before I'd indulged? But *indulged?* That implied
Some perverse enjoyment —I'd thought temptations
Were supposed to appeal to one's body & mind,
Not strip one of appetite & the other petrify...?

Indigestible images seeding indelibly
In my brows' ploughed furrows —I, a glum scarecrow,
My straw-innards burst like a stuffing-clocked pillow...
What unreasonable hybrid of bird with such putrid
Appetites was pecking crumbs from my mind's
Stagnant gutters? Would there ever be a verdict?
A reveal? A naming of this imp inside spinning gold
Thoughts into ungraspable straws, which might,
As according to rumoured gramarye, diminish
The powers of this interpolating Rumpelstiltskin—

Break the dark spell of its magical thinking?
Would any conclusion be pinned-down by
The pad-tapping proctor? Something less opaque
Than the insouciant pout of his cryptic mauve lips
Refusing to unseal & whisper *Open Sesame,*
Dispel the vague shibboleth: *"Intrusive thoughts"*—
That thorny almost-motto that held my soul hostage...
I chomped at it... (It seemed, for the time being,
It was open season for interpretations
& symptoms, & every thought for itself)...

Would the mirror's insiders ever unveil themselves?
Step out from behind the hermetic glass wall
Of their sealed-in Aladdin's Cave plunged in dimmers
& enter the light? Let the bottled Genie out?
Explain what my cloudy metamorphosis was about?

No—*Nothing*; no elucidation was forthcoming;
No enlightenment to right me; no insights ignited;
No exorcism performed; no bell, book & candle;
No magic wand waved to an abracadabra &
A rabbit out of a hat; no blessing, absolution, or hope
Of a prayer... Nothing as prosaic as an explanation
To help me escape this Sphinxian cantrap,
This eclipse of the will, & dispel the Pepper's
Ghost warping my head... They kept me in
The riddling dark—under strip-light glare,
Strapped to my thoughts in a cold plastic chair,
Stumped by blank notepad slanting towards me
From a trouser-creased lap, & the sculptured Delphic
Spandrel arcing over Dr Vorster's divaricated visage
& vague glazed gaze—mind-archimandrite
With mandarin grin, marble hands arched in a prism,
Spectacles glinting intransigently,
Merely refracting my questions pressed up
Like speechless lips against the tinted glass
Of the two-way mirror's un-telling reflections...

## THE SCARECROW ABANDONS HIS POST

*Nerves*—euphemism for the mental scarring of a vague
Genetic heritage fastening keenly as mucilage
Or tags on the mossy furs of malachite awakenings—
Kept me back from school, routinely, for the lion's
Share of a whittled year that misted to an age
Of mind-abandonment; psychical truancy...
Phantasmagorical summer lanes absorbed me...
Thoughts whispered past like absent butterflies
As I daydreamed on a sun-parched verge, the milk
Glove of my hand bathing in the tar-black warmth
Of Max's straggly coat—my fellow mongrel wonderer,
Jet truant & deserter, animal-shadow, dark familiar...

But then another shadow intruded, threw over us,
Cast by a flushed-faced grimacing farmer whose
Straw teeth hatched rhetorically: *Shouldn't you be
At school today?* The unexpected chill in the cloudy
Pool of his censorious shadow startled Max &
Shook me awake from daydream; I gazed up,
Timorous contempt filling me at this unannounced
Presence: *No, not today*, I replied, glum as a sack-
Headed scarecrow, seed-lipped but mouthless,
A rope of apprehension tightening round my neck
As my fist clenched on Max's lead, then slackened
Again as the rustic inquisitor hovered away... At
That moment—one which passed without incident,
But left the treacly menace of his curiosity behind it,
& a sour sting on my tongue like a tensing bit—
I thought of adding: *I should be out in the fields today,
Stiff on a post, only crows supposed to notice.*

# TWO GLOUCESTERSHIRE MAUVES

## 1. TWIGWORTH YEWS
*i.m. Ivor Bertie Gurney* (b. Gloucestershire, 1890–d. London, 1937)

Impact of mustard gas, *"no worse than catarrh"*—from a gurney's
Vantage, Nurse Drummond drew his heart's triage—invalided love,
Over in advance—then over the nervous verge; wires strung too
Rigid—*Boing! 'Bloomingest'* urge's suicidal leitmotiv...

Brancepeth Castle *'basket case'*: tinkling wonky ivories
Echoing on an old piano's *'boiler factory in full swing'*;
Rev. Cheeseman, sisters Hunt & Marion Scott nurtured his
Tuneful gifts, grown to songs of sprung green ranges rising
In glissandos—from rag traders' son to composer of the five
*Elizas*; wounded-shouldered, shell-shocked Housman settings—this

Gloucester lad flung *Severn & Somme* by howitzer mood-swings;
'Unteachable' to Stanford—might have bloomed brighter than Ireland,
R.V.W., Bridge, but for his *'bolshiness'*... Poems' embers
Numbed asylum years—a bloodied cough unhinged the creaking
Escritoire of his chest... Buried humbly by Twigworth's puttied
Yews: no stripes for Privates of verse, no chevrons for severed nerves.

## 2. LITTLE GIANT
*i.m. Isaac Rosenberg* (b. Gloucestershire, 1890–d. Arras, 1918)

Immigrant to imagination's melting regions—parentage
Salvaged from pogroms of Dvinsk, saved by the *"Mauve Decade"*;
Anglicised identities: Hacha & Dovber changed to Anna
& Barnett; but Isaac's remained—a sickly boy, brought up on
Cable Street, in a poor district, schooled at St. Paul's Whitechapel

Round the corner from Wellclose Square; then Baker Street, Stepney—
Out at fourteen, apprenticed to an engraver; then Slade's
Studios: dovetailed talents, like David Jones, mortised between
Easel—alongside Marsh, Bomberg, Carrington, Binyon, Nash—&
Nib; but it was verse which carved his visage—along with chronic
Bronchitis—to a whittled gnome; though his shadow, once thrown,
Eclipsed the other Jewish *'Whitechapel Boys'* —Gertler, Leftwich,
Rodker... Attached to a *'bantam'* battalion, giants at five foot two,
Goat of a Suffolk Folk Ranker, dropped by a sniper at Fampoux.

## GUNS OF ANGUISH

Harold, our grandfather of the distaff side,
Of lunging gait, agitations, twitching thumbs,
Sudden surges & beetroot-faced rages
When he'd punch his own head, was barely held together
By brown-rimmed glasses, feathered trilbies,
Affectionate *Old China*-s, an impish sense of humour,
& self-neglecting generosity; he was the youngest
Of six Parkers (no relation to the pen manufacturers,
Although he'd always used one, an avocado-coloured
Ballpoint primed for football pools & word searches):
Uncles Frank, Sid & 'Lol' (Laurence), & aunties
'Doff' (Dorothy) & Olive—but there was a phantom
Seventh sibling, our mother's ghost-uncle,
After whom Harold had been named, as if by
Sentimental replacement; this first Harold
Was killed while spiking the guns of a German dugout
In the First World War; a blunt-pencilled note—
Acknowledging his rummy luck at having so far
Been spared while so many of his comrades had bitten
The clay—the only fragment left of him...

The second Harold's second-hand name weighed heavily
Upon his rock-shoulders, proved more of a jinx,
For he was never lucky, nor had any peace of mind
After four years cooped up in a Prisoner of War camp
During the Second; he'd been tortured for escape attempts,
Hit over the head with rifle butts, made to stand outside
All night in the Bavarian snow, naked—naturally,
We'd always assumed these were the causes of his
Shaking tempers, restless fingers, jolting limbs
& fogginess... Once our endearingly garrulous
But domineering grandmother had passed away,
Quandaries arose surrounding Harold's 'accidental'
Overdoses—doubtful clouds swelled like cotton wool
Stoppers in his pill-bottles; he was haunted by
Dry-rot landlords & damp problems, & sometimes
By grandma whose ghost he'd argue with on the edge
Of the bed for his widowed remainders; he'd been
So devoted to Beryl, had acted as her arms & legs
For those last years she'd held court swollen-shinned
In an armchair, regaling us with sagas of her
Colonial girlhood in Roaring Uganda,
Over scooped avocado halves she'd drench in vinegar—

Two Massai paddles, a mould-spotted safari helmet
& an elephant-foot gamp-stand for props,
*The Flame Trees of Thika* stirring up all those old
Memories on television: her mother biting snake venom
From a servant's rump, her Staffordshire father
Putting up telegraph poles to help keep the Empire
Gossiping up to sunset... Harold needed no wires
To keep up cross-correspondence with his spectral
Beryl, but it led him into greater agitations
During periods of poorer reception when lines
Crackled & frequencies shifted—until he lost
The connection altogether, turning gradually
Greyer round the gills, occasional cuts & bruises
Splotching his bald pate, little strips of bloodied
Tissue stippling his stubble where he'd cut himself
Shaving—*Oh Daddy... I'm worried about you*,
Mum would say in an anguished voice wrung-out
Like a dishcloth; his daughter & only child,
Whom he used to tease as *mop head* for her unruly
Curls when she was a girl, tomboyish like Haley
Mills in *Tiger Bay* (grown by then, that child star,
Portraying pith-shaded Elspeth Huxley)—but
By then Harold barely recognised his Helen...

What spiteful Furies chose to hound such innocent
Quarry as this tortured man who'd never thought
Of himself...? O, but he'd go out fighting in a fit
Of blind rage, last gasped stage of a strange
Pathology we'd later learn, through throes of our
Mother's atrophy, was part of a pattern of faulty
Repeats, Huntington's mutant proteins, with a fifty-
Fifty chance of being passed on to offspring,
All hinging on whims of rogue genes' trigger springs,
A nail-biting game of prussic roulette (for
Some surgeons say the brain smells a little bit
Like bitter almonds), until by some providential
Rapture it's snatched up & captured by fate,
Sparing all future scions, for it can't skip generations...

But if it can suddenly *stop*, then surely some way
Back in our foggy genealogy it must have had
A *start*? & there must have been a *nothing-huntingtin*
Before that...? We *all* have the Huntington gene,
But something has to trigger its rampant mutation—
Not good enough to vaguely frame it as '*hereditary*':

That only obfuscates an inevitable beginning;
The mutant gene couldn't have begat *itself*,
It must have come from *somewhere*—the old
Chicken-or-egg paradox; did this disease
Originate in Harold—could it have been triggered
By a rifle jolt? Or war camp traumas? None of his
Siblings ever showed such graphic symptoms—
Frank, Sid, 'Lol', 'Doff', Olive—all apparently spared
Its repeating pincers! Their deaths put down to
*Natural causes*—& anyone who's witnessed
The twitching witch's cantrap of the psyche,
The choking exsufflations of Huntington's, knows
There's nothing natural to its malicious scouring...

& who knows whether Harold's phantom namesake
Would have developed the disease had he lived to
His middle age & not been blown to smithereens
When barely out of his teens (& our grandfather
Christened by a different name belonging only to him,
Something all his own, not the borrowed shadow-
Handle of a dead-soldier brother, a repeat prescription,
Death-prompted tradition, but something starting,
& stopping, with him)...? If so, perhaps those guns
The first Harold spiked, which backfired on him,
Spared him from worse shrapnel splintering the head
Inflicted on the youngest brother he foreshadowed:
The nail-bomb of *huntgintins*, slowly exploding,
Silent as a depth-charge, eating whole hemispheres
Until moth-eaten with shell holes, spiking the basal
Ganglia & petrifying the split celery
Of the brain-stem—he'd not live to know the most
Fundamental thunder rumbling from the cerebellum
Until all spongy about the bore; not Heaven's
Artillery, but more Hell's bat-winged battery
That blasts from Huntington's stentorian foundry;
Though had phantom Harold survived the trenches
He still might have been struck by shell shock,
That strange neurological jinx of trauma-sprung
Twitches, motor jolts, tremors & tics thrust up
To surfaces from plate-scraping tectonics
Of the nervous fabric—a kind of khaki Huntington's...

The guns of anguish might be silent for a time,
Rusted into obsolescence, or spiked with sponge-rods;
Or might simply be waiting primed & dormant

Until the average age of onset, for fuses
Of faulty gene repeats to be triggered again
With ignition, pound remorselessly into another
Hunted generation... Meantime, we sit tight,
& hope for some pharmacological breakthrough,
A miracle cure—since it will take more than a wish
Or prod of a sponge-rod to spike those guns of anguish...


## THE RAGE

*An extended villanelle on Huntington's Disease*


How does a gentle soul go out in rage?
Most enter in a tantrum, part in tears,
But some—again—rave as they disengage.

This isn't only dread of end, some sage
Saccadic catching up with spooling years,
It's just some quiet souls go out in rage.

Nor is it tempered by steepness of age,
Or paucity of time—youth's abject fears
Of blackness—some rave as they disengage.

But nature of departure can presage
The loss of all composure as the biers
Quake beneath the narrow house—then rage,

Rent from bile of sickness, takes the stage
To shattered laughter at warped puppeteers
Threading tripwire strings through balisage.

Corporal of the Buffs in wartime cage
Tortured on & off for four barbed years—
So came as no surprise he went in rage:

But yesterday's tempers traced the first stage
Of a disease which robbed his demobbed years
To a snared hare the priest could not engage.

Autopsies thumb the brain's each cabbaged page,
Leaf flimsy onion-skins obscure as smears;
Neurons scoured this gourd, & caused the rage,

But postmortem's obfuscating beige
Botched 'blood-poisoning'—a fib that blears
& marbles readiness to disengage

In a daughter outraced past grasping stage
By a basal ganglia's burnt rubber gears;
Her eyes' repeats replay that glint of rage

No whispered reassurances assuage;
What she grasps abruptly disappears
To shadow's dislocated cartilage.

Memories clump into one turgid page—
Her mind can't turn the untouchable years
Gummed together with time's thick mucilage.

My threatened stem pre-empts a shaping swage
That may trap me in same warping veneers
Coating her wooden bones for saxifrage

Of rotting lobes; her arms are plumbed to gauge
Depth & space, swaying trunks that steer
A trumping body—limbs bolt, disengage.

A blunted line's elephant in her cage...
The hunted gene knows few test-volunteers:
Why trace the cureless thunder at this stage;

Pre-empt the protein-pogrom to rampage
Before it has to?   Will my punished ears
Prepare me *more* for when I disengage?
Will augurs fail? Will *I* go out in rage?

## THE HEAD MAPPERS

El Galician, castaway abroad in rumbled Brighton—
Worn-out cod-bohemia of scoring binges—
Would I were as bronzed by this snagging summer sun
But I'm better off entombed in curtains at the fringes

Of coffee-fuelled festivities; occasionally you call
To catch your night-friend in his vampire anaemia;
Recluse of Clyde Road; un-listened-to oracle
Steeped in beatific tea & nicotined acedia

But obese with ideas by the fingers' shadow-tug
To brushed rumbas on lettered ebonies—you knead
& pull the battered map of your face, a tanned lung,
Then thumb back to your bulbs of phrenology heads;

We agree in patches: flamenco's fuelled on *duende*;
We live on through the grapy genes of lumbered progenies—
Even then, we felt the fibre & nerve of ancestry
Groping through our abstract-grasping phalanges...

But according to you, only genes survive our death—
That's no option for my slow-dissembling brain,
So I conjure a soul in the oblivion of a breath
To absorb on-coming doubt, jump a passing train

Of trackless optimism... We both sub-let the dead—
But I don't believe everything is labelled on the head.

# GOOD MIDNIGHT, TIGRESS

*i.m. Jean Rhys* (1890-1979)

*For Alexis Lykiard*

Partly prompted by an extract from Olivia Lang's *The Trip to Echo Spring:*
*Why Writers Drink* published in *The Guardian* 13 June 2014

With compliments to Charlotte Brontë, but also apologies,
*Jane Eyre* would never read the same again since this
Pale-eyed tigress, Jean Rhys—born Ella Gwendolyn Rees
Williams—took her claws to Mr Rochester,
Smoked him out by letting Antoinette vent her spirit
From that mystifying attic into the pyromaniacal light
Of a former life prior to her descent into ignited
Madness of some ambiguous hereditary gene—
Rescued by the flannel-suited Englishman whom
Renamed her 'Bertha', betrothed to him & betrayed
Red-eyed in green retreat, she was Rhys's shadow
Creole castaway, her Dominican familiar—
But more, as Jane was a substitute for a former wife,
Jean was a replacement child for a dead sister;
Alternated her identity: Mrs Hamer, Ella Lenglet,
Ella Gray the chorus girl, Jean Rhys, writer;
Yesterday here, tomorrow somewhere else,
An inveterate recluse, she escaped from public view
For sixteen years or so, resurfacing by '56
In a Sargasso lagoon before Jane came on the scene,
Before there was even a '*first* Mrs Rochester'...

*After Leaving Mr Mackenzie, Voyage in the Dark*
& *Good Morning, Midnight* had already beguiled
A generation of endangered female souls,
But *Wide Sargasso Sea* would be the *raison d'être*,
Buoyed on imbibing choicest poisons, a life-raft
To belated greatness, not unlike the slow crawl
Of *The Yellow Wallpaper* for Charlotte Perkins
Gilman; survivor of two nerve-eroding couplings,
Always on the verge of everything & nothingness,
She sat in wait at intervals as marital bait for
Another hauling before a priest & mauling
By sharp paws of inappropriately striped husbands,
For tigers were better-looking to her... Drink-sodden
Survivor of an abortion, the death of one daughter,
& the survival of another, Maryvonne, who was

Removed to another country altogether, Rhys
Removed herself several times over, south-westerly
As the whitethroat flies, first to darkest Cornwall—
*A la* Daphne Du Maurier whose *Rebecca* echoed
Charlotte Brontë's much-loved novel, which Rhys had so
Brilliantly illuminated in a gasping prequel,
Right down to the shadowy former wife (the late
Mrs de Winter), the metaphorical *'mad woman
In the attic'*, & a flint-faced maid obsessed by
Her memory right up to a conflagrating end...

Obscurity beckoned like a bookend: fifteen years
In her rickety bird-hide at *'Bude 'the Obscure''*,
Most of which Rhys spent in silence off the literary map,
Faceless, noseless, though sometimes spotted,
Like a rare black brant, grey egret, or white-tailed
Tropicbird (a plumed Creole) taking a tip from
The temporarily amnesiac Agatha Christie
In absentia (a mystery to flap Poirot or Marple),
Who vanished for eleven days in 1926
During a nervous breakdown—but protracting it
To sixteen winters (typical of Rhys's thirst for excess)—
Then, towards pink sunset, she sank down anchor
At Landboat Bungalows, Cheriton Fitzpaine,
In Red Devon, along with her nervous third husband,
Max Hamer, where, as vindictive local rumour
Had it she'd been witnessed chasing away nosey
Neighbours with the dousing lances of a pair
Of scissors, whose gossip pilloried her as *"a witch"*—
Poverty & despair finished her, & neither
The friendships of Sonia Orwell or Francis Wyndham
Nor the intoxicating afterglow of late-coming fame,
Which sank in like a delayed hangover prolonged
After a hair of the dog that lasted a decade's absence,
Could save her from a fate like her washed-up,
Mascara-smudged, estaminet-haunting, aperitif-
Tippling spinster-drifter of the Thirties Parisian
Demimonde, *"Dum vivimus, vivamus ..." (while we
Live, let us live)*, *'Drink, drink, drink ...'* So went
Sasha Jansen's slurring pledge while toasting
*Good Morning, Midnight*—might have been her
Creator's own pitted-olive epithet of cocktails
& smoky paradoxes (Rhys's personal motto
Once mooted to a close friend: *Dum spiro, spero:
While I breathe, I hope*): *'Her past tormented her*

*So she had to write about it; & then writing*
*Tormented her: she had to drink to write, & she*
*Had to write to live'*, so Carole Angier diagnosed
In her biography of Rhys—&, with a double
Negative, her old friend Diana Athill said:
*'No one who had read her first four novels would*
*Conclude that Rhys was very good at life; but*
*No one who never met her could know how very*
*Bad at it she was'*—but those who never met her
Knew for having read her, for Rhys breathed her
Own life through Bertha Mason, Sasha Jansen,
Anna Morgan & suicidal Julia Martin,
More than merely alter egos, they were her
Fictive avatars of alternative narratives,
Vents for her nervous swerves when on the verge
Of downward swoons, even fainting fits, but always
Brought herself up short by doses of nose powder
Wafted from pomanders, or nasal waves
Of vinegarettes, no self-pity for her, never
That, only prescriptions for fillips, pills, pick-
Me-ups, sips, pitiless critiques—she drowned
In wishing-wells of submerged genteel illusions
Brined in bitter absinthes of her devastating novels...

## NIGHTBIRD

Past one in the morning
on a hibernating week night
suddenly a girl was singing
out in the moonlight—

plangent, melodic, her siren voice
parting the dark—early-to-bed
neighbours stirred—not from choice:
their night was interrupted.

Floor-boards creaked, windows shushed
open—slammed grumpily shut.
The girl's singing—no more to be heard.
Silence reclaimed it—*Goodnight, nightbird.*

## NIGHT OF THE PEGASUS

Limbs calcified to stiff pillars of stone,
Human stone, stunned to virtual catatonia,
Blunted, unsmiling mouth bolted, clink-clunk,
Under keyless lock, metastasis of gesture,
Frozenness of stare; sapping of basal ganglia;
Paralysis of thalamus; the cabbage-lobed brain
As a cauliflower ear, a beaten & pummelled
Cerebrum, spoking each clock & corpuscle
Of a body Chinese-boxed in Chorea...

A twitching-tissue hair-shirt stitched not to fit,
But encumber, de-armour the motor, trip up
Movement; insatiably itch like a bee-sting,
Skin-crawling urticaria, allergy of the will,
Inflammation of the soul, the Spirit's Hives,
A riddle Sphinxing the tongue till it swells up
Like Oedipus' curious foot, marble-numb...

Automatic motor punctiliously stumped,
Plumbed until unable to function, spoilt
Of all spontaneity—jerky, disjointed,
Jolting as stop-motion footage—the jittery
Movements of Ray Harryhausen's horned
Cyclops in *The Seventh Voyage of Sinbad*
Which scared her as a schoolgirl of nine,
Cinema-truant from the shadow of a nun...

Now her impulses pared down to dumb miracles
By thimble-rule of thumb; swallowing wrung,
Lungs bunged, masticating mimed *ad nauseam*
To Bruxism's ivory grind—*& there is much
Gnashing of teeth*, we find... The light-trick of sight,
Satirical shadow theatres flickering flames
Of darkness *in flagrante*; Furies chasing
Furies through mesmerised eyes' magic lanterns...

The Scaramouch puppetry of sleep—now all
Is deconstructed to jolts, bolted joints stiff
As wood, the strings pitilessly exposed; ghosts of lost
Thoughts metamorphosing into optical masques
Of insights in day-nights that contract in spasm;
Phantasms no chalky cornea can fathom:
Glimpses of grotesques—could be the Gorgon,

Hair of asparagus snakes like Sargasso
Thickly writhing in mantis-green shallows,
No more submerged in the deep sea dive
Of air-tight mind; the petrified spirit pinned
To the spot; the coral-toothed spine welded to
Peach-duvet vertebrae spotted with ammonic
Pinto blotting to a future Turin reef...

Throbbed eyes pronged with salty splinters
Sweating tears & trembling bells of memories
Dismembering, nerves & neurons dumbly
Ebbing with repeats of mutant proteins—
Freeze of reflexes, de-fragmentation of ego—
O those drowning months of stooped posture,
Improbable limb-locked aplomb, hunched shoulders,
Arms plunged like pendulous elephant trunks
Swung numbly through the air, O Dumbo,
O Nelly, steering clumping leaden shins
Galumphing *trumpety-trump-trump-trump*—
Now all packed back in a circus trunk...

No pills can prolong jealously guarded agonies
Of hope, nor recover the broke economics
Of macro-fracturing; metabolisms melting down;
From acid reflux to wither & brux—no redux:
Nothing can staunch the slow creeping of stone
Through ducts of a capsized vessel, cementing;
Thumped & spun on a whirling potter's wheel
To the spiteful sculpting of Huntington's rhumb;

No antidote to the numbing sting of its suicidal
Incubus, after hatching; a noisome grub sprouting
Black wings of waxing shadows scouring the lobes,
Honeycombing the porous membranes, eclipsing
Personality, de-grouting ego, plunging the soul
Into cloudy ponds in moss-choked groves
Of sunken gardens plumbed without mind or
Number, where thorny statues twitch & wince,
Gasp last answerless solicitations,
Then recline in despondent glooms like punished
Cactuses wilting on shuttered window-sills
Of the will's remorseless chill—only mould
& Gorgons grow in the night of the Pegasus...

## 'SCORCHED CARPET': *LEPIDOPTERA CHOREA*

I kiss her forehead, faintly scented with ammonia
Like a baby's milky scalp, stroke her moth-soft cheek;
Altered brown pools hoist up unfocusedly
With a snared doe's powerlessness, a bovine innocence,
Then throw their gaze star-ward at the ceiling
Trying to trace a way back in cracks amassing
To an anguishing maze; locked limbs penned in
By metallic fulcrum on a bed's grazed acre
Where she ruminates on the mangold-vague
In a pitiless light's amaranthine gaze...

Her hard-starred husband sits chipped & beaten,
Glass-eyed with tiredness, biting cussed nails in
A war of attrition between gum-bone & doomed tooth—
Curded gold ingots with gaps in-between,
Gnarled markers against the dark of his laugh—
Alternately: puzzling his gingered moustache/
Cradling his bald dome's freckled Dodo-egg
In olive-brown hands' torn curatorship...
*She just lies there & says 'I'm going to sleep now',*
*& that's it, the same pattern every day;*
*& I sit there reading the paper; & if she isn't*
*Sleeping, she's staring aimlessly at the ceiling,*
*Not talking, just staring into space, listening*
*To the rustling of my supplement cryptic;*
*It's as if she's continually waiting... But for what?*
*There's nothing to wait for anymore... Is there? Except...*
*Maybe, my next visit... tomorrow... the day after...*

A plunge of the gut tugs me back to wracked pasts;
Mutters in austere summers by the charred
Carcinoma of the fireplace as to how our life—
Prior to stowing away in that granite hold
Of mortgaged purgatory—pitched into night,
Swum off to nostalgia's pinched margin... All since,
Dreamlike, unreal-seeming, adrift on a splintering
Sea's dismembered memory-debris, us clinging
To furniture bits like slicked-back rats; a limbo
Stormily jolting us into spent nerves, withering
Spirits, automatic pilots, vaguely thrown echoes
Of ourselves, a crop of broken shadows amok
On stone floors of a rug-sprung cottage sprouting
Tumours of dry-rot, variegated thought-funguses,

Damp-patch arabesques, ghosts of hectoring
Heirlooms carved out from the tortoiseshell dark,
& angst-cracked vases fraught with petrified flowers
Plucked copiously from days' sunken gardens...

Out in the sticks of Kernow's obscure-delving veldts
& bleak-skied disenchantments, we fell under
A spell amid fishermen's seaweed-tangled creels
Of twisting hillsides—restricting us, intercepting
Escape; my mother now snagged in its slippery
Lobster-cage; won't let us dispatch past mistakes,
Just patch up a boat's rotting frame, still trapped
In chartless waters, un-navigable fogs, our
Compass submerged as the spoon in her pureed food—
Drinks chalky with thickeners: solids & fluids sink
Quick in her lungs like wrong-downed anchors...

Dad called our downward spiral *A jinx*—
& in spite of uprooting from ill-wishing Cornish
Superstitions, horseshoes & pixies, he thinks
Our bloodline's congealed by a gypsy's swart curse—
Or the Irish rebel's whose shillelagh-thick skull
Dented the gist of a forebear's cudgel—
That branch rooted to the spot in the singe
Of his ashy lounge, against a wall's tar-orange...

But if it's a curse, it's Huntington's grotesque
Olive-skinned dress-rehearsal for the grave;
Punctilious scouring of bulb, lobe & body—
A moth's clumsy lamp-clunking chorea
That hovers on my mother's wood-tongue: she:
A puppet suspended on the bed's lunging knee,
Legs lolling hollowly, clenched smile's bruxed teeth
Thrown with a screened ventriloquist's wheeze...

Did a harbinger's cudgel club an albatross?
Who knows the source for this coursing sorcery?
That trapped past has latched us in its narrative,
Snatching at us when we can least resist;
A mushrooming thought-form smothering our sights,
Netting us in its shadowy web—each time
We resurface in blinks of wakefulness,
It prises our eyes open to another warped twist...

Before the door whispers shut on that carpeted tomb,
I glance back at her drooping dormouse lids
Screwed tight as a child's incanting a wish;
This abrading disease, a knuckled fist
Kneading interminable brass-rubbings of her brain's
Fibrous butternut—a vast Rembrandtian wall
Diminishing her shadow to a signature scrawl
At the foot of a blank canvas, bare, biblical
(*O how she'd obsess on those Dead Sea Scrolls...*)
But for a small wooden cross nailed to its plaster—
A chrysalis trying to hatch out unnoticed,
Or a bulb-singed, clenched-winged, crouching moth—
Scorched Carpet's imago camouflaged as a cross...


[* *Scorched Carpet* is the name of a species of moth]


## THE ROOKS OF BARNHAM

Our monthly pilgrimage to Bognor Regis on a triage
Of carriages brings its brief stop-off point of beatific
Interlude as we wait on the platform at Barnham
For our change of train en route to that rundown
Edwardian seaside resort of Victorian rest cures
& curvaceous art deco relics, then deep into
Its incubated suburban interior, by foot, on bumpy
Pavements, leaf-soft, shoes feeling more like slippers
Tripping pile, past well-trimmed privets & penny-
Pinched porches, towards a sleepy Poets' Corner—
SHELLEY ROAD, KEATS WALK—but stop just before,
On Sylvan Way, to visit the ammonia-fumed
Nursing home for old stuffing-knocked rag-dolls,
Obsolete Bagpusses, my mother among them,
Withered bird, grey-green woodpecker struck rigid
Like a bookend carved from birch, all *yawfs* but
No *yaffles*, craning in bedridden nest,
Skin waxier with each encounter, stretching thin
Over a tightly drawn avian-like skull, so fragile,
Eyes sinking further into shadowed sockets,
Wishbone arms winged angularly, mouth opening
Eagerly like a chick's beaked rictus, for thickener-

Feeding, a luminous soup barely distinguishable
From the hurdy-gurdying phlegm grinding deep
Within the wheezing vaults of her chest—
A numinous slime, like ectoplasm,
Strange gruel, pea soup, mushily nourishing...

Before we arrive at her bedside, we have our brief
Pause for reflection, pastoral respite, on the leaf-
Shaded platform of Barnham's raised bird hide,
Thoughts loitering near to the quaint station tearoom
Mothballed since Doctor Beeching's time,
A rumbled place of scotched encounters,
Stale scones, dishwater tea, doilies, frilled curtains
& protracted departures... We gaze over beige-
Gravelled tracks to dappled shadows playing on sun-
Captured pastures of uncluttered Sussex countryside,
& listen to the caws of the rooks conducting
Councils high up in the soporific wood-orchestras
Of swishing, swaying alder-sails—something
In the rook-call reassures me, its croaky oldness,
Nostalgic, transports me to summering churchyards,
Brambles & blackberries, Geoffrey Bayldon's
Rookish vicar in *Sky West & Crooked*, or his
Raven-voiced avuncular Crowman, scruffy
Jackdaw of a warden in crumpled crow-feathered hat,
A hobo-pallbearer, his mittens stuffing straw back
Into Worzel 'Hedgerow' Gummidge—a name he'd
Intone with flint & pity: his mischievous but
Lachrymose charge, a mud-caked, carrot-nosed
Scarecrow who'd habitually abandon his post
To woo wooden-jointed, unyielding Aunt Sally...

Then my thoughts turn to the Victorian macabre
Of the Potter's Museum we'd visit in my childhood
After its transplanting from Bramber to always-
Sunny Arundel (long since relocated to
The inhospitable bleakness of rumpling Bodmin,
Upstairs at Jamaica Inn, above the Daphne du
Maurier exhibition, simply a replica of her writing
Room sealed behind glass, desk central as an altar,
Rackety typewriter placed upon it like a saintly relic—
It was as if this weird museum was following us,
Since not long before it was moved there we'd
Uprooted from Sussex to Cornwall; visiting it
Again in that different setting felt like returning

To our past through a portal): morbid curiosities,
Stuffed animals, glass-partitioned taxidermies
Dressed to seem picturesque: pinned rabbits in
Cricket whites on an idyllic village green; petrified,
Bead-eyed kitten bridesmaids congregating
Around a whiskery groom in coattails; the squirrel
Orchestra; a schoolroom piled with studious guinea-pigs;
& the air-tight burial of Poor Cock Robin—
A flock of floridly plumed mourning birds arced
Overhead at a churchyard; the small grey coffin
Pulled to the grave's edge by an auburn dwarf-bull
Pallbearer, implausibly tied by a rope through
Its nose-ring to the Lilliputian church; the cream
Barn owl gravedigger, one claw propped on the handle
Of its triumphant spade; & the blackly shining
Rector Rook, dark parson, perched mid-obsequy,
One claw clutching his holy book, croaking his
Way through an Anglican sermon from Ezekial,
Clerical collar stark white against anthracite plumage...

O how rooks evoke halcyon country: chiaroscuro
Clouds on cows, softly tolling belfries of coolly
Summoning chapels crouched amid tilting headstones
Of sleeping parishioners, afternoon sun casting
Oblongs of shadow between stone-silent tombs,
Trees arched prayerfully by wooden porches...
My mind winds on shady hidden ways when I hear
The churchly caws of these darkly warming curates
Of the trees, their calls, my aural 'cure', my soul's
Restorative; dry woody sound like tree-bark
Brushing my ear, soothing me, smoothing out
My shadow to full length, willowing, letting go
Of the light, the wilting light, a moment's shadowy
Flight from thoughts too deeply planted,
Recharging beleaguered energies until
The signal-box clicks me back into stop-motion
Narratives long-strained but now more becalmed
By the cawing of those rooks perched high up
At their creaking, branching lecterns at Barnham.

## REGAL MARGIS

Broke, they were brought to Bognor: the buy-to-bet
Boom's mortgage balloon meant this derelict cove
Of custardy art deco, lobster pots, upturned boats,
End-of-the-pier phantom Punch & Judy men,
Blue plaqued obscures, where stamp-collecting
George V sojourned to take his water cure,
Was the closest they could moor to Brighton
& their sons... Such limbo of burnt-thumbed suburbs
So close to tide-ebbing blood-ties mumbling
Repeatedly nearby on beaches of recrudescent,
Shored-up memories swelling & collapsing
On the sands, roiling more with shingle as
They crept back, simmered in her mind until her
Surging thoughts popped like seaweed pods, one by one;
The leathery tentacles of time's narrative torn
Apart by the muscular churn of gaunt waves'
Sardonic applause, margins blurred beyond Regis,
Now bruised on damp pages, her rubbery limbs
Bouncing on strings of jolting puppetry, malign
Legerdemain for a jaundiced audience invisible
As jellyfish in this strange, dream-merging, graspless
'Regal Margis' on West Sussex's Westphal arm...

His half-happy short-lived retirement of months,
Hovered-over by his wife's moth-eaten thoughts
Before they tripped & hit those treacherous lights,
Throbbing bulbs; in the false calm he'd nurtured
A habit—as if adumbrating a storm ahead—
Of tapping Morse code (recalled from his Royal
Marine Signaller days) on the warm rusty switch
In the pottered nostalgia of the two-roomed Museum
Next door to a porchway with blue plaque marking
The spot where a beer-soaked Blake was once stung
By Bognor bobbies in Eighteen-O-something-
Or-other... those legendary green song lines
Of 'Jerusalem', from *Milton*, sprang from his pen
When he briefly lived nearby in sleepy Felpham—
The cottage still there with its slope of black thatch,
The wooden door latched, undoubtedly haunted,
& the road's named after him, but the village,
Long absorbed into barely publishable suburbs,
Once aired like a 'Ladder of Angels' to Blake,
Now petrol-coated outskirts of parked Satanic cars...

Brief soporific months slept off in the town's
Unannounced Poets' Corner: the pause before
Her mind's trapeze collapsed into the sawdust ring
Of delusions' unexpurgated Grand Guignol;
The Chorea's grotesque routines of circus tumbling;
Leaving her husband a pale washed-up clown,
Face-tugging, fuddled by juggling of diagnoses
& ever-switching prescriptions, trick-unicyclists
Passing on batons of appointments between them,
Until the last port of call hit upon the mutant
Gene by a smudging margin: this degenerative
Germinal seed might be passed on... & on...
Far out across the circular sands & seaweed
Links to distant tides... Hardly time to process
The garbled messages since she'd tripped on
Slippery steps in the public toilets, twisting
One foot back anticlockwise at the ankle—ever
Since then, nothing could be put right again...

Slumped by her barred bed, a peach crib,
His fogged ghost struggles to decode her vague signals,
Cryptic as Tongues; nonplussed, his blunt fingers
Tapping indecipherable Morse on his scrambling brow:
*Dit dah dah   dit dit dit dit   dah dit dah dah/ dit dit dit dit dit*
*Dit dah dit   dit dit dah dah dit dit...? Dit dah dah   dit dit dit dit*
*Dah dit dah dah/ dah dit   dah dah dah   dit dah dah...?*

...traipsing back to the pigeon-cooing glooms
Of Bognor Station, following vague hours holding
Her frail hand & stroking her thinning ashy hair,
The automated tannoy reminds passengers
In aggressing greasy-spooned English
Of a consciously articulated estuary accent:
*It is anti-so-shawl to put your feet up on the seats—*
Then the curt instruction's followed by a sprinkling
Of glockenspiel, like a holiday camp jingle
(No doubt still deployed at the local *Butlin's*)
As if by way of apology at such prior abruptness,
An upward-sliding chromatic solfège pitching...

*&—did—those—feet...?*

[Transcription from Morse Code: *Why / her? / Why / now?*]

## BRITTLE TWIGS

So fiercely defensive of your sons—Dad used to say
You were like a ferocious lioness protecting her cubs—
Such delicacy of soul, such gentle talons, & sharpness
Of tongue all the more deadly for its edge of kindness;
Ardently devoted to loved ones, you spared nothing
Of yourself in the cause of the family—daughter, wife,
Mother, martyr, self-sacrificing clotheshorse to chores
Of an unforgiving cottage, scrubbing clothes in cold
Water in lieu of a washing machine, just a primitive
Contraption called a wringer to aid your pink-raw hands;
Or sweeping dust-coated floors with brooms for not being
Able to afford a Hoover—but all the while your doubts
Collected like stubborn cobwebs thick as birds' nests
Up in the furthest rafters of bough-beamed bedrooms,
Brown blooms of morbid obsessions; the brittle fibre
Of your nerves wilting like tightly bound twigs gripped
In a besom; no more the fearsome Margaret of Anjou
As our father depicted you by contrast to his saturnine
Henry VI, monkish scholar-king not cut out for hand-
Wringing money worries, constant fighting to keep
The wolf from the door, fend off bailiffs & guard
Against snaggletooth dragons of mortgage lenders;
Nor were you anymore a feisty storm-hearted mother
To his temperamental heirs presumptive—now you were
More an anxious lioness, something was altering you,
A gradual gauntness carving out your visage to a vaguer
Engraving of a living mediaeval tomb; shrivelling
Of vim, blunting of optimism, fogging of defiance,
Dwindling of vigilance—now it seemed you were
Struggling to protect something far more fundamental
Than a roof & family, silently battling to defend it
Against formidable odds of flaming arrows that flared
Over you in hot flushes (we'd thought, symptoms
Of menopause, perhaps, but you'd refused to see
The doctor); you fought gallant & alone for as long
As you could hold out, dumbly besieged by spillages
Of your own boiling oil pouring inwards, your defences
Melting down—in those first skirmishes there was no
Sign so alarming to draw our attention, except
A clenching of the drawbridge of your jaw, a bracing
Of your brow's stormed battlements, a grinding of your
Turreted teeth at the clattering of panic's portcullis,
& the lowering of your visored gaze gradually

Resigning beneath the tousled mantling of your
Mouse-brown hair, as if avoiding your own reflections;
& that something you were fighting to defend
Was your self, your essence, personality,
Which you felt slipping piece by piece like brittle
Twigs loosening from a besom; you kept fighting
Right up until there were barely any twigs left
Bound tight enough for your thoughts to keep their grip—
Then, the last glass of resistance in your voice
Shattering as you whispered on the phone through
Sobbing breaths almost echoing, as if you'd
Plummeted down a bottomless well, *I think...*
*I'm losing... my mind*, & I tried futilely
Reassuring you in a soothing tone, *Mum,*
*You're having a panic, take deep breaths—*
I didn't grasp then that I was faintly catching
The last brittle twigs of the besom slipping...


## SHADOWS WALTZ HALTINGLY

*Hesitation, Change, Drag, Twitch, Hesitation, Drag,*
*Twitch, Fasciculation, Change, Drag, Twitch Again,*
*Judder, Halt, Akinetic-Rigid, Unsteady Gait, Rapid*
*Progression, Jerky Movements, Arms Flailing, Halt,*
*Posture Stooping, Drag Trunk Slanting, Halt, Jerk,*
Wobble on the balls of the feet, *repeat, repeat—*
Thus goes the Hesitation Waltz of Huntington's,
St. Vitus' Dance, known by other bitter sobriquets—
The Terpsichorean Chorea, the Misfold Fandango,
The Westphal Shuffle, the Basal Ganglia Tango,
The Akinetic-Rigid Jig; & the pattern is repeated
In strange mutations of proteins singed to huntingtins,
Faulty gene repeats, hereditary, as with all
Extraordinary Houdini-esque contortions of the body,
Or jerking Nijinsky-like choreographies *a la*
The spasmodic jerks, rigid twitches, jolting fits,
Ungainly angular poises of pagan Russian peasants
In *Le Sacre du printemps*—repeat, repeat;
But the trick with this imbalanced balletic feat,
This preternatural *paso doble*, tripping quickstep,
Stuttering foxtrot, rubber-limbed rumba, juddering

Jitterbug, jittery jig, apart from the glide upon
Flat feet, glissades of fallen arches, is in anticipating
Its unpredictability, so that it seems an effortless,
Almost automatic, puppet-like extemporisation
Of motor & cognitive faculties, no strings visible,
No single move seeming smooth in progression,
Since there's no rhythm, no tempo of which to speak
That can be tapped out from a prompt-box, no pattern
To its stilted freestyle steps, this grotesque burlesque
Of jerky movements, no conscious coordination,
Nor even improvisation, nothing deliberate or
Spontaneous about this irruption in mind & body
Snatched up so completely in atrophic raptures—simply,
No terpsichorean preparation, no special spicing
Of rosin to help propulsion, no tutoring that can
Anticipate the shape-changing gradations &
Transmogrifications of Chorea's choreography;
It's a jinx in the genes that germinates rigorously,
Turns nerves to jelly, bones to rubber, the skeleton
To inhibiting crib—unsympathetic magic,
Muscular sorcery, which enchants destructively,
Drives proteins to top themselves prematurely,
Mocks the body, rocks it into darkly shaking
Hokey-cokey—St. Vitus Dance progresses in stages
Of gradual descent, back arching, head stooping,
Arms lunging lower & lower, down & down,
As if descending a downward flight of warping steps,
Collapsing coping stones, each slab of body gradually
Giving way; each stage, jaggedly degenerative,
A path of splintered paving ingravescent, strange
Mutations & dismantling neurotransmitters;
A series of irreversible leaps, phantasmagoria
Of grimaces, cryptic gestures, unrehearsed changes,
Strangely angular entanglements of ligament
& muscle spasms, until the trunk & branches
Seize up, limbs numb to rigid umbrages no sudden gusts
Can sway; but this grimacing dance, this Gammaldans
Of milk signs, this huntingtins jig, keeps going
Uninhibited by atrophy of spirit, mind, body,
An unforgiving whirligig... It's then the backdrop warps
& the scenery transmutes as the stage switches
From the sparseness & lassitude of that last afflicted
Lavender-fragranced room, out onto the languishing
Lawn framed through demure French windows,
Where the late autumn light is fractured, fragmentary,

Like shards of stained glass tinged with glimmerings of green,
Miracles of harlequin, chartreuse—but shrubberies
Rumble the daydream as they rustle in the galleries,
Not applauding but fidgeting, & the grass agitating,
As a limbering breeze whips up from nowhere,
& sudden clouds scud across a cream October sun
Translucent & vague as a tranquilizer, a primrose
Sphere of Diazepam, a gauze for anaesthetising,
A fog-light smudging off & on—then a change from
Gloom-plunged mood-lighting back to daylight vagary,
& on the dancing grass, shadows waltz haltingly...


## BLUEBELLS

Lives blue-rinsed, marriages engrained,
Doily-stitched brows un-knit to Masefield
& Housman's nostalgic crumbs from the cake-tin...

Old Granny Time winds us down the lane
Of her girlhood's buttery patina—
Kiss-in-the-haystack lass, buttercup-under...

Grown four words to sow their own poems
—'joy', 'wood', 'spring' & 'flowers'—each one
Summons in bluebells, hidden in thought's wood:

*'Bluebells brushed by the April balm';*
*'Bluebells twinkling in the cool dark wood';*
*'A Spring wood filled with a joy of bluebells'...*

A bloom of old dears whose petals lose fade
Colourful for moments in the shady sway
Of a tree-beamed Church's creaking boughs...

Bluebells, twinkling in the cool dark wood...

## JAPANESE GARDENS

If I could take you
to those Japanese gardens

throw your worries
to the orange blossoms

I'd lead you back
up those humbling stones

that stooped your head
till it drooped like a lily...

We'd drop bad thoughts
in the lotus well,

catch the koi fish
of your wishes back,

the splash of your last
laughter... *if*...

orange blossoms... stones...
laughter... splashing ... throw...

no *if*... I would... I'd
follow you in...

## CHINESE ECHOES

I used to feel as if I'd disappear
to memory ambered in a mother's tear—
strange how thoughts carry, distort in time's ear:
now I'm mourning you while you're still here.

## *from* AUTUMN GLADE

I remember us visiting this same Crematorium
Every so often when we were children,
& while dad went to pay his respects to his parents
In a patch of bluebell wood where their ashes slept
Amid an uncanny hush punctuated only by
The soothing coo of woodpigeons, my brother & I
Would run across the long lawns towards the strange
Red-brick emplacement bedecked with blossoms,
Something almost out of *Alice in Wonderland*
(Foundations of a long-demolished manor house),
Similar to those strange sloping chalk gardens
We'd explore on other weekends, where we'd
Skip across stepping stones on a pond mantled
With lily pads, dragonflies droning overhead...;
& there was a time we came across a gnarled old
Woman clasped in a shawl, a wicker basket
Hanging on her arm as she picked blackberries
From the thorny autumn brambles, how gullibly
We shuddered as Dad told us she must have been
A witch out collecting nettles to fill up her cauldron...

Many traumatic autumns on, in a chill November
Morning lit by a miraculous sun, we've watched
Our mother's coffin glide along silent shoulders
Of white-gloved pallbearers, through the Chapel of Rest,
Then settled on its biers on a green-curtained platform
Where to sad English strains of 'Greensleeves'
The drapes whispered shut like a canopy of leaves
As a wind dies down... We knew our thoughts would
Commemorate her every waking moment hence,
& more poignantly than any hollow-worded eulogy
On the scrolling Roll of Souls in the Chapel of Memory,
Indulgence arranged for privileging fee—but we
Knew she was not one for ceremony, having
A fuss made, least of all on her behalf; she shunned
The limelight, hugged the shade, preferred to fade
Into the background... especially when we had
Friends round, whose only glimpses were of a pair
Of phantom hands settling down mugs of tea
At the top of the stairs, then disappearing
Suddenly to the slightest creaks of the wooden
Flight too narrow for banisters—that mousy
Shyness which shooed her away from visitors,

We'd thought, had grown around her soul like a gloomy
Wood through too many years of cottage withdrawal,
A time-stilled atmosphere's draughty inwardness,
Was just the beginning of her Dido-like drift
Into a Shade of her former life-loving self,
Already bereft while still living; a once-dauntless
Soul rehearsing her future haunting...
                                     Only hours
After she was scattered to rest, Dad later told me,
He'd suddenly been aware of her presence all around
As he sat alone in his armchair that afternoon
After the funeral, he sensed her everywhere,
A presence on a vaster scale than in life, her soul
Filling the room & atmosphere—he felt she was
Complete & herself again, younger & lighter
(Sundry clairvoyants have reported independently
Of how our spirit bodies recapture our earthly
Primes) after fifteen years of whittled existence,
As her mind & body gradually dismantled—
Now cured of the disease that had afflicted her
Almost as long as we could remember, until it
Seemed almost impossible to picture her as she
Used to be before the whirlpool churn of Chorea,
A malicious spell to bewitch vital proteins,
Fragment her grasp of the real into nightmarish
Realms, ghoulish hallucinations, horrendous
Delusions: convinced she was to be *"burnt as
A witch"*—as if the punishment itself bestowed
The status—& was awaiting sentence to be
Carried out, nurses furtively collecting kindling
Hidden under piles of linen; to innocently drown,
Or guiltily float & so be burned: no kind option
For hapless occupants of Huntington's ducking-stool...

Now those horrors were over—she woke up refreshed
& freed, as if after a long recuperative sleep,
The weight lifted from her, now able to breathe freely,
To move with such ease, as if gliding, so light she
Could fly—except this was in another place we
Couldn't compass or appreciate, on the other side
Of a spirit-partition; yet now Dad remembered,
For moments that felt like hours, how she used to be,
For better or worse over forty years, for she was
Herself & everywhere so vividly he spoke to her,
Saying he knew she was there but couldn't see her—

Almost felt as if she was trying to nudge him to go
With her outside the room & out into some
Wonderful infinity of world, she wanted him
To share her rapture—in her visiting spirit he
Detected excitement, restlessness, a tingling
Energy that verged on agitation, but brilliant
& liberating, he felt as if she was trying
To tug him out of his chair... to... somewhere...
Just as in life she'd always wanted to *"get out"*
As much as possible, not wanting to be rooted
To the spot unless she was too sleepy to care,
Opposite to his homebirdish nature—almost
Always out to a café where she'd sit & sip her
Tipple of innocuous coffee (decaffeinated
In her later years though we never told her)...
After that, Dad only had one other visitation,
When he was lying in bed, eyes shut, but still awake,
His mind, as ever, ticking, when he suddenly
Heard her voice crystal clear, bright as daylight,
As if she was beside him in the room, by the bed,
& he *knew* it was *her* voice, disembodied but
So true to how it once sounded, now reconstructed,
Calmer, kind, piercingly clear, intact again,
& all it said was his name, *"Andrew"*...

Now all those tears & terrors, fears & phobias,
Phantasms, obsessions, delusions, paranoias
& choking fits no spoon-fed mush or potions
Could fix—vanquished; together with those
Twilight figments of her besieged imagination,
The mind she knew she was losing, which she
Broached in sobs of trembling timbres on the phone,
& when she cried out, petrified, at familiar
Phantoms coming up the driveway, false shadows
Darkening her net-curtained hide—that brandied
Draught of agonised tones still swills around
The anguishing glass of her younger son's
Ganglia, cuts through him like a blade—
All these Furies have been burnt & scattered
As ashes in a peaceful woodpigeon-cooing
Crematorium, on a patch called Autumn Glade...

## CIRCLING THE YEW

In a brambly churchyard, the kind Thomas Gray
Might have spun into steeples of poems perched
On a bench in a tree-arced corner sketching
The teetering headstones through cemetery tropes
In dove twilights, we circled an ancient yew,
Broad & gnarled, large scarecrow eyes scored
By woodpeckers, trunk smoothly scooped out
To a cavernous hollow—a half-opened wound
Enterable through a narrow wedge—you managed
To fit inside, being so thin, your broken
Chuckle echoing in the wood-womb of smooth
Curvaceous bark twinkling with mucilage
Of snail spoors, willowing gossamers like strands
Of saliva catching the brandied autumn light,
Refracting it to strings of miniscule rainbows...

We wondered how long ago this ancient yew
Sprang here—this thick misshapen hand of grasping
Branches balancing seepages of greenery;
How many human stories had played out in the shadow
Of its insuperable pose, swollen with wisdom,
So solid of purpose, so rooted of repose,
Surrounded in chiselled summaries of bygone lives...?

Perhaps *'Happy Lepperd'*, the buried child—mound
No bigger than molehills pocking each yard
Of mousy churchyard grass—had come of spirit-age
& kept growing in the afterlife, weaving
Daisy chains under a parallel shade...?
& maybe the eighteenth century farmhand
Who'd slept off his scrumpy in a sun-pounded field
& never woken up for thundering sunstroke,
Had sat up under this age-hewn yew's
Ripped umbrella on the shadier side
& wondered at the villagers all gathered together
Like damp jackdaws around a freshly-dug grave:
What terrible blow had thrown those weepers
Into simpers like patters on the yew...?

You told me yews are drawn to churchyards
As hungrily as worshippers to pews; have always
Sprung from powdery nutrients of disintegrated bones—
That without these mounds, these tipping grounds,

279

Many yews might not have grown, nor rooted
In our mossed imaginations with a grasp beyond
Our gasping sermons; been left unappreciated
In their tapering poetries of twining boughs
& shooting tongues of deeply irreligious green...

Are our souls—assuming we have any—in a way
Also yews: to blossom so improbably from clay?


## MEMORY'S EGG TEMPERA

Clutching his hands sat on the edge of her bed
Like that broken down man with drooping head
In Walter Sickert's *What Shall We Do for the Rent?*
There are many questions, few can be answered—
& so it is also with this painting: is the naked
Woman sprawled behind him asleep or dead?
Is the man remorse-stricken for something he did,
Or worse, tormented by something he never said
To reassure her that he could see a way ahead?
Is the nude simply sleeping, a suicide, or murdered?
& what is he contemplating in that stooping head—
Has the shine on a crown ever been so expressed?
& then, at this distance, I'm suddenly reminded
Of another problem picture so many times coated,
*'& when did you last see your father?'* by Frederick
Yeames, a depiction of a small boy in impossible
Blue being questioned by crop-haired Cromwellians
As to the whereabouts of his absent Royalist father:
It's some time since I visited after the bereavement;
So many scenes & moments so deeply impressed
Yet applied slapdash, fast-drying, like egg tempera—
Why, if composed with such carelessness of brush,
Should memories take on textures so permanent,
Especially the ones we most wish to forget—
The tragedies, dramas, storms, traumata, regrets—
Which worry & grow as turgid works-in-progress,
While gentler moments are the least remembered?
How slow we are to remember our Time's on rent,
& each payment simply goes to pay the mortgage
On a forgetful god's long-neglected nest egg.

# THE AMATEUR BLUEMANTLE

He traced the family name to sift ancestral grains
But only from the lines of his father's & mother's
Sides all the way back to doubleted Tudor times,
But he'd neglected to put his genealogical gifts
To the test of tracing back his wife's side—
Not her mother's, the Shoesmiths, whom he'd followed
All the way to the fourteenth century—but
Her father, Harold's, who'd died of a hereditary
Disease carried through mutant genes misdiagnosed
At the time of his death as blood poisoning—
& then further back to try & trace any pattern
That might shed ghoulish light on the gene's origins,
Since these repeats of faulty proteins later surfaced
In his wife, Harold's daughter, broken down in body
& mind by only sixty-five; & so the cloud
Now hung over his heirs, who'd no incentive
To find out if they'd inherited the defective gene
Before the time of its symptoms' onset, to hunt
Out the Huntington's, for there's no cure, nor
Even treatment—nothing but sublime ruminations,
Fear of signs of its nascent neurodegenerative
Devastation—he'd never thought his hobby, his
Sacred pastime in humdrum life could have become
So cruelly symbolic of the horrendous erosion—
Before her natural time—of the woman he loved,
With whom he'd spent most of his life, nine years
His junior yet predeceasing him unexpectedly,
& of this latest catastrophic entry in the family
Tree of a mortal threat which might be passed on
Like an unwanted baton to his progenies, & even
Beyond, to the end of the line... He'd always
Suspected some obscure family curse had thwarted
Their chances of happiness for years, but only now
He'd come to comprehend its true nature, extent,
Its pathology, & that it was not visited on
His own line, but his wife's: Curse of the Parkers...

& yet, even now, in the raw absence of his
Recently departed wife, he still finds strange
Consolation in his hobby of remembrance,
Tracing family traits, archiving Parish Records,
Birth, marriage, death dates, & sees no reason
To prorogue such grim cataloguing, nor to probe

Autopsies, thumb postmortems, but, oppositely,
Prolong such brown studies, expand on them,
Let the leads of primogeniture germinate
& make new links of kinship—at his computer
Night & day tapping into distant pasts
& making charts of ancestries replete
With coats of arms, heraldic crests, lambrequins
& trappings, for many pastimes are bedfellows
To self-harm; & none more so than in the case
Of this ash-singed knight, this chivalrous scribe,
A graveyard ranger perched on the leather cantle
Of slanting desk chair—the amateur bluemantle.


## THE DOG & THE WIDOWER

His life-bitten father with teeth like wet dog-ends,
Wrung-out & widowed, shadowed by his worried dog
Almost glued to his heels, his vigilant familiar,
Or canine reincarnation of a once feisty but
Latterly nerve-shattered wife—this is no cupboard love,
For Pip skips some meals, or simply nibbles at the edges,
She has a nervous stomach, diabetes & a habit
Of anxious fasting, difficulty trusting, ever-
Vigilant, she flinches whenever a human hand hovers
Over her miniature head to lovingly mould her
Delicate skull in its warm palm—Pip was mistreated
In a past she can't articulate, least of all express,
So the human sculpting of her traumatised pathology
Simmers in mystifications of anxious growling,
Faint whining, shivers & strange moist-eyed silences,
Caliginous signs open to interpretation
For fonder ownerships—but as with all relationships
Of any species with potentials for developing souls,
Expressions & responses are best kept at their simplest,
While deeper glimpses should be left to slip
Into postprandial sleeps in net-curtained antechambers,
Upholstered tombs of warping rugs & half-contented
Armchairs like soft tree stumps grown out from carpets
With two stout branches truncated by crinkled greying
Antimacassars, toes capped in slippers; bereft,
His father roots his thoughts down for a late
Afternoon nap before another early turning in,

For dusk is better slept through, human beings' lowest ebb,
Time for misty dreams, lachrymose recollections
Of distant mystical ties, fading mythologies
Of dollhouse families in foggy daguerreotypes,
Faint mutters & chinking tea-things, moth-hands
Aflutter about spectral cake-stands, his cut-glass
Granny crimped in high-necked grey summer blouse,
How she & that genteel garden seemed such permanent
Fixtures back then, when everything felt certain,
Seemed unending, delicately predictable;
While strangely, everything since—the Main Act
Of his life, all its trials, tribulations, loves,
Vicissitudes & children, & his vanished wife
Whose life now flashes past him like a mayfly's flitting—
All dissipates in the ray-lit dust's fractured sprinkling...
Pip peeps open her wet pebbly eyes, & he sighs
& strokes her back to sleep & the cradling
Silence of teacup-&-warm-palmed companionship...

## AT COTEHELE

When she announced to her husband as they took
Tea outside Cotehele's Tudor promontory
Of halcyon habitation (bar spectral occupancy),
*I think I'm going to die soon*, he must have been
Shocked, since she looked well back then, if a little
Peaky from her early morning shifts—but no
Obvious symptoms, it was just something she
Seemed to sense, an indeterminate decline;
True, he must reflect now, it had felt as if she'd been
Slipping away from him in some sense, piece by piece,
Layer by layer, for a vagueness of years, but he'd
Thought it was just a phase, a harmless metamorphosis...
His absent sons had also sensed something amiss
For some time, but had assumed it was tiredness
Mixed with mystical anxieties that adumbrated
Her pained smile's misting grimace; or, in male
Ignorance, supposed it was menopausal, this
Oblique tidal-shift, restlessness, tendency
To dwell on local deaths a little too personally,
As if others' losses took something of herself away—
Karma of a macro-empathy... Or might portend

Something closer to home, the imminent departure
Of a shadowed relative... About that period,
The spread of foot & mouth had prompted
A holocaust of cows, the once tranquil Cornish
Baizes suddenly ablaze with macabre beacons,
Signals of black smoke, as if those derelict chimneys
That sprouted up from the grassed-over graves
Of filled-in tin mines had been resuscitated back
Into phantom industry, pumping out resins
Incongruously across unfathomable blue skies
Bruising with smog, inky clouds like tousling
Funeral plumes—bonfires of contaminated bovine,
Of sacrificial cattle razed to patches of ash,
Tumours of mortality stippling the landscape
With scorched horns, charred carcasses, burnt tails
Like fired blasting caps, black jagged stumps
Of trees after a forest blaze (or the last graze
Of Pompeii)—it was as if she'd sifted these sights
Reflectably into her self-perception, as if she
Sensed in their propinquity some prophecy...

Just a matter of years until she'd be sitting on
The edge of a lunging bed at Graylingwell,
Petrified with fear, sobbing uncontrollably,
Convinced the nurses were planning to burn her
For being a witch—uncanny association:
Up to the seventeenth century countless victims
Of St. Vitus Dance, & its cousin Huntington's
Chorea, in times of febrile Bibles had been judged
As witches, ducked under water, flung onto pyres,
Or locked up in straw-filled asylums to rot in
Cabbaged miasmas with writhing mystifications
Of gripping, grasping hands' milk signs, so-called
*Fasciculations*... Huntington's strange, almost
Onomatopoeic pathological tag—for it's
A hunting gene repeat—waited in the wings
To elucidate her obscure condition beyond
The point of honeycombing the brain's parched fabric
To a brittle washed-up sponge, a globed bouquet
Of coral, a greenfly-infested cauliflower
Catered with wider ventricles of symmetrical
Chasms, like Rorschach blots hinged in the middle,
The shadow of a butterfly spreading black wings;
A moth night-singed... No doubt, as her sense
Of personal doom had sobered the mood amid

The obscure blooms of the rose arbour at Cotehele
That day, he would have drawn in a long tug of his
Cigarette, puzzling at this strange augury
Of coffee grain issuing through the mousy whisper
She deployed in public (so as not to draw attention
To herself), sighed, then pressed his freckled fingers
Against the rusting cattle-grid of his wrangling brow,
Trying to fathom the moment's incomprehensibleness—
Casting a gaze away from her, over the rugged
Gardens & steep-shelved rockeries of Cotehele's
Plunging grounds; something tugging his thoughts
Like an anchor over the cliff-edge of the gardens'
Indeterminate end, down, down, deep under
The periwinkle depths of the Cornish wreckers' sea...


## A STUDY IN BROWN

Is the body, at the last, akin to a kidney, liver or
Viscera left behind as vestigial gristle, shed after
The spirit's departure? Descartes might have said so,
But not Thomas Aquinas who thought soul & body
Were one, so Platonists impeached him as a heretic
For apportioning disproportionate importance to
The expressive dummy-mechanism of the human body;
& I'm inclined to their view, at least as a way to
Accommodate that shell left behind that looked faintly
Like my mother, yet almost mummified, only hours
After her spirit's departure; it seemed like a replica
Or effigy sculpted on a marble tomb; a hollow
Sarcophagus rigid as her spasm-gripped oesophagus
During those final choking years; the ridge of her nose
Arched higher in repose, more pronounced than in life,
Brow slightly tensed in earnest, temples arced like
Inscrutable spandrels, as if even in death she
Was still fathoming some imponderable—& yet,
She seemed at peace, at least, far beyond any hopes
We had of seeing her in life for that remorseless
Erosion of her motor- & thought-faculties,
The tautness of her frame strapped into Huntington's
Intractable straitjacket; but now, observing this
Nerveless thing lying there, it wasn't my mother,
Not by a slightest brush of fingertip against ice-skin—

Wherever she was now it was no longer here,
But elsewhere—*Where*...? Such dry-throated questions
Have haunted countless thinkers since ancient times,
Harried some like Furies to early graves—
As with Robert Burton, lepidopterist collector
Of the moths & butterflies of human moods,
Manias, traumata, distempers; mercurial
Curator of psychical wounds, nuances, patterns,
Tones & winged variations: the Phlegmatic Green,
The Rare Black Bile, & other species... Undone
In the end by brown studies & morbid obsessions:
The date of his predicted death pencilled in on
The calendar, & dutifully signed off in suicide....

If the lens of the eye is, as some suspect, a recorder
Of the last death-stung moments, then isn't it ironic,
Ultimately frustrating, & yet so fitting, so
Typical of our confused earthly condition that they
Cannot impart to the beholder anything,
Seemingly no longer seeing, lightless films of warped
Imitation tinctures representing what were once
Such brighter, bolder colours, now faded & muddied
Like dead moth's wings; pale chalky postage stamp
Clippings, the stilled unblinking blind witnesses
Linking our riveted living eyes to fast-fading
Desperate hereafters; spiritless eyes are simply
Eyes become more fully themselves after
The personality's departure; figments left behind;
Faint traceries, barely visible adumbrations
Of colour on Roman marble, brass rubbings:
They return to what they've always been, had we
Recognised it: glutinous symbols washed up
On the shores of a dream, gelatinous organisms
Like winkles or cockles, vestigial glimpses
Marinaded in brine, mere emblems of true eyes,
True faces, true bodies over which no shadows
Of temporality hover in the realm of ideal presences,
Divine individualities of afterlives;
For life is shadow-theatre, pretend-play, a dress
Rehearsal for something far realer, never glimpsed
Through the portal of the grave, but we will all end
Up there in the end & be blind no more—so
Platonists once thought, ever optimistic as
To something far more perfect, comforting &
Illuminating awaiting us after the body's stilling—

Something more fully itself, more complete &
Complementary than the mere shadows of our
Flat-packed world, just so many empty-paned
Frontages under raised awnings of our eyelids...

## CLICKING THE LIGHT FANTASTIC

Mother, Catholic, harrowed with doubt
& inexplicable guilt, housed mysteries
In her mousy soul—Lourdes-deep;
Father, Anglican, more practical,
Romantic but no truck with superstitions,
Heart steeped in English histories,
Soul sourced from dour Scottish crofters
Of tartan ancestries lubricated
On liberal swigs of fermented barley—
Mother, teetotal, abstinent apart
From the periodic lapse of chocolate...

Scarcity, their marital cloth, nourishing
That unexplored hemisphere of the spirit
Inflated on fasting, that unpeels the senses
To a sharper light of unleavened perceptions,
Symbolic sight of thriving invisibles
Microscopically crawling like recusant lice
In mouldy bread-bins; spilt rice of priest-hole
Eucharist... Father traces the line
Of ancestors passed onto other sides—
Euphoric seconds pounce on the compass-
Point of his thoughts as he thinks he charts
A vital link that stitches our lapsed lineage
To an illegitimate purple thread,
Blackberry juice trickles nettle-let veins...

Mother genuflects as she thaws the fridge...

The electric meter purges its last indulgence—
An all-encompassing click like a bleak epiphany
Plunges the kitchen into faithful darkness;
We pilgrims do penance for fifty pence...

## THE CHURNING

*No Grand Inquisitor has in readiness such terrible tortures as has anxiety*
                    —Søren Kierkegaard, *The Concept of Anxiety*


Ever since I can recall, there's been the Churning—
It wasn't born, but aborted; it was there before me,
But adumbrated my being, ebbed into me as shadow,
A caliginous grub incubated in my botched body,
My metabolism's overspill of bile... I hope I'm not
An embryonic Robert Burton trying to lance the boil
Of chronic colic, clot the blood, curb the toil
Of scotched bucolic, plough cognitive clods
To maladaptive pulses, wormwood-groping crops,
Strangling thought's green shoots, swamping growth,
Suffocating bulbs & lobes of sound-mindedness
Through morbid studiousness, a clutching at roots
To try & twist them into shrubs of fascination,
Only to be tugged further under by their reedy binds,
Sinuous thick Sargasso; prompt fulfiller of a predicted
Date's departure: to die punctually, with compunction...

Ever since The Fall, Adam felt the churning in
The pitch-dark snake-pit of his writhing belly;
An indescribable edge, a ploughing of the gut,
A knotting, wrenching, retching—abrupt as the sharp
Tang of that apple; but more violently nauseating,
Like a fork of lightning thrust in the navel, then twisting;
A bolt of thunder—almost recumbentibus;
A drenching of inextinguishable Dread... but of *what..?*
What might befall? What might lie ahead? This abdominal
Treadmill kept dredging its interminable message—
Something must have happened to trigger this...

The shadow of an answer formed his soul's core
& slowly wormed out from the bitten apple of his
Head's corrupting gourd—something ominous
& moist insinuated itself, something slippery
& serpentine, bruising before his eyes; he swore
He'd glimpsed this movement once before—
In the corner of his soul, but which vanished at his turn,
Or so he'd thought, leaching his numinous innocence,
Damping out immanence; clammy, ungraspable
Thing—Guilt, Conscience, incubus of sublimation...

Even before he'd bitten from the fruit he felt this
Churning inside, vertiginous wheeling of mind,
Mental dizziness, shivering, stretched skin prickling,
Mouth parching, gut churning with a kind of hunger
That gnawed, as with tapeworms in the bowels;
But this time he recognised what this feeling was,
Unpalatable as apple pips, rudimental disruption,
Deep disturbance, scrape of consciousness'
Tectonic plates, sudden edge, strange verge,
Grave craving, apprehension spiking appetite—
It was more than mere vigilance: *angst, anxiety*,
An anti-feeling that precedes the sins it thus
Precludes, pre-empts through proleptic penance,
Perpetual anticipation of... *nothing*; inflicts
A churning punishment in the pit of the stomach
For sins uncommitted—Guilt's gristle, undigested...

## ANGST IN AUGUST

After long silences the Spanish say *An angel passed*,
But during the thorny quiet of my late summer trance
It was a dark angel that came, & lingered, hanging
Its black wings over me like a giant jackdaw's shadow
As I curled up on that cold sepulchral sofa
In a lounge suddenly rangier, formidably roomier,
Plunging anguish—that dark angel passed,
With agonising gradualness, & only once it had
Outstayed its unwelcome sojourn in the gaping absence
For what seemed an age, its cloven visitation
Dovetailing with Pan's silent hooves pattering
On the carpet to pipe up panic; not for the first
Time in my life's flight I'd come to grasp what
Kierkegaard meant by Dread, or Angst, & its strange
Reflecting agent, Guilt—for things only imagined,
Played out in the head, but which might yet be spilt
From it—& there's the hinge: a pre-reflective
Preventative against impulsive evil, against the will,
Even—avenging nerves, sprung triggers of conscience,
Subsumed into our souls' inbuilt obsolescence;
No rhyme or reason to this sudden guardedness,

This sense of something terrible about to happen,
Spontaneous catastrophe; the prickle before thunder;
A treadmill laced with eggshells—transgression,
& no way back to forgiveness afterwards;
During that dark blazing August I buried myself away
In that shady basement flat, a gloomy antechamber
At the base of a damp pyramid, for days on end,
Unable to eat, rest, or trust myself to be alone in
Such boundless space of freedom's open prison,
For fear I'd be driven through some vertigo of thought
To rid myself of World, abandon being—I needed
The reassurance of another presence to keep me
Anchored to the moment, take the edge off my
Sudden vigilance against strange nervous urges
To uproot the present, wrench out the future,
Dig up my thoughts & feelings & melt them
Into memory graves of aggressive sadness;
To ever remain yet be elsewhere, mourn my own
Absence by eavesdropping on relatives' bereaved
Reminiscences; I had to save loved ones from my
Heart's destructiveness, all living things seemed
Vulnerably inviolate, imperilled by my impulses,
My hands not trusting themselves to grasp anything
Among so many fragile glass-valuables, photographs'
Captured souls—tragedies in gradualism...
Valiumed vagueness mingled with exhaustion's
Natural analgesic brought this violent nerve-
Fever down; the wing-tip of a light angel mopping
My brow—or was it my future ghost drifting in
On the draught, returning to prevent its advent,
Perform its own exorcism?    A sudden gust
Of unbridgeable insight surged through angst in August.

## RAGGED ANGEL (IN RED CABBAGE)

*i.m. Søren Aabye Kierkegaard* (5 May 1813–11 November 1855)


Argonaut of Angst—Søren Aabye Kierkegaard;
Forty-two years in the blink of an eye, *øjeblikket* of Being...
Under rustic cloak of outward sternness his haggard
Father contained earthquakes of Yahweh's wrath,
Tectonic plates of a neurotic God scraping against
His biblical conscience: he believed an Abrahamic
Curse predestined his children to predecease him as
Punishment for blaspheming in a moment of green rage,
& a prenuptial spilling of his seed; but his hen-wife,
Ane, clasped her chicks close, especially Søren
& his brother Peter, the only two of seven
To outlive the parents... Young Søren, a proto-Törless,
Determined his own Bildungsroman by exploring
The crooked streets of Copenhagen's cramped-in
Poor districts, Knight of Faith against conventions
Of his well-heeled class, he'd not shun society's
Outcasts, but would roam among them, greeting
Each as his equal... As a boy he'd been nicknamed
*'Fork'* for his excoriating tongue & proneness
To quips—yet he looked so fragile, a ragged angel
Always wearing the same red cabbage-coloured coat...

Grown up, he wore a mask of haunted beauty, gloomy
Handsomeness, a dourer Adonis with a shock
Of blond hair & almond-shaped eyes beset
With cloudy pools—grey-paned soul-windows;
But he spurned temptations heaped upon him by
Amorous admirers of the pulchritudinous sculpture
His spirit occupied, & sipped the sour potion
Of Keats's gallipot—the tonic of bachelorhood:
Broke off his engagement to the girl he loved, Regine,
A stranger he'd recognised at first sight, felt he'd
Always known—*'like all knowledge love is recollection'*;
But he felt bound, as Abraham with Isaac (& Keats
With Brawne), to sacrifice his fiancé of finitude
& their future for the infinite resignation
That would bring him closer to his cold-shouldered God—
Or Goddess, demiurge, Gaia, anima, Muse:
The shadow-woman dormant in Man, shrub of His
Inner-rib, incubus of His aborted womb,
Overwhelming for sensitive men, demanding of them

Heart-sacrifices; so it was for Kierkegaard, as for
Keats before him, mythical archetypes, Aeneas
& Orpheus—Regine & Francis, their Dido
& Eurydice... Søren was only able to *'swim in life'*,
&, if needs must, upstream, splashing against
The rapids (for all humans are salmon, always leaping
Forward back to brackish origins), but he felt
*'Too heavy'* to levitate for long in love's *'mystical*
*Hovering'*—its luxurious prison brought out
A chthonic Houdini in him, keen to break the chains,
Untie the knotted sleeves, swim back up to the surface—
Gasping escapology; so he released Regine from her
Obligation (she'd become, in time, Schlegel née
Olsen), & by so doing released his spirit
From its submergence—& with this purgation
Gushed aphorisms, speculations, philosophical
Discourses, much gnashing of teeth, *Fear &*
*Trembling*; he felt too angst-ridden for marriage,
Too melancholic for children; his celibate pledge:
*'To find the idea for which I can live & die'*...

Adam's Sin adumbrated him, & all humankind,
Infinite guilt rooted in the shadow of Eden—
Pumpkin of compunction; & Guilt, the wrinkled gourd
Of that apple, a grating rind, the grind of Angst,
For which the only analgesic he could alchemise
Was Hidden Inwardness, his own Negative Capability
Of reflective grief & resignation, since God dwelt
Within us, so we must nurture the inner-life;
*'To be or not to be'*, as Hamlet, that other angsting
Dane, had put it—to act or not to act, according
To Kierkegaard; the *Either/Or* of existence,
The choice between the World or God; & it was
In this hinterland most of us dwelt, in realms
Of resignation, free-floating grief, & anxiety
That springs vertiginously from freedom's *'dizziness'*—
Such chronic indecision made up the path of broken glass
Trod by Adam's scions—though in most it slept, blunted,
But still splintering, festering in necessary recesses;
In more ruminating minds it swung as giant pendulums,
&, had Kierkegaard realised, pounded as loud in
Another Copenhagener of the pen, Hans Christian
Andersen, who trod his intrusive thoughts through
Marshy fairy tales, galoshes anguishing...

Critics soaked in the backwash of Kierkegaard's fractious
Heteronyms, a species of punning nom de plumes—
Victor Eremita, Johannes de Silentio, Nicolaus
Notabene, Constantin Constantius, Vigilius
Haufniensis, Hilarius Bookbinder, Anti-Climacus,
Inter et Inter, et al—who answered back in variant tones,
Although their reclusive creator resorted to
His own name during the protracted *'Corsair Affair'*,
A periodical spat of splitting hairs with Meïr Aron
Goldschmidt; then, later, in the posthumous *Judge for
Yourselves!*, Kierkegaard targeted the Danish Church,
Declaring the pyrrhic triumph of Christianity
For having *'completely conquered'* the world & thereby
*'Abolished'* itself! (How ironic his name, Kierkegaard,
Was Danish for Churchyard)—on completing this last
Parting-shot manuscript, exhausted, Kierkegaard
Collapsed on a Copenhagen street, unable to be
Resuscitated due to some *'complication'* incubated
Since a childhood accident, some inner-bruising
On the brain harboured there ever since his little
*'Fork'* fell out of a tree... Had he been attempting
To reach an apple atop another imbroglio
Of knowledge-boughs before he toppled? If so,
Presumably the apple had been left unbitten,
Albeit slightly bruised... & a bit less forbidden...?

---

*Øjeblikket*: the moment/instant from *øjeblik* 'blink of an eye, moment' (Danish),
also the title of a treatise against the Danish Church by Kierkegaard.
*Törless*: *The Confusions of Young Törless* by Robert Musil (1906).
*Bildungsroman*: novel of formation/education/culture (Germanic).

## THE ANXIOUS LIONS

Flat & cream-white against the hatchbacks of the street,
Like a giant Staffordshire Flatback turned back-to-front
On a mantelpiece, leaning slightly, strikingly
Unremarkable—few notice it, unless one points out
Its scrollwork of empurpled shadows almost regal against
The austerity of twilight—or for its crooked shabby-
Classical portico—which somehow supports itself
Like a half-developed premise, in spite of a weighty,
Protruding stucco firmament, to all appearances,
In defiance of gravity, re-sculpting physics—over
Which lounges one white moulded lion, reclining,
Its glazing faintly crazed, paunch perceptibly peeling,
Marble mane moulting, while underneath glare
Two smaller leonine heads captured mid-roar atop
Each near-symmetrical pilaster, like bookends either
End of a faded-elegant, faintly unloved, almost-
Ornate mantelshelf (like those stone resin bookends
I purchased for next to nothing, a lion & a unicorn,
To keep my books from spilling off the shelf);
& either side of its flaky black door the nouns LION
& HOUSE shout out—or rather, roar—in large
Black lettering under the glowering lions,
My mangy guardians—this is my refuge at the fag-
End of a year besieged by bereavements, both
Of the dearly departed & still-living but alighted;
My haggard refuge from a hollow howling world
Of bygone goodness but dependable belligerence,
Boisterousness, avarice, acquisitiveness, greed
& disregard, judgement & stigma; this winter we
Are in Narnia in Aslan's absence, a white-coated
Realm ruptured with hoar frost, petrified at its heart
By a pallid Chancellor with whom pleas of mercy
Cut no ice, Baronet-to-be of Ballentaylor though
It might as well be Ballantrae or Baskerville Hall,
All he's missing is his powdered wig; meanwhile
Mythological growth pokes through the green-
Concealing snow, though mostly only tiny tufts
Chewed by fleecy ruminants as cud—& the crudely
Moulded but boldly coloured Staffordshire Flatback
Of tricorned Dick Turpin clip-clopping astride Black
Bess stares sinisterly from my high-stacked bookcase,
Polite clodhopper, oblivious from its vantage-point
Of 18th century Potteries, a rustic antique

Of proletarian craftsmanship, sculpted in naïf-
Relief by artisans' uninstructed hands, baked,
Then painted gauchely in un-integrated colours,
& finally dipped in glaze; but in this humble-
Tumble shabby-boho rabbit-hutch flat halfway
Down this car-humming through-street, I have my
Proud if sloughing lions guarding me close by
The bruised embrasure of my front window where
I sit, write & remember—though the wind
Remembers for me, boisterously; howls through
Milton Road, howls with the sea, a wassailing
Of salty Brighton banshees inland-bound—only
The roaring of the guarding lions can drown
The howling of the southerly wind funnelling
Through this side-thought of a street, where it tumbles
Up against northerly gusts... I'm still here, just
About, but nagging doubts gnaw me, tug at my gut
Like the numbly plumbing umbilical hernia
Caused by long months coughing-up pea-soup sputum
Brought on by black mould on a basement flat ceiling,
Prompting a rupture in my stomach lining;
& now this cumbersome shrub in my belly
Strains like an incubus, a sprouting damp-fungus
Of the gut—strange how it buds during this
Bereavement from my mother's autumn passing,
As if something nudges in me to be near her again,
Re-establish bonding with a womb now buried in
The lime with worms; perhaps it's best to have it
Nipped in the bud, sown up, & thereby snip
The numinous cord that still ties me to her memory
Like a thread of ectoplasm... How is it the festive
Time glitters with tinselled thoughts on death...?
Each day I try to quantify how likely I am to stay
Alive for the foreseeable future, all my many
Ailments, afflictions, nicotine addiction, taken
Into account; & how to catch ahead my thoughts
On future compositions, poems, narratives, to trail
Up to my ultimate turning... How we word-worms
Burrow down, how we poet-caterpillars cocoon
Ourselves in anticipation of posthumous wings...

But at least for now I feel safe & guarded by
Those leopards *couchant guardant* outside my window,
Those Shelleyan lions holding vigil over my
Unvanquishable doubts: they guard the redoubt

Of my embattled thoughts, obsessions—the Latin:
*Obsessus, to be besieged*—blunting the edge
Of these digs for my Didymus, an emplacement
For my displacement, unhampered by damp
& black mould as the bird-hide of a basement
Backroom I clambered from to moor here in
A studio flat's brown studies... No mauling
Of the winds can knock those lions down, no howls
Drown out their roar louder than the storms
Tossing in from the sea... Though sometimes,
Stalked by Kierkegaard, I think I see my own
Grimacing face, harassed & faintly menaced,
In place of their fiercer expressions,
Fulminating visages, stone ovals surmounted
By flaming manes, ever-vigilant lions...

I hope I am protected too by the namesake
Of this Road, whose once darkening sights
Turned to permanent shadow under the ample
Brim of his charcoal-black Puritan capotain—
Milton, such a solid name, so rooted, as the stone
He used to sit on by a roadside to escape
Nuptial pandemonium, planted deep as an
Ancient stump whose roots hook themselves
Immovably into the black loam—& so I
Might just come to think of this cramped studio
Of shadows honeycombed in Lion House,
As more than simply a stopping-point—I
Might come to call it *Home*... But for the time
Being it will be my proto-tomb, an antechamber
To future feeling, a marble mausoleum
Guarded by those anxious stucco lions
Until I'm ready to re-emerge, be born again,
Roar back from the womb of my howling rooms
For another mauling of World...

## DESK SHUTTERS

I glanced at your eyes after you'd departed,
Could hardly avoid the way your filmy eyelids
Refused to stay shut after father's blunt fingertips
Eased them down each time: almost imperceptibly
They sprang back up like two tiny desk shutters—
Your foggy brown-grey eyes: coins sinking in a well,
Blurry & vague; pebbles just beneath the surface
Of a stream—even from the initial distance
Of the doorway, when my eyes first roamed across
The room to your peach-duvet tomb, your eyes were open,
Blankly staring up at the ceiling, petrified by
What I desperately hoped was some divine insight,
An elevating revelation, anything but oblivion—
*God*, hopefully, *Whom* you'd not long before
Murmured you wanted to see; so eager, you seemed,
But humble, asking permission just before you
Passed away: *Can I go now...?* As if you'd been
Patiently waiting, checking beforehand that you'd
Seen everyone there was to say goodbye to,
But were now keen to go... Moving closer:
Your flat brown pupils, dimensionless, seemed almost
As if pretending to be pennies—two bisected
Moth-wings camouflaging themselves as tender once
Placed upon them to *'pay the ferryman'*, as was once
Custom, though, likelier, to weigh the lids down...

How to describe your emptied eyes? Chalkier, vaguer,
Mere impressions rubbed off onto bone-china domes
Of yellowing sclera, delicate, perishable
To the slightest brush like butterflies' flimsily
Filmed wings; or, to mix metaphors, a mackerel's
Stymied stare on ice at a fishmonger's, vague glare,
Stygian astigma—globed adumbrations; the glint
That lit them, dimmed, misted, caliginous, no longer
Seeing anything, turning in on themselves,
Discarded optics, un-telling, unreflecting;
Gummy mementoes seeming as if they could simply
Be unpeeled like stamps or transfers, come off
On the fingertips as gossamer; no longer
Inhabited, light-extinguished, rinsed of purpose,
Mere after-prints of something lifted out from them—
*Spirit*? Some spark which once illumined them,
Now elsewhere, relinquished; released from the irises,

As a zephyr of air escaping silently through
A pin-puncture; this body, this shell, this husk,
This wax simulacrum, this sculpture of your
Priceless essence, pale impression of personality,
Spirit, your *You*, now decanted into an invisible
Vessel still-living eyes aren't privy to... We arrived
At your bed-ridden shore shortly after your departure;
Your deskbound husband, our newly shadowed father,
Told us you'd passed calmly, your scalp delicately
Cradled like a fragile egg in his warm brown hands;
We came too late for you to look on us one last time,
Your sons whom you barely recognised, but who'd
Followed your guide through the dwindling light
Of *Wuthering Heights*—its whispers brushed off
On us like hoarfrost in our youths, inspired us
To write—but now we stood wordless, our shadows
Thrown upon your small crumpled form, witnesses
To the last part of your narrative vanish before us—
Was that why your eyelids refused to stay closed
& kept springing open like tiny desk shutters...?


## CHANCTONBURY RING

*For James*

We hurled our shadows forward as our legs galloped along
The rumpling ridgeway launching from the Downsmen's dew pond,
Past the phantom Roman hill fort's spiral of stone stumps
(The 'Ring' that hung on Chanctonbury), up to the beckoning
Thickets of the hilltop wood of wordless knowledge gods—
Wind-children of Woden, we, *scops* of the beech copse,
Opposite personalities, but all partitions melted as we
Explored our sprung imaginations, minds conjoining,
Co-pilots of cloudless scopes, whispered impossibilities,
Inseparably apart, laughing against the wind;
Our shadows tripping to catch us up as we hurtled round
The white enchanted trees near Chanctonbury Ring—
But we never dared to challenge girding legend
By running round the wood seven times anticlockwise,
As folklore proscribed, to see if the Devil would appear
& offer us two bowls of soup to replenish our appetites
In return for our souls—numinous soups of our barely

Containable bodies that felt inexhaustible back then,
Imperishable even; but so much boundlessness
Of being & mind imbued in us by ever-approving
Parents would prove almost intolerable in troubled
Future moments impossible to foretell; come close
To spilling over for our bottling up of subtle doubts
Sown in whistling childhood, bedding down to sediments;
Seeds exploding into riotous blooms once our souls
Clouded over from boys to men, & those past spells
Of childhood boredom so simply dispelled by play-acting,
Now more complicated, requiring painstaking
Coping apparatus, vital installations in the nerves;
A mightier vigilance against bamboozling
Imbroglios of agitation at tingling cramps
In weightier arms tightening, pounding hearts,
First blips in pulses, sudden thunder-claps of panics,
Galloping thoughts breaking into stampedes
Of imponderables; the honeyed wonder of younger
Green allegiances souring to fatiguing gruels of age,
Other bonds & obligations, our shadows gradually
Gaining ground, almost outpacing us—now disenchanted
Children still up there hiding on that wooded hill,
Exploring, or stick-fighting as Robin Hood & Little
John knocking quarterstaffs together, arches of our
Feet gripping the slippery moss of a sloping log,
Like tightrope-walkers, anoraks clasped on our
Backs as capes, or Plantagenet mantels with
Empty arms dangling, tall antics catching on
The amaranthine thickets, near Chanctonbury Ring...

## THE BLOOM

You who have seen the beauty in the poem
    Are its most essential part:
The depth & meaning you see in it
    Pollinate its anther-heart;
Pump the valves that bloom the blood
    That make its letters start—
Without your plumbing eye the poem
    Calcifies to art.

# SUPPLEMENTAL POEMS

## (1991-2021)

# THOUGHTS OF TREES

*MINE*

As my thoughts cloud over
I long for the sun to return,
& as soon as wished for out it comes
To light my cloudy brow's slow burn.

I look out from the sunken window
& the solitary tree
Swaying in the subtle breeze
Waves green gloves at me.

*ITS*

Who is that who's staring out?
Is it me his eyes traverse?
I might scratch words on his cold look
Composed in rhyming verse.

Shall I flower with cherry blossom
Whose petals' pinkish glow
Echo the tone of his complexion?
Why does he stare from his window?

## MISPLACED

Sat, lacklustre, 'mid the din
Of the ortho-orators—
Am I me, or was I him,
Stooped by the radiators?

Deep, deep down, I always did
Knot my sickly stomach—
Others dared defy & carp,
Others slouched like hammocks.

I silent, timid, lachrymose
Allowed my mind to stray—
I faked alertness, mimicked zeal,
While my thoughts were far away.

I'd frown, I'd sigh, inside I'd die,
I'd plan a strategy
To cough my way through sleepless nights
So I'd stay off next day.

While some would be ashamed of this
I'll simply end to say
That duty was for me a drain,
Numbing, day to day.

# TRUST

Trust—where did I mislay you?
You were left outside when it rained,
A bitter torrent of ferocious love,
& like a corrugated-iron roof
You rusted & refrained—
A crow-shadow stole your daylight dove.

Trust—how did I mislay you?
You were my father's friend who lied,
Tricked him, broke him, stole his crust,
As I, a boy, witnessed the feud
He drank & cried, & my tears dried—
We all suffered as you abused his trust.

For moth-months, dull-winged years since
Your treatment of him, of us all,
You disappeared under Time's dust—
Father survived your sordid stint
& his Myrmidons, though one missed school
For he saw his Achilles' heel was trust.

# FEARS OF VANISHING

## I

I walked the leafy, dim-lit pathways
Where moon-cold colours cast by night
Bleached pavements mauve, grass-blades grey:
Columns of molluscs like concrete blight
Glistened the ground I traipsed in haste
Skirting gastropods' trails of white.

I fell into a furlough from the light—
Allowed the dark to furl me in
Its arms of ink, blot me out from sight,
Trees clawed the air like cats' paws, dripping
Paint-brush branches on the canvass of night
To reveal red verges of russet leafing.

I traced my footsteps back into the dark,
The duty-dousing dark from where I come;
A rip of pitch-black peeling back like bark
To the stripping of an axe; revealing the stark
Flood of the moon like a nocturnal sun.

## II

I wonder reader whether you've dwelt
In such a twilight, having sipped
Dark nectar, swaying about in the veldt
Of midnight countryside of lush loam lipped
By bolder buds, where ink-thick night's trees
Spread like hands slid in gloves of black felt.

Each branch sharp as a feather-quill's nib
Dipped in black ink, thick in pitch as treacle,
The pen which scratches out these lines—rosehip's
Healing tang hallows grim steeples
Of tall, crooked witch-hat trees that tip
To & fro: halyards to Hecate's squall.

I, a wastrel wayfarer, waded, sopping wet,
As if through dream-dosed slumber, or waist-deep
In rushing waters, roaring rivulets,
Through the wind-raged rain lashes' sweep,
Till in a grove sheltered from the elements
I found a stout fork-tine tree, rooted deep.

In this grove, a scythed-out shrine, I caught
The raucous, squawking howl of a ghostly crow
Whose rancorous wail in the static air wrought
Chilling airs with shudders—scurrying low
Rodents, roused by noctambular rapture, sought
Hollows of husk-trees scored by beaked foes.


III

Sleet speared down in sharp shooting splinters
As I hobbled up the hill, invisible
But for dashes falling where the road ghost winters—
Sudden winds mustered to tumble
While, on the wintry ridge, I, bedraggled, lingered
On the road which, then empty, there sprawls.

Fleets of traffic flitted past my presence,
Dancing dodgem-lights like spitting pyres,
Or cats' dilating irises, iridescent,
Which, while awaying, shed flecks of red that mires
The dark like hellish eyes, then lambent
Beacons die fast like storm-tossed fires.

Like these lights, I fear sometimes
I may be swallowed up by night
To find myself fastened in an air-tight brine,
To disappear from all-else's sight,
Preserved in my fermenting youthful prime,
Restrained in the sour milk of worldly spite,
Suspended like olives in a jar to fork tine—
I've felt a spectral wayfarer where hedgerows wind—
Fears of vanishing I've had every time.

IV

To this bleak night I return:
Along winding lanes I, gibbous, traipsed,
Burdened by a dorsal feather-fern
Which weighed heavy on me, chaste
By restricting binds like knots in churn
In a stomach starved by bitter taste.

A harrowed face of twisted penitence
Crafted by the cutting cold a goblin
Made faces at the wind for admittance
Into a twilight realm where lamp-lights burn
In the fog with unremitting resentment—wished
To spill from the swinging of my fastened urn.


V

Longing to spill into could-have-beens
He treads, still sopping wet, back home
To the empty house encasing stale dreams,
Of sunken stance set back from the road
In a hamlet of glum roofs propped on rotting beams
That bid for betterment with winks of light
& nods of chimney smoke...

# IN THE ORCHARD BOWERS

I've seen what seems like many suns
& slept through dreams of many moons;
It's easy to cast your mind back clearly
When you've only known two rooms.

Still I remember wading through pastures,
Deep seas of waving, tumbling sward,
Knowing so little, thinking so much,
Unready for what I was treading toward.

Yet all I've ever done in truth
Is let stagnation catch me in its swath;
Pray alone unalloyed under a roof;
Resign with fading colours like a moth.

I think I've thought all thoughts to think,
Toiled & loitered, & self-tortured—
In dandelion-clocking dreams I drift
Into an autumnal orchard...

I recall brooding by murky waters,
Passing through wilting garden flowers,
Paled by a white sun's light-bulb glow—
I've sat alone in the orchard bowers.

# BLUE ALDER MONODY

## I

Dreams lie dormant in winter trees
But most disown them, so they discolour,
Though there are still some timeless thieves
Who breathe life into minds far duller:
The Myrmidons of Morpheus
Whose melodic words live brief, then die,
Like palsied buds in deep woods, sunless,
Or the life-span of a butterfly:
Of the breath of a day... So poets mourn
The demise of their songs in the dank gloaming
Prolonged only by the danderous storm
Which swiftly follows the wind's moaning
When mossý hollows offer fonts to mollify
Fits of passion to innocuous sigh.

## II

Life's sent to a breathless inanimacy
Shown in the doze of cloud-lumbered skies
With a thick pillowing of intimacy
That in morning gloom suffocates sunrise;
Fogs smother the trees & cobweb boughs,
Blanket the swards until the mists lift
Unveiling perches of amber-eyed owls
Silent in their sights' swivelling shift;
Who dilate their fathomless pupils in size
Diluting to colours of numerous name,
&, in so doing, come to hypnotize
The soul's misting portholes as senses drain—
Torments torn asunder by swiftness of mission
Glimpse the rare gift of ubiquitous vision.

III

Still searching numbers stumble here
Struck by the sonorous organ grind
Of thunder shudders through bulrushes near
Slumberless shallows of the mind;
The fomenting fonts of Nature's Church
Overspill their brims in bubbling purge
Of curdling currents whose sinuous surge
Unsettles the stills shadowed by the birch;
This place is restless, so full of surprise—
Phantoms shelter here who haunt the trees
Which, as young ideals bid old men goodbyes,
Shake off their rusty armours of leaves...
As the dreams of dreamers cease to be
We drift into shallow sleep morbidly.

# THE LAST WARMTH OF AUTUMN

When the last warmth of autumn's breath
Breathes on the wintry air
You will remember me once again
Though my shadow no longer falls there.

When the last warmth of autumn's breath
Breathes on your restless soul
You will potter through my forgotten things
As memories take their toll.

When the last warmth of autumn's breath
Breathes on your haunted mind
You will no longer be haunted by me
But will leave all thoughts of me behind.

When the last warmth of autumn's breath
Breathes on the bitter air
You will find the place where shadows lie
& your shadow will join mine there.

## OVERGROWN

We lost ourselves here years ago
escaping brick & mortar lives
where lawns were always mown;
we broke away
from old suburban moulds
to find all overgrown.

No neat lawn, just tendrils
of untamed, trailing wilds
cramping the light
with thick nettles & brambles;
a dilapidated greenhouse
trembled in the night.

A bare apple tree
dropped blossom on the path
into a filled-in well;
the tired house crouched
beyond repair
in its crumbled garden wall.

Deep in this brittleness
a time-bitten cottage
of wind-gnarled Cornish stone
glared at us
with deep-set windows—
how could we make this home?

In those cottage glooms
we would later come
to live in disrepair;
to colonise rooms
that had known no sun
& breathe the cold damp air.

Slaves to a mortgage,
possessors of a sunken roof
of wilting slates—
for some change of fortune
the moaning wind
waits & waits.

## GORGON STONE

Staring back I see it
as a Gorgon's cottage for
everything about the place
stood breathless as stone;
the twisted apple tree,
a tortuous sculpture
brittle to the bone.

Slate-grey stone, solid
more than solidness I'd known;
rough to touch, ingrained
as father's face inside it;
frame of sturdy, chalky brick
old & unshakeable
as rustic superstitions.

The sprawling rubble-garden
had a trampled sadness
as if granted one last lease of life
before timelessness set in
to fade its tumbled green,
distil its balding grass into
the still life of a dream.

## THE HAUNTED GHOSTS

A face peered through the two-way window
Of our shadow-cottage, squinting in
With sun-shade hand, it shook back as
The dogs claw-scraped up to the ledge        /
Barking ferociously as Cerberus
At the gates of Hades —I, Orpheus
With my shrinking father (Oeagrus)
Quickly stirred, blinking & startled at
Being discovered in our rustic squat
(The limbo we Shades haunted)—
*'I'M SORRY'* called the trespasser
Through the starved glass, gingerly
Retreating, *'I DIDN'T THINK ANYONE
LIVED HERE'* —& nor did we...

## OLIVE STONES

How will you haunt me? Will I meet your
ghostly face through the window or
will you tap your nails on my bedroom door?

Will I hear the shuffle of your slippered feet
on the carpeted living room floor
entering to find it empty but for

a different feel, a chill, a fleet
shadow as moonlight pours in—swear I saw
something, but what, I can't be sure?

Will I detect the subtle creak
of a recently-left seat,
or catch an ungraspable glimpse of you
counting days in olive stones as you used to?

## INKY-DINKY-DINK, FLEUR-DE-LIS, FLEUR-DE-LIS

Sat by a lip-singed fag-bandaged lady
On the bench by the entrance to the hospital
That glues & re-glazes cracked terracotta dolls,
Dragging at the sun, tapping ash in the bin,
Licking thought-sores' salty nicotine
She rasps, *I used to recite poetry*, then sings:
*INKY-DINKY-DOO-DA, INKY-DINKY-DEE,*
*INKY-DINKY-DOO, FLEUR-DE-LIS, FLEUR-DE-LIS...*

*I'm Scatty Hattie, everyone knows me*
*INKY-DINKY-DOO-DA, INKY-DINKY-DEE*
*I knew you was a poet soon as I clapped eyes*
*On you DINKY-DOO I used to like poetry,*
*I used to WRITE poetry INKY-DINKY-DEE,*
*FLEUR-DE-LIS, FLEUR-DE-LIS—*
*I'm not for the sunshine normally*
*Just gettin' a taaan you see INKY-DINK*
*They're always cadging cigs off me*
*Even though I don't smoke*
*FLEUR-DE-LIS, FLEUR-DE-LIS*
*I know I've got my back to you,*
*Just braanin' it you see—DINKY-DOO*
*I'm not ignoring you... DINKY-DEE*
*Am I? I'm just 'avin' a smoke FLEUR-DE-LIS,*
*I 'ope it ain't boverin' you—*
*Is my smoke boverin' you? DINKY-DOO*
*'cos it's boverin' me—me' lungs that is,*
*Welllll, by now they'll be all charred*
*INKY-DEE Black as two malt loafs I 'ave*
*Na daabt FLEUR-DE-LIS, FLEUR-DE-LIS...*

I thought to her: one day in the future
When I'm wrung of the last vestiges of *me*
Scrunched beside you on this bench again,
A shadow misshapenly cast, will you
Recall our first sojourn *DINKY-DEE*
& how much more *DINKY-DOO*
Intact that light was back then
*FLEUR-DE-LIS, FLEUR-DE-LIS...?*

## THE LADY IN THE CABINET

*for V.S.*

I gave you *The Yellow Wallpaper* to read—about
A woman who imagines another woman trapped
Behind the walls of an attic bedroom sequestered
For a quaintly termed *'rest cure'* from her *'temporary*
*Nervous depression'*, a woman trapped in the patterns
Of a damp attic's musty sulphur wallpaper...
I suppose part of my hope in bringing you here
To this quiet Thirties-built rented maisonette
Was to help you heal, take your *'rest cure'*, but there's
No real cure for the years of abuse you endured
That sometimes seem to you unreal & ambagious
As bad dreams, nor for the drip-drip residue
That endures ever since & leaves a mustardy aftertaste,
A sting in everything, reverberating to numbness
On your tongue whenever you attempt to articulate
Anything relating to it, verbally relive it
In alternative versions trying to find one which
The soul-moving-on can almost-accommodate;
The chronic psychical scars that can only be patched up;
The punishing repeated lashes of flashback;
The scratching rut of trauma; the mental stains
That catch on fabrics of the present, tarnishing
All textures, scratching & scarring them...

After crawling halfway through Charlotte Perkins
Gilman's unsettling tale (almost a prose poem
On menopause warped, phantasmagorical Gothic
Psychological allegory—O how grotesquely
Inadequate these hermeneutical terms just as
Those psychiatric plaster phrases applied to your scars—
*'Emotionally unstable personality disorder'*—
Terms that trap us behind nursery bars,
Or brocaded wallpaper creeping with damp
& blotchy with mould spores, bloated with dust
& moisture, an appalling poultice pressed
Against our lips, smothering our mouths, or,
Salted, wrapped around your red-scarred arms),
You latching on particularly to that part depicting
The wallpaper patterns as tangents plunging
Into nothingness, hurling themselves off
Their own scrolled edges, committing suicides
In curlicues (metaphorically speaking, of course),

But then abruptly truncating it, partly for lack
Of concentration, partly for it being written
In your third language—after German, Arabic—
& pitched in baroquely expressed maple-dripped prose
So typical of Yellow Nineties literature (the Mauve
Decade in Gilman's America), cryptic turns of phrase,
You spoke about *"the lady"* you saw who was *"trapped"*
Inside the wooden cabinet I'd bought from a charity
Shop to house my accidental collection of porcelain
Miniatures, refugee figurines—cheap replica
Furstenberg, Meissen, chipped serendipities;
You spoke of how the lady was menacing, of how
She faintly knocked on the cabinet's glass at night,
Wanting you to let her out; so, draping the throw
From the couch over the cabinet at least kept her
Strange gray face from sight, although you'd
Still hear her tapping faintly on the glass in spite,
A faint knocking slightly muffled through the woollen throw;
Then, when I asked you to explain in what sense
You *"saw"* a lady in the cabinet you said you
*"Saw her"* in your *"mind"* & that she was you,
Not your reflection but a nocturnal doppelganger
With independent spontaneous expressions,
Trapped behind the glass, trapped inside the cabinet
Of your mind, as if you were on display, confined,
A rigid figurine in your own right, reified—
Yet it felt cheapening, such a figure of speech,
A pathetic attempt to capture spiritual disfigurement...

In spite of how deeply I pitied your difficult tilt of mind,
Tried to help you catch the pieces of your splintered
Consciousness, some too sharp to pick up, how much I
Sympathised, how my heart broke like the Gothic clock
You bought me for my bereft birthday that glum
Summer plunged under shadowy boughs of dark thoughts,
Black heavy leaves of bereavement, stung until
Numbed by nettled nerves, festering mental burns
Of a breakdown which shook me to my core,
The broke clock whose pendulum just couldn't keep
A soft enough rhythm to sustain its rusty swing,
Its brittle rocking, still echoing... faintly knocking...
I couldn't help appreciating the metaphor...

## BROWN STUDIES

I've spent so much of my life to date
Immersed in brown studies of the mind;
There was never a choice—I came late
In the evening of world, & always find
My mood is cooler at night on the prowl
Of silence's chill holiness—owl

Alert & twitching in moon hours, calm
As I never am in daytime, sharply aware
Of the stillness & its magical balm
That soothes & transports me anywhere
But where I am; brown studies embalm me
In comfortable numbness; thoughts pitch free

Into oceanic consciousness—I'm happy
When unhappy, or somewhere in between
Contentedness & sadness; moonlight-tipsy;
Sedated by time & numbness—morphine
Compares to brown studies' ambrosial bowl
Lips sip, soup of respite, residue of soul.

## JUNE HAUNTING

In lockdown I visit my father the anchorite
Crouched like a gnome in the smoky glooms
Of his dingy singed living room-cum-grotto
In front of his half-open window,
A birdwatcher shielding inside a hide;
Or it's as if he bides behind an unreflecting two-way mirror
Since the sun behind me blinds me to him
Though he sees me clearly, perhaps clearer than before,
&, as always, I'm pale as milk, especially after
An epic interior spell, which, even with my
Reclusiveness has been a revelation of nerve...

Am I a revenant paying him a visit,
A revenant who thinks I'm still living, a ghost
His woozy thoughts have unwittingly brought out
From the cobwebbed boughs of his mind's shadow wood...?
His youngest son grown from shadow who somehow
Survived well into adulthood, now middle-aged,
Against all augurs, gray in daylight, a wraith, a waif,
Frail Linton, fraught Hartley, brow-knitted Little Time
Who ripened in spite of expectations, a deep
Sense of emptiness, unspotted on the spectrum,
Problems put down to nerves, a strange vagueness,
Something missing... Or maybe that was all a dream
& my father's Allan Quatermain mourning his son...?

Isn't haunting just a sublime absentmindedness?
A soul's shadow-throwing? Astral ruminating...?

Back at the flat I sit in my green leather chair
In the backroom overlooking the long-neglected garden,
& think on my father, how much he has shrunk,
Seemingly in the drag of a cigarette, ash-tapped,
Crookbacked, brittle, but the warmer image
Of him long-summered in my mind is still rooted,
Gentle-strong, a gnarled trunk, browned by the world,
An anchored Capricorn, his large tanned hands,
& I sit back & listen to the wind in the garden
Moaning then roaring, & the warped old wooden
Shed creaking & groaning as gusts disfigure it,
So long neglected as the garden, the overgrown,
Overwrought garden, its agonised grass
Going over & over the same ground again...

By the Same Author

*Anxious Corporals*
(Smokestack, 2021)

*Gum Arabic*
(Cyberwit, 2020)

*Shabbigentile*
(Culture Matters, 2019)

*Tan Raptures*
(Smokestack, 2017)

*Shadows Waltz Haltingly*
(Lapwing Publications, 2015)

*Odour of Devon Violet*
(www.odourofdevonviolet.com, 2014)

*Blaze a Vanishing /*
*The Tall Skies*
(Waterloo, 2013)

*Captive Dragons/*
*The Shadow Thorns*
(Waterloo, 2011)

*Keir Hardie Street*
(Smokestack Books, 2010)

*A Tapestry of Absent Sitters*
(Waterloo Press, 2009)

*Picaresque—*
*The Pirates of Circumstance*
(chipmunkapublishing, 2008)

*The Mansion Gardens*
(Paula Brown Publishing, 2006)

Also available from Caparison

*The Brown Envelope Book—*
*Poetry & prose on the experiences*
*of unemployment, the benefits system,*
*disability & work capability assessments*
(318pp, 2021)

*Mermaids in Wormwood*
Christopher Moncrieff
(160pp, 2021)
Illustrated

*Earth Talk*
Peter Street
(54pp, 2020)

*Restless Voices*
Alan Price
(56pp, 2020)

*Tabac Blond*
Christopher Moncrieff
(136pp, 2019)
Illustrated

*The Huntington Hydra*
Bruce Harris
(100pp, 2019)

*Waters of the Night—*
*Collected Poems 1974-84*
Howard Mingham
(68pp, 2014)

*The Robin Hood Book—*
*Verse Versus Austerity*
(512pp, 2012)

As well as a selection of e-books

www.therecusant.org.uk/caparison-books

BV - #0087 - 130223 - C0 - 234/156/18 - CC - 9781838496623 - Gloss Lamination